The Bible speaks today

Series Editors: J. A. Motyer (OT)
John R. W. Stott (NT)

God's new society

The message of Ephesians

D0412814

Other titles in this series

Songs from a Strange Land
Psalms 42–51
John Goldingay

A Time to Mourn, and a Time to Dance
Ecclesiastes and the Way of the World
Derek Kidner

The Lord is King
The Message of Daniel
Ronald S. Wallace

Love to the Loveless
The Story and Message of Hosea
Derek Kidner

The Day of the Lion
The Message of Amos
J. A. Motyer

Christian Counter-Culture
The Message of the Sermon on the Mount
John R. W. Stott

The Saviour of the World
The Message of Luke's Gospel
Michael Wilcock

Only One Way
The Message of Galatians
John R. W. Stott

Fullness and Freedom
The Message of Colossians and Philemon
R. C. Lucas

Guard the Gospel
The Message of 2 Timothy
John R. W. Stott

Christ Above All
The Message of Hebrews
Raymond Brown

I Saw Heaven Opened
The Message of Revelation
Michael Wilcock

God's new society

The message of Ephesians

John R. W. Stott

Rector Emeritus of All Souls' Church
Langham Place, London

Inter-Varsity Press

Inter-Varsity Press
38 De Montfort Street, Leicester LE1 7GP, England

© John R. W. Stott, 1979

Unless otherwise stated, quotations from the Bible
are from the Revised Standard Version of the Bible,
copyrighted 1946, 1952, © 1971, 1973 by the
Division of Christian Education of the National
Council of the Churches of Christ in the USA,
and used by permission.

First published 1979
Reprinted 1982

ISBN 0 85110 597 1

Set in 10/11pt Garamond
Printed in Great Britain by
J. W. Arrowsmith Ltd, Bristol

*Inter-Varsity Press is the publishing division of the
Universities and Colleges Christian Fellowship
(formerly the Inter-Varsity Fellowship), a student
movement linking Christian Unions in universities
and colleges throughout the British Isles, and a
member movement of the International Fellowship
of Evangelical Students. For information about local
and national activities in Great Britain write to
UCCF, 38 De Montfort Street, Leicester LE1 7GP.*

General preface

The Bible speaks today describes a series of both Old Testament and New Testament expositions, which are characterized by a threefold ideal: to expound the biblical text with accuracy, to relate it to contemporary life, and to be readable.

These books are, therefore, not 'commentaries', for the commentary seeks rather to elucidate the text than to apply it, and tends to be a work rather of reference than of literature. Nor, on the other hand, do they contain the kind of 'sermons' which attempt to be contemporary and readable, without taking Scripture seriously enough.

The contributors to this series will all be united in their convictions that God still speaks through what he has spoken, and that nothing is more necessary for the life, growth and health of churches or of Christians than that they should hear and heed what the Spirit is saying to them through his ancient—yet ever modern—Word.

J. A. MOTYER
J. R. W. STOTT
Series Editors

Contents

Contents

Author's preface

Those of us who call ourselves 'evangelical' Christians are claiming by this epithet to be gospel people, who hold fast the authentic Christian evangel. It is a bold claim, and sometimes resented. In order to sustain it, we need constantly to return to the Scriptures in which alone the normative statement of the gospel is to be found. Measured by this standard, it has to be admitted that many of our formulations of the good news are defective. One of our chief evangelical blind spots has been to overlook the central importance of the church. We tend to proclaim individual salvation without moving on to the saved community. We emphasize that Christ died for us 'to redeem us from all iniquity' rather than 'to purify for himself a people of his own'.[1] We think of ourselves more as 'Christians' than as 'churchmen', and our message is more good news of a new life than of a new society.

Nobody can emerge from a careful reading of Paul's letter to the Ephesians with a privatized gospel. For Ephesians is the gospel of the church. It sets forth God's eternal purpose to create through Jesus Christ a new society which stands out in bright relief against the sombre background of the old world. For God's new society is characterized by life in place of death, by unity and reconciliation in place of division and alienation, by the wholesome standards of righteousness in place of the corruption of wickedness, by love and peace in place of hatred and strife, and by unremitting conflict with evil in

[1] Tit. 2:14.

9

place of a flabby compromise with it.

This vision of a renewed human community has stirred me deeply. At the same time, the realities of lovelessness and sin in so many contemporary churches are enough to make one weep, for they dishonour Christ, contradict the nature of the church, and deprive the Christian witness of integrity. Yet increasing numbers of church members are seeking the church's radical renewal. For the sake of the glory of God and the evangelization of the world, nothing is more important than that the church should be, and should be seen to be, God's new society. Towards the fulfilment of this vision Ephesians gives us a strong and steady stimulus.

During the past five years and more I have been studying the text of Ephesians, absorbing its message, feeling its impact and dreaming its dream. It has been a great practical help in this period to attempt to expound the letter to various groups and to receive their reactions. I began with the responsive and long-suffering congregation of All Souls Church, and continued with conferences in India, Nepal, Canada and Mexico, and in July 1975 with the memorable Keswick Centenary Convention. No audience is more alert and critical than one composed of students; I have therefore found it specially profitable to share with student groups in India, America, Europe, Australia and Latin America, and to be challenged by the more sustained exposition required in 1976 by the Summer Study Institute at the University of Maryland, USA, and by the Summer School of Regent College, Vancouver. I am extremely grateful for the intellectual and spiritual stimulation of these experiences.

I am also grateful to several individuals who have given me personal help in various ways in the writing of this book, especially to Roy McCloughry for tracking down some useful references, to Myra Chave-Jones for reading a portion of the MS and to Tom Cooper for reading it all, and for their comments, and to Frances Whitehead and Vivienne Curry for the strenuous labour of deciphering my scribble and converting it into beautiful typescript.

JOHN R. W. STOTT

Chief abbreviations

AG   *A Greek–English Lexicon of the New Testament and Other Early Christian Literature* by William F. Arndt and F. Wilbur Gingrich (University of Chicago Press and Cambridge University Press, 1957).

Armitage Robinson   *St Paul's Epistle to the Ephesians, with Exposition and Notes* by J. Armitage-Robinson (Macmillan, 1903).

AV   The Authorized (King James') Version of the Bible, 1611.

Barclay   *The Letters to the Galatians and Ephesians* in the *Daily Study Bible* by William Barclay (The Saint Andrew Press, 1954. 2nd edition, 1958).

Barth, *Broken Wall*   *The Broken Wall: A Study of the Epistle to the Ephesians* by Markus Barth (1959. Collins, 1960).

Barth, *Ephesians*, I, II   *Ephesians, A New Translation with Introduction and Commentary* by Markus Barth, in the *Anchor Bible* (Doubleday, 1974. Vol. I, Eph. 1–3; Vol. II, Eph. 4–6).

Bruce   *The Epistle to the Ephesians, A Verse-by-verse Exposition* by F. F. Bruce (Pickering & Inglis, 1961).

Caird   *Paul's Letters from Prison* by G. B. Caird, in the *New Clarendon Bible* (Oxford, 1976).

Calvin	*Sermons on the Epistle to the Ephesians* by John Calvin (delivered 1558–9, first published in English in 1577, revised translation by Banner of Truth, 1973).
Dale	*Lectures on the Epistle to the Ephesians, its Doctrine and Ethics* by R. W. Dale (Hodder & Stoughton, 1882; 5th edition 1890).
Findlay	*The Epistle to the Ephesians* by G. G. Findlay, in the *Expositor's Bible* (Hodder & Stoughton, 1892).
Foulkes	*The Epistle of Paul to the Ephesians* by Francis Foulkes, in the *Tyndale New Testament Commentaries* (Inter-Varsity Press, 1963).
GNB	The Good News Bible (Today's English Version), NT 1966, 4th edition 1976; OT 1976 (The Bible Societies and Collins).
Gurnall	*The Christian in Complete Armour, or a Treatise of the Saints' War against the Devil* by William Gurnall (originally published in 3 sections, 1655, 1658 and 1661: 3 volumes, 8th edition, London, 1821).
Hendriksen	*Exposition of Ephesians* by William Hendriksen (Baker, 1967).
Hodge	*A Commentary on the Epistle to the Ephesians* by Charles Hodge (1856. Banner of Truth, 1964).
Houlden	*Paul's Letters from Prison* by J. H. Houlden, in the *Pelican New Testament Commentary* series (Penguin, 1970).
Hunter	*Galatians to Colossians* by A. M. Hunter, in the *Layman's Bible Commentaries* (1959. SCM, 1960).
JB	The Jerusalem Bible (Darton, Longman and Todd, 1966).
JBP	*The New Testament in Modern English* by J. B. Phillips (Collins, 1958).
Lightfoot	*Notes on Epistles of St Paul, from*

12

	unpublished commentaries by J. B. Lightfoot (Macmillan, 1895). The notes on Ephesians cover only 1:1–14.
Lloyd-Jones, *God's Way*	*God's Way of Reconciliation, Studies in Eph. 2* by D. Martyn Lloyd-Jones (Evangelical Press, 1972).
Lloyd-Jones, *Life in the Spirit*	*Life in the Spirit in Marriage, Home and Work, An Exposition of Eph. 5:18 to 6:9* by D. Martyn Lloyd-Jones (Banner of Truth, 1974).
Lloyd-Jones, *Warfare*	*The Christian Warfare, An Exposition of Eph. 6:10–13* by D. Martyn Lloyd-Jones (Banner of Truth, 1976).
LXX	The Old Testament in Greek according to the Septuagint, 3rd century BC.
Mackay	*God's Order: The Ephesian Letter and this Present Time* by John A. Mackay (the 1948 Croall Lectures; Nisbet and Macmillan, 1953).
Mitton, NCB	*Ephesians* by C. Leslie Mitton, in the *New Century Bible* (Oliphants, 1976).
Moule, *Ephesians*	*The Epistle to the Ephesians* by Handley C. G. Moule, in the *Cambridge Bible for Schools and Colleges* (Cambridge University Press, 1886).
Moule, *Grace*	*Grace and Godliness, Eight Studies in Ephesians* by Handley C. G. Moule (Seeley, 1895).
Moule, *Studies*	*Ephesian Studies* by Handley C. G. Moule (Hodder & Stoughton, 1900).
Moule, *Veni Creator*	*Veni Creator* by Handley C. G. Moule (Hodder & Stoughton, 1890).
Moulton and Milligan	*The Vocabulary of the Greek New Testament* by J. H. Moulton and G. Milligan (Hodder & Stoughton, 1930).
NEB	The New English Bible (NT 1961, 2nd edition 1970; OT 1970).
NIV	The New International Version of the Bible (Hodder & Stoughton, NT 1974, OT 1979).
RSV	The Revised Standard Version of the

13

	Bible (NT 1946, 2nd edition 1971; OT 1952).
RV	The Revised Version of the Bible (1884).
Salmon	*History of the Roman World from 30 BC to AD 138* by Edward T. Salmon (Methuen, 1944).
Simpson	*Commentary on the Epistles to the Ephesians and the Colossians* by E. K. Simpson and F. F. Bruce, in the *New International Commentary on the New Testament* (Marshall, Morgan & Scott and Eerdmans, 1957).
Thayer	*A Greek–English Lexicon of the New Testament* by J. H. Thayer (4th edition, T. & T. Clark, 1901).
TDNT	*Theological Dictionary of the New Testament* ed. G. Kittel and G. Friedrich, trs. into English by G. W. Bromiley (Eerdmans, 1964–1974).
Westermann	*Between Slavery and Freedom* by W. L. Westermann, in *The American Historical Review* (Vol. 50, No. 2, January 1945).
Yoder	*The Politics of Jesus* by John Howard Yoder (Eerdmans, 1972).

Ephesians 1:1–2

Introduction to the letter

The letter to the Ephesians is a marvellously concise, yet comprehensive, summary of the Christian good news and its implications. Nobody can read it without being moved to wonder and worship, and challenged to consistency of life.

It was John Calvin's favourite letter. Armitage Robinson called it 'the crown of St Paul's writings'.[1] William Barclay quotes Samuel Taylor Coleridge's assessment of it as 'the divinest composition of man' and adds his own dictum that it is 'the Queen of the epistles'.[2]

Many readers have been brought to faith and stirred to good works by its message. One such was John Mackay, former President of Princeton Theological Seminary. 'To this book I owe my life', he wrote. He went on to explain how in July 1903 as a lad of fourteen he experienced through reading Ephesians a 'boyish rapture in the Highland hills' and made 'a passionate protestation to Jesus Christ among the rocks in the starlight'.[3] Here is his own account of what happened to him: 'I saw a new world . . . Everything was new . . . I had a new outlook, new experiences, new attitudes to other people. I loved God. Jesus Christ became the centre of everything . . . I had been 'quickened'; I was really alive.'[4]

John Mackay never lost his fascination for Ephesians. So, when invited to deliver the Croall Lectures in Edinburgh

---

[1] Armitage Robinson, p. vii.
[2] Barclay, pp. 71, 83.
[3] Mackay, p. 24.
[4] *Ibid.*, p. 21.

15

University in January 1948, he chose Ephesians as his topic. He wanted to anticipate the formation of the World Council of Churches in Amsterdam later the same year. The theme of its inaugural assembly (subsequently modified) was to have been 'The order of God and the disorder of man'. So he entitled his lectures *God's Order*. In them he referred to Ephesians as the 'greatest', the 'maturest' and 'for our time the most relevant' of all Paul's works.[5] For here is 'the distilled essence of the Christian religion, the most authoritative and most consummate compendium of our holy Christian faith'.[6] Again, 'this letter is pure music . . . What we read here is truth that sings, doctrine set to music'.[7] As the apostle proclaimed God's order to the post-Augustan Roman era which was marked by 'a process of social disintegration', so Ephesians is today 'the most contemporary book in the Bible',[8] since it promises community in a world of disunity, reconciliation in place of alienation and peace instead of war. Dr Mackay's enthusiasm for the letter raises our expectation to a high point as we begin our study of it.

Paul, an apostle of Christ Jesus by the will of God,
To the saints who are (at Ephesus and) also faithful in Christ Jesus.
²Grace to you and peace from God our Father and the Lord Jesus Christ.

Three introductory matters confront us as we read these two opening verses of the letter. They concern its author, its recipients and its message.

1. The author

In keeping with the convention of his day the author begins by announcing himself. He identifies himself as the apostle Paul.

Now the Pauline authorship of Ephesians was universally accepted from the first century until the beginning of the

[5] *Ibid.*, pp. 9–10. [6] *Ibid.*, p. 31.
[7] *Ibid.*, p. 33. [8] *Ibid.*, p. 36.

nineteenth. Why is it, then, that German scholars from the 1820s onward began to question the letter's authenticity, and that this scepticism about Paul's authorship of Ephesians is widespread today? To quote only one example: 'There are many grounds for thinking that it comes neither from his hand nor even from his lifetime.'[9]

Most commentators draw attention to the letter's distinctive vocabulary and style. They tot up the number of words in Ephesians which do not occur in Paul's other letters, and the number of his favourite words which are not found in Ephesians. His style, they add, is far less impassioned than usual. Markus Barth, for instance, has written of the author's 'pleonastic, redundant, verbose diction' and of his 'baroque, bombastic or litany-like style'.[1] But this is a largely subjective judgment. Besides, linguistic and stylistic arguments are notoriously precarious. Why should we expect such an original mind as Paul's to stay within the confines of a limited vocabulary and an inflexible style? Different themes require different words, and changed circumstances create a changed atmosphere.

Two other and more substantial arguments are advanced, however, to cast doubt on the letter's authenticity, the first historical and the second theological. The historical argument concerns a discrepancy between the Acts account of Paul's longstanding and intimate acquaintance with the Ephesian church and the entirely impersonal and 'hearsay' relationship which the letter expresses. Although his first visit had been brief (Acts 18:19–21), his second lasted three years (Acts 19:1 – 20:1,31). During this period he taught them systematically both 'in public and from house to house', they came to know him well, and at his final parting from the church elders their affection for him had been demonstrative, being accompanied by tears, hugs and kisses.[2] It comes as quite a shock, therefore, to discover that the Ephesian letter contains no personal greetings such as conclude Paul's other letters (no fewer than twenty-six people are mentioned by name in Romans 16). Instead, he addresses his readers only in generic terms, wishing peace to 'the brethren' and

---

[9] Houlden, p. 235.   [1] Barth, *Broken Wall*, p. 12.
[2] See Acts 20:17–38, especially verses 18, 20, 34 and 36–38.

grace to 'all who love our Lord Jesus Christ' (6:23–24). He alludes to his own situation as a prisoner (3:1; 4:1; 6:20), but makes no allusion to theirs. He urges them to live in unity and sexual purity, but he gives no hint of any factions or of an immoral offender such as he mentions in 1 Corinthians. He refers in general terms to the craftiness of false teachers (4:14), but he identifies no particular heresy as in Galatians or Colossians. Moreover, he gives no indication that he and they know one another personally. On the contrary, he has only 'heard' of their faith and love, and they of his stewardship of the gospel (1:15; 3:2–4).

This impersonal character of the letter is certainly surprising. But there is no need to deduce from it that Paul was not its author. Other explanations are possible. Paul may have been addressing a group of Asian churches rather than just the Ephesian church, or, as Markus Barth suggests, 'not the whole church in Ephesus but only the members of Gentile origin, people whom he did not know personally and who had been converted and baptized after his final departure from that city'.[3]

The second argument which is raised against the Pauline authorship of Ephesians is theological. On this subject commentators make a wide variety of different points. It is emphasized, for example, that in Ephesians as distinct from the letters of unquestioned Pauline authorship, the role of Christ assumes a cosmic dimension, that the sphere of interest is 'the heavenly places' (a unique expression occurring five times) in which the principalities and powers operate, that the focus of concern is the church, that 'justification' is not mentioned, that 'reconciliation' is more between Jews and Gentiles than between the sinner and God, that salvation is portrayed not as dying with Christ but only as rising with him, and that there is no reference to our Lord's second coming. None of these points is more than a comparatively minor shift of emphasis, however. And there can be no mistaking the letter's essentially Pauline theology. Even those who deny its Pauline authorship are obliged to admit that it is 'choc-a-bloc with echoes of the undoubted writing of Paul'.[4]

[3] Barth, *Ephesians*, I, pp. 3–4.   [4] Houlden, p. 242.

18

In addition, there is the foreign 'feel' of the letter which some readers get. Nobody has expressed this more vividly than Markus Barth in his earlier study (1959) entitled *The Broken Wall*. He calls his first section 'Paul's puzzling Epistle', and presents it as 'a stranger at the door'. What is the 'strangeness' of Ephesians? He lists the doctrine of predestination, the emphasis on intellectual enlightenment, 'superstition' (by which he means the references to angels and demons), an 'ecclesiasticism' which divorces the church from the world, and in his teaching about home relationships a 'moralism' which he calls 'patriarchal, authoritarian, petit bourgeois' and lacking in originality, breadth, boldness and joy. This is how he sums up his initial impression of Ephesians: 'This strange fellow resembles a fatherless and motherless foundling. He uses a tiresome baroque language. He builds upon determinism, suffers from intellectualism, combines faith in Christ with superstitious demonology, promotes a stiff ecclesiasticism, and ends with trite, shallow moralism.'[5]

When I first read this evaluation, I wondered whether it was really Ephesians which Dr Barth was describing, so divergent was his reaction to the letter from mine. But as I read on, it became clear to me that he was not satisfied with his own judgment. First, he concedes that he may be guilty of a caricature, then he explains that he wanted to shock his readers into feeling what non-Christians feel when approached with a caricature of the gospel, and finally he redresses the balance by depicting 'the charm of acquaintance' which people experience who get to know Ephesians better. The letter endears itself and its author to us, he suggests, by three characteristics.

First, Ephesians is intercession. More than any other New Testament epistle, it 'has the character and form of *prayer*'. When somebody *argues* with us, he may or may not persuade us; but when he *prays* for us, his relation to us changes. 'So it is with the stranger at the door. Ephesians has gained a right to enter because its readers have a place in the intercession of the author.'[6]

Secondly, Ephesians is affirmation. It is neither apolo-

---

[5] Barth, *Broken Wall*, p. 22.   [6] *Ibid.*, pp. 23–24.

getics, nor polemics. Instead, it abounds in 'bold' and even
'jubilant' affirmations about God, Christ and the Holy
Spirit. 'Ephesians makes itself welcome and is a charming
document just because it dares to let shine nothing else but
God's love and election, Christ's death and resurrection,
and the Spirit's might and work among men.'[7]

Thirdly, Ephesians is evangelism. In his survey of the
letter's contents Markus Barth emphasizes its 'bold asser-
tions' about God's saving purpose and action (chapters 1
and 2), about 'God's ongoing work in his self-manifestation
to and through the church' (chapters 3 and 4), and about
'the bold and joyful ambassadorship of the Christians in
the world' (chapters 5 and 6). All this, he says, gives
Ephesians 'pecular significance for all concerned with the
evangelistic tasks of the church today'.[8]

What, then, is the state of play in scholarly circles
regarding the authorship of Ephesians? Many sit on the
fence. They would agree with J. H. Houlden that there
is 'no consensus of expert opinion', for 'argument answers
argument without clear outcome'.[9]

Others still deny that Paul was the author and propose
elaborate alternative theories. Perhaps the most ingenious
is that of the American scholar E. J. Goodspeed. He
speculated that about the year AD 90 an ardent devotee of
the apostle Paul, dismayed by the contemporary neglect
of his hero's letters, went the rounds of the churches he
had visited in order to collect and later publish them. But
before publication he saw the need for some kind of
introduction. So he composed 'Ephesians' himself as a
mosaic of materials drawn from all Paul's letters, especially
Colossians (which he had memorized), and attributed it to
Paul in order to commend him to a later generation. E.
J. Goodspeed went further and hazarded the guess that
this author and publisher was none other than Onesimus,
the converted slave, since somebody of that name was
Bishop of Ephesus at the time. Although this reconstruction
has gained some popularity in the United States and has
been adopted in England by Dr Leslie Mitton, it is almost
entirely speculative.

[7] *Ibid.*, p. 29.
[8] *Ibid.*, p. 30.   [9] Houlden, p. 236.

Other scholars are coming back to the traditional view. A. M. Hunter rightly says that 'the burden of proof lies with those who deny Paul's authorship'.[1] Markus Barth uses the same expression and applies the maxim 'innocent until proven guilty'.[2] For myself, I find even these judgments too timid. They do not seem to give sufficient weight to either the external or the internal evidence. Externally, there is the impressive witness of the universal church for eighteen centuries, which is not to be lightly set aside. Internally, the letter not only purports to be written by the apostle Paul throughout, but its theme of the union of Jews and Gentiles by God's gracious reconciling work through Christ is wholly appropriate to what we learn elsewhere about the apostle to the Gentiles. I do not think G. G. Findlay was exaggerating when he wrote that modern scepticism about the Pauline authorship of Ephesians will in future come to be regarded as 'one of . . . the curiosities of a hypercritical age'.[3] The absence of any satisfactory alternative is rightly emphasized by F. F. Bruce: 'The man who could write Ephesians must have been the apostle's equal, if not his superior, in mental stature and spiritual insight . . . Of such a second Paul early Christian history has no knowledge.'[4]

After this brief survey of some modern viewpoints it is a relief to come back to the text: *Paul, an apostle of Christ Jesus by the will of God.* Paul claims the same title which Jesus had given to the Twelve,[5] and whose background in both Old Testament and Rabbinic Judaism designated somebody specially chosen, called and sent to teach with authority. For this ministry he had not volunteered, nor had the church appointed him. On the contrary, his apostleship derived from the will of God and from the choice and commission of Jesus Christ. If this be so, as I for one believe, then we must listen to the message of Ephesians with appropriate attention and humility. For we must regard its author neither as a private individual who is ventilating his personal opinions, nor as a gifted but fallible human teacher, nor even as the church's greatest missionary hero, but as 'an apostle of Christ Jesus by the

[1] Hunter, p. 45.   [2] Barth, *Broken Wall*, p. 41.   [3] Findlay, p. 4.
[4] Bruce, pp. 11–12.   [5] Lk. 6:12–13.

21

will of God', and therefore as a teacher whose authority is precisely the authority of Jesus Christ himself, in whose name and by whose inspiration he writes. As Charles Hodge expressed it in the middle of the last century, 'The epistle reveals itself as the work of the Holy Ghost as clearly as the stars declare their maker to be God.'[6]

2. The recipients

In the second part of verse 1 Paul uses several epithets to describe his readers.

First, they are *the saints*. He is not referring by this familiar word to some spiritual élite within the congregation, a minority of exceptionally holy Christians, but rather to all God's people. They were called 'saints' (that is, 'holy') because they had been set apart to belong to him. The expression was first applied to Israel as the 'holy nation', but came to be extended to the whole international Christian community, which is the Israel of God.[7]

Next, they are also *faithful*. The adjective *pistos* can have either an active meaning ('trusting', 'having faith') or a passive ('trustworthy', 'being faithful'). RSV chooses the passive here, but the active seems better since God's people are 'the household of faith',[8] united by their common trust in God through Jesus Christ. At the same time, J. Armitage Robinson may be right in suggesting that 'the two senses of *pistis*, "belief" and "fidelity", appear to be blended'.[9] Certainly, it is hard to imagine a believer who is not himself believable, or a trustworthy Christian who has not learned trustworthiness from him in whom he has put his trust.

Thirdly, Paul's readers are *in Christ Jesus*. This key expression of the letter thus occurs in its very first verse. To be 'in Christ' is to be personally and vitally united to Christ, as branches are to the vine and members to the body, and thereby also to Christ's people. For it is impossible to be part of the Body without being related to both the Head and the members. Much of what the epistle later develops is already here in bud. According to

[6] Hodge, p. xv.　　　　　　[7] Gal. 6:16.
[8] Gal. 6:10.　　　　　　　[9] Armitage Robinson, p. 141.

the New Testament—and especially Paul—to be a Christian is in essence to be 'in Christ', one with him and with his people.

Fourthly, some manuscripts add that Paul's readers are *at Ephesus*. Originally a Greek colony, Ephesus was now the capital of the Roman province of Asia and a busy commercial port (long since silted up). It was also the headquarters of the cult of the goddess Diana (or Artemis) whose temple, after being destroyed in the middle of the fourth century BC, had gradually been rebuilt to become one of the seven wonders of the world. Indeed, the success of Paul's mission in Ephesus had so threatened the sale of silver models of her temple that the silversmiths had stirred up a public outcry.[1]

Paul's description of his readers is thus comprehensive. They are 'saints' because they belong to God; they are 'believers' because they have trusted in Christ; and they have two homes, for they reside equally 'in Christ' and 'in Ephesus'. Indeed all Christian people are saints and believers, and live both in Christ and in the secular world, or 'in the heavenlies' and on earth. Many of our spiritual troubles arise from our failure to remember that we are citizens of two kingdoms. We tend either to pursue Christ and withdraw from the world, or to become preoccupied with the world and forget that we are also in Christ.

The words 'at Ephesus' are not to be found, however, in the earliest Pauline papyrus (Chester Beatty 46) which dates from the second century. Origen in the third century did not know them, and they are absent from the great fourth-century Vatican and Sinaitic codices. The matter is further complicated by the fact that Marcion in the middle of the second century referred to Ephesians as having been addressed 'to the Laodiceans'. Since Paul himself directed the Colossians both to see that his letter to them be read 'in the church of the Laodiceans' and that they themselves 'read also the letter from Laodicea',[2] some have thought that this so-called 'letter from Laodicea' was in fact our 'Ephesians', and that he was instructing the churches to exchange the two letters which they had received from

[1] See Acts 19:23 ff.　　　　[2] Col. 4:16.

23

him. Certainly Tychicus was the bearer of the two letters.[3]

How then can we reconstruct the situation which led to these variants, some copies having 'in Ephesus', others having no designation and one referring to Laodicea? Near the beginning of this century Adolf Harnack suggested that the letter was originally addressed to the church in Laodicea, but that because of that church's lukewarmness and consequent disgrace,[4] the name of Laodicea was erased and that of Ephesus substituted.

An alternative explanation was proposed by Beza at the end of the sixteenth century and popularized by Archbishop Ussher in the seventeenth, namely that Ephesians was originally a kind of apostolic encyclical or circular letter intended for several Asian churches, that a blank space was left in the first verse for each church to fill in its own name, and that the name of Ephesus became attached to the letter because it was the principal Asian city.

Somewhat similarly, Charles Hodge thought that perhaps the letter was 'written to the Ephesians and addressed to them, but being intended specially for the Gentile Christians as a class, rather than for the Ephesians as a church, it was designedly thrown into such a form as to suit it to all such Christians in the neighbouring churches, to whom no doubt the apostle wished it to be communicated.'[5]

Such a more general readership would explain not only the variants in the first verse but also the absence from the letter of all particular allusions and personal greetings.

All the same, the circular letter theory is entirely speculative. No manuscript carries an alternative destination. And Colossians, which Paul says he intended for another church as well (Col. 4:16), nevertheless includes some personal greetings. So the mystery remains unsolved.

3. The message

The letter focuses on what God did through the historical work of Jesus Christ and does through his Spirit today, in order to build his new society in the midst of the old.

---

[3] Eph. 6:21–22; Col. 4:7–8.
[4] Rev. 3:14–22.   [5] Hodge, p. xiii.

24

It tells how Jesus Christ shed his blood in a sacrificial death for sin, was then raised from death by the power of God and has been exalted above all competitors to the supreme place in both the universe and the church. More than that, we who are 'in Christ', organically united to him by faith, have ourselves shared in these great events. We have been raised from spiritual death, exalted to heaven and seated with him there. We have also been reconciled to God and to each other. As a result, through Christ and in Christ, we are nothing less than God's new society, the single new humanity which he is creating and which includes Jews and Gentiles on equal terms. We are the family of God the Father, the body of Jesus Christ his Son and the temple or dwelling place of the Holy Spirit.

Therefore we are to demonstrate plainly and visibly by our new life the reality of this new thing which God has done: first by the unity and diversity of our common life, secondly by the purity and love of our everyday behaviour, next by the mutual submissiveness and care of our relationships at home, and lastly by our stability in the fight against the principalities and powers of evil. Then in the fullness of time God's purpose of unification will be brought to completion under the headship of Jesus Christ.

With this theme in mind, we may perhaps analyse the letter as follows:

1. The new life which God has given us in Christ (1:3 – 2:10)
2. The new society which God has created through Christ (2:11 – 3:21)
3. The new standards which God expects of his new society, especially unity and purity (4:1 – 5:21)
4. The new relationships into which God has brought us—harmony in the home and hostility to the devil (5:21 – 6:24)

The whole letter is thus a magnificent combination of Christian doctrine and Christian duty, Christian faith and Christian life, what God has done through Christ and what we must be and do in consequence. And its central

25

theme is 'God's new society'—what it is, how it came into being through Christ, how its origins and nature were revealed to Paul, how it grows through proclamation, how we are to live lives worthy of it, and how one day it will be consummated when Christ presents his bride the church to himself in splendour, 'without spot or wrinkle or any such thing . . . holy and without blemish' (5:27).

The contemporary relevance of this message is obvious. Karl Marx also wrote of 'the new man' and 'the new society'. And millions of people have caught his vision and are dedicating themselves to its realization. But Marx saw the human problem and its solution in almost exclusively economic terms. The 'new society' was the classless society which would follow the revolution, and the 'new man' would emerge as a result of his economic liberation.

Paul presents a greater vision still. For he sees the human predicament as something even deeper than the injustice of the economic structure and so propounds a yet more radical solution. He writes of nothing less than a 'new creation'. Three times he uses creation language. Through Jesus Christ God is recreating men and women 'for good works', creating a single new humanity in place of the disastrous Jewish-Gentile division, and recreating us in his own image 'in true righteousness and holiness'.[6] Thus according to Paul's teaching the new man and the new society are God's creative work. Economic restructuring has great importance, but it cannot produce these things. They are beyond the capacity of human power and ingenuity. They depend on the fiat of the divine Creator.

This message of the church as God's new creation and new community is of particular importance for those of us who call ourselves or are called 'evangelical' Christians. For by temperament and tradition we tend to be rugged individualists, and are thought to care little about the church. Indeed, the expressions 'evangelical' and 'low church' are generally supposed to be synonymous. Yet they should not be. The true evangelical, who derives his theology from the Bible, will be bound to have the very 'high' view of the church which the Bible has. Today more

---

[6] 2:10,15; 4:24.

than ever we need to catch the biblical vision of the church. In the West the church is in decline, and urgently needs to be renewed. But what form of renewal do we desire? In the communist world the church is always stripped of privilege, often persecuted and sometimes driven underground. Such situations prompt the basic question: what is the church's essential being, without which it would cease to be the church? Then in several regions of the third world the church is growing rapidly, and in some places its growth rate is faster even than the population growth rate. But what kind of churches are coming into being and growing? Thus in all three worlds—the free world, the communist world and the third world—we need to be asking radical questions about the church. And Ephesians will supply us with answers. For here is Christ's own specification of his church, the church for which once he 'gave himself up' (5:25), the church 'which is his body', and even his 'fullness' (1:23).

Much of the message of Ephesians is adumbrated in the apostle's opening salutation: *Grace to you and peace from God our Father and the Lord Jesus Christ* (verse 2). True, this was the customary greeting with which he began all his letters, a Christianized form of the contemporary Hebrew and Greek greetings. Yet we may safely say that nothing from Paul's pen was ever purely conventional. On the contrary, both these nouns are particularly appropriate at the beginning of Ephesians—'grace' indicating God's free, saving initiative, and 'peace' what he has taken the initiative to do, namely to reconcile sinners to himself and to each other in his new community.

'Grace' and 'peace', then, are key words of Ephesians. In 6:15 the good news is termed 'the gospel of peace'. In 2:14 it is written that Jesus Christ himself 'is our peace', for first he 'made peace' by his cross (verse 15) and then he 'came and preached peace' to Jews and Gentiles alike (verse 17). Hence his people are to be 'eager to maintain the unity of the Spirit in the bond of peace' (4:3). 'Grace', on the other hand, indicates both why and how God has taken his reconciling initiative. For 'grace' is his free and undeserved mercy. It is 'by grace' that we are saved, indeed by 'the immeasurable riches of his grace' (2:5,7,8),

27

and it is by the same grace that we are gifted for service (4:7; *cf.* 3:2,7). So if we want a concise summary of the good news which the whole letter announces, we could not find a better one than the three monosyllables 'peace through grace'.

Finally, before leaving the introduction to the letter, we must not miss the vital link between the author, the readers and the message. It is the Lord Jesus Christ himself. For Paul the author is 'an apostle *of Christ Jesus*', the readers are themselves *in Christ Jesus*, and the blessing comes to them both from God our Father and *from . . . the Lord Jesus Christ*, who are bracketed as the single spring from which grace and peace flow forth. Thus the Lord Jesus Christ dominates Paul's mind and fills his vision. It seems almost as if he feels compelled to bring Jesus Christ into every sentence he writes, at least at the beginning of this letter. For it is through and in Jesus Christ that God's new society has come into being.

I New Life

Ephesians 1:3 – 2:10

1. Every spiritual blessing

The opening section of Ephesians (1:3 – 2:10), which describes the new life God has given us in Christ, divides itself naturally into two halves, the first consisting of praise and the second of prayer. In the 'praise' half Paul blesses God that he has blessed us in Christ with every spiritual blessing (1:3–14), while in the 'prayer' half he asks that God will open our eyes to grasp the fullness of this blessing (1:15 – 2:10). We shall be concerned in this chapter with the apostle's expression of praise.

*Blessed be the God and Father of our Lord Jesus Christ, who has blessed us in Christ with every spiritual blessing in the heavenly places, *4*even as he chose us in him before the foundation of the world, that we should be holy and blameless before him. *5*He destined us in love to be his sons through Jesus Christ, according to the purpose of his will, *6*to the praise of his glorious grace which he freely bestowed on us in the Beloved. *7*In him we have redemption through his blood, the forgiveness of our trespasses, according to the riches of his grace *8*which he lavished upon us. *9*For he has made known to us in all wisdom and insight the mystery of his will, according to his purpose which he set forth in Christ *10*as a plan for the fullness of time, to unite all things in him, things in heaven and things on earth.*
*11*In him, according to the purpose of him who accomplishes all things according to the counsel of his will, *12*we who first hoped in Christ have been destined and appointed to live for the praise of his glory. *13*In him you also, who have*

heard the word of truth, the gospel of your salvation, and have believed in him, were sealed with the promised Holy Spirit, [14]which is the guarantee of our inheritance until we acquire possession of it, to the praise of his glory.

In the original Greek these twelve verses constitute a single complex sentence. As Paul dictates, his speech pours out of his mouth in a continuous cascade. He neither pauses for breath, nor punctuates his words with full stops. Commentators have searched for metaphors vivid enough to convey the impact of this opening outburst of adoration. 'We enter this epistle through a magnificent gateway', writes Findlay.[1] It is 'a golden chain' of many links,[2] or 'a kaleidoscope of dazzling lights and shifting colours'.[3] William Hendriksen likens it to 'a snowball tumbling down a hill, picking up volume as it descends',[4] and E. K. Simpson—less felicitously perhaps—to 'some long-winded racehorse . . . careering onward at full speed.'[5] More romantic is John Mackay's musical simile: 'This rhapsodic adoration is comparable to the overture of an opera which contains the successive melodies that are to follow'.[6] And Armitage Robinson suggests that it is 'like the preliminary flight of the eagle, rising and wheeling round, as though for a while uncertain what direction in his boundless freedom he shall take'.[7]

A gateway, a golden chain, a kaleidoscope, a snowball, a racehorse, an operatic overture and the flight of an eagle: all these metaphors in their different ways describe the impression of colour, movement and grandeur which the sentence makes on the reader's mind.

The whole paragraph is a paean of praise, a doxology, or indeed a 'eulogy', for that is the word Paul uses. He begins by blessing God for blessing us with every conceivable blessing. More particularly, he makes what seems to be a deliberate reference to the Trinity. For the origin of the blessing is *the God and Father of our Lord Jesus Christ,* who is also 'our Father' (verse 2); its sphere is God the Son, for it is *in Christ,* by virtue of our union

[1] Findlay, p. 21.   [2] Dale, p. 40.   [3] Armitage Robinson, p. 19.
[4] Hendriksen, p. 72.   [5] Simpson, p. 24.
[6] Mackay, p. 75.   [7] Armitage Robinson, p. 19.

with him, that God has blessed us; and its nature is spiritual, *every spiritual blessing*, a phrase which may well mean 'every blessing of the Holy Spirit', who as the divine executive applies the work of Christ to our hearts. As Charles Hodge put it, 'These blessings are *spiritual* not merely because they pertain to the soul, but because derived from the Holy Spirit, whose presence and influence are the great blessing purchased by Christ'.[8]

It is partly this trinitarian reference which has made some scholars comment on what they call the 'liturgical' feel of the paragraph. It is a 'great benediction', writes Markus Barth, 'an exclamation of praise and prayer, resembling those pronounced in Jewish synagogues and homes', and it 'may . . . have come to Paul from the living stream of oral, probably liturgical, Christian tradition'.[9] Some commentators have gone further and detected in the paragraph a trinitarian structure like that of the Apostles' and Nicene Creeds—the Father electing (verses 4–6), the Son redeeming (verses 7–12) and the Spirit sealing (versus 13–14), each stanza concluding with the refrain 'to the praise of his glory' (verses 6,12,14). Although this is rather too neat to be probable, yet the trinitarian content of the paragraph remains obvious.

First, God the Father is the source or origin of every blessing which we enjoy. His initiative is set forth plainly, for he is himself the subject of almost every main verb in these verses. It is he who 'has blessed us' (verse 3), who 'chose us' (verse 4) and 'destined us . . . to be his sons' (verse 5), who 'freely bestowed on us' his grace (verse 6, literally 'graced us with his grace'), indeed 'lavished' his grace upon us (verse 8), who also 'made known to us' his will and purpose which he 'set forth in Christ . . . to unite all things' (verses 9–10). Further, he 'accomplishes all things according to the counsel of his will' (verse 11). Turning from the verbs to the nouns, Paul refers in quick succession to God's love and grace, to his will, his purpose and his plan. Thus the whole paragraph is full of God the Father who has set his love and poured his grace upon us, and who is working out his eternal plan.

[8] Hodge, p. 28.   [9] Barth, Ephesians, I, pp. 97–98.

Secondly, the sphere within which the divine blessing is bestowed and received is the Lord Jesus Christ. In the first fourteen verses of the Ephesian letter Jesus Christ is mentioned either by name or title ('Christ', 'Jesus Christ', 'Christ Jesus', 'the Lord Jesus Christ', 'the Beloved') or by pronoun or possessive ('he', 'him', 'his') no fewer than fifteen times. And the phrase 'in Christ' or 'in him' occurs eleven times. Already in the first verse the apostle has described Christians as 'saints' and 'believers' who are 'in Christ Jesus'. Now in the rest of the paragraph he draws out the implications of this pregnant expression which denotes a new principle of human solidarity. Formerly we were 'in Adam', belonging to the old fallen humanity; now we are 'in Christ', belonging to the new redeemed humanity. It is 'in Christ' that God has blessed us in time and chosen us in eternity (verses 3–4). It is 'in the Beloved' that he has bestowed on us his grace, so that 'in him' we have redemption or forgiveness (verses 6–7). It is 'in him' that the first Jewish believers became God's people (verses 11–12) and 'in him' also that Gentile believers were sealed as belonging to God (verses 13–14). It is also 'in Christ' that God has set forth his plan to unite all things 'in him' or under his headship (verses 9–10). Once we Gentiles were 'separated from Christ' and therefore hopeless and godless (2:12) but now 'in Christ' we have been overwhelmed with blessing.

Thirdly, there is the Holy Spirit. Although in this paragraph he is mentioned by name only in verses 13 and 14, his activity is assumed throughout, and his varied work is described in later chapters. What Paul stresses here is that the blessing God gives us in Christ is *spiritual*. A contrast is probably intended with Old Testament days when God's promised blessings were largely material. Perhaps the most striking example is to be found in Deuteronomy 28:1–14, where the blessings promised to an obedient Israel were many children, a good harvest, an abundance of cattle and sheep, and leadership among the nations. It is true Jesus also promised his followers some material blessings. For he forbade them to be anxious about food, drink and clothing and assured them that their heavenly Father would supply their needs if they put the

[left margin — curled page fragment]

the divine blessing
esus Christ. In the
ter Jesus Christ is
st', 'Jesus Christ',
'the Beloved',
s') no fewer than
r 'in him' occurs
the apostle has
ers' who are 'in
graph he draws
pression which
y. Formerly we
humanity; now
new redeemed
sed us in time
n the Beloved'
t 'in him' we
It is 'in him'
eople (verses
were sealed
'in Christ'
ngs 'in him'
ve Gentiles
peless and
erwhelmed

h in this
es 13 and
ried work
s here is
itual. A
nt days
naterial.
und in
d to an
est, an
ng the
some
xious
their
t the

[main column]

s nature is
ch may well
as the divine
ur hearts. As
e *spiritual* not
because derived
influence are the

which has made
call the 'liturgical'
benediction', writes
praise and prayer,
vish synagogues and
o Paul from the living
Christian tradition'.[9]
ner and detected in the
ke that of the Apostles'
lecting (verses 4–6), the
the Spirit sealing (versus
with the refrain 'to the
14). Although this is rather
ne trinitarian content of the

he source or origin of every
s initiative is set forth plainly,
of almost every main verb in
'has blessed us' (verse 3), who
destined us . . . to be his sons'
towed on us' his grace (verse 6,
his grace'), indeed 'lavished' his
who also 'made known to us' his
he 'set forth in Christ . . . to unite
Further, he 'accomplishes all things
sel of his will' (verse 11). Turning
nouns, Paul refers in quick succession
race, to his will, his purpose and his
le paragraph is full of God the Father
ve and poured his grace upon us, and
his eternal plan.

[9] Barth, *Ephesians*, I, pp. 97–98.

33

Secondly, the sphere within which
is bestowed and received is the Lord J
first fourteen verses of the Ephesian let
mentioned either by name or title ('Chr
'Christ Jesus', 'the Lord Jesus Christ',
by pronoun or possessive ('he', 'him', 'h
fifteen times. And the phrase 'in Christ'
eleven times. Already in the first verse
described Christians as 'saints' and 'believ
Christ Jesus'. Now in the rest of the par
out the implications of this pregnant e
denotes a new principle of human solidarit
were 'in Adam', belonging to the old fallen
we are 'in Christ', belonging to the
humanity. It is 'in Christ' that God has ble
and chosen us in eternity (verses 3–4). It is 'i
that he has bestowed on us his grace, so th
have redemption or forgiveness (verses 6–7).
that the first Jewish believers became God's
11–12) and 'in him' also that Gentile believers
as belonging to God (verses 13–14). It is als
that God has set forth his plan to unite all thi
or under his headship (verses 9–10). Once
were 'separated from Christ' and therefore h
godless (2:12) but now 'in Christ' we have been ov
with blessing.

Thirdly, there is the Holy Spirit. Althoug
paragraph he is mentioned by name only in vers
14, his activity is assumed throughout, and his va
is described in later chapters. What Paul stresse
that the blessing God gives us in Christ is *spi*
contrast is probably intended with Old Testam
when God's promised blessings were largely
Perhaps the most striking example is to be f
Deuteronomy 28:1–14, where the blessings promise
obedient Israel were many children, a good harv
abundance of cattle and sheep, and leadership amo
nations. It is true Jesus also promised his followers
material blessings. For he forbade them to be a
about food, drink and clothing and assured them tha
heavenly Father would supply their needs if they p

34

concerns of his rule and righteousness first. Nevertheless, the distinctive blessings of the new covenant are spiritual, not material; for example, God's law written in our hearts by the Holy Spirit, a personal knowledge of God, and the forgiveness of our sins.[1]

In order to put this beyond doubt Paul adds to his adjective 'spiritual' the clause *in the heavenly places*, or better—since no geographical location is implied—'in the heavenlies' (*en tois epouraniois*). This is the first occasion on which he uses this remarkable expression, which occurs five times in Ephesians and nowhere else in his letters. What does it mean? The word 'heaven' is used in Scripture in several different senses. Ancient authors used to distinguish between 'the heaven of nature' (the sky), 'the heaven of grace' (eternal life already received and enjoyed by God's people on earth) and 'the heaven of glory' (the final state of the redeemed). But 'the heavenlies' is to be understood differently from all these. It is neither sky, nor grace, nor glory, nor any literal spatial abode, but rather the unseen world of spiritual reality. The five uses of the expression in Ephesians indicate that 'the heavenlies' are the sphere in which the 'principalities and powers' continue to operate (3:10; 6:12), in which Christ reigns supreme and his people reign with him (1:20; 2:6), and in which therefore God blesses us with every spiritual blessing in Christ (1:3).

The teaching of verse 3 is thus seen to be extremely important. Christians are trinitarians. We believe in one God, the Father, the Son and the Holy Spirit. We affirm with gratitude and joy that God has blessed us (*eulogēsas*, an aorist tense) in Christ with every spiritual blessing. That is, every blessing of the Holy Spirit has been given us by the Father if we are in the Son. No blessing has been witheld from us. Of course we still have to grow into maturity in Christ, and be transformed into his image, and explore the riches of our inheritance in him. Of course, too, God may grant us many deeper and richer experiences of himself on the way. Nevertheless already, if we are in Christ, every spiritual blessing is ours. Or, as the apostle

[1] *E.g.* Je. 31:31–34.

puts it in Colossians, we 'have come to fullness of life in him.'[2]

Having stated the general principle, Paul moves on to the particulars. What are these blessings with which God has blessed us in Christ? In the rest of the paragraph he unfolds them. They relate to the past (*before the foundation of the world*, verse 4), the present (what *we have* in Christ now, verse 7) and the future (*the fullness of time*, verse 12). The past blessing is 'election', the present 'adoption' to be God's children, and the future 'unification' when all things will be united under Christ.

1. The past blessing of election (verses 4–6)

Paul reaches back in his mind *before the foundation of the world* (verse 4), before creation, before time began, into a past eternity in which only God himself existed in the perfection of his being.

In that pre-creation eternity God did something. He formed a purpose in his mind. This purpose concerned both *Christ* (his only begotten Son) and *us* (whom he proposed to make his adopted sons, and indeed daughters, for of course the word embraces both sexes). Mark well the statement: *he chose us in him*. The juxtaposition of the three pronouns is emphatic. God put us and Christ together in his mind. He determined to make us (who did not yet exist) his own children through the redeeming work of Christ (which had not yet taken place). It was a definite decision, for the verb *he chose* (*exelexato*) is another aorist. It also arose from his entirely unmerited favour, since he chose us *that we should be holy and blameless before him*, which indicates that we, when in his mind he chose us, were unholy and blameworthy, and therefore deserving not of adoption but of judgment. Further (Paul repeats the same truth in different words), *he destined us in love*[3] *to be his sons through Jesus Christ, according to the purpose of his will, to the praise of his glorious grace which he*

---

[2] Col. 2:10; *cf.* also 1 Cor. 3:21–23.

[3] AV, RV and NEB put the expression 'in love' immediately after 'holy and blameless before him', because they understand it as referring to the love which God wants to see in us. Thus holiness is defined in terms

36

freely bestowed on us in the Beloved (verses 5–6).

Now everybody finds the doctrine of election difficult. 'Didn't I choose God?' somebody asks indignantly; to which we must answer 'Yes, indeed you did, and freely, but only because in eternity God had first chosen you.' 'Didn't I decide for Christ?' asks somebody else; to which we must reply 'Yes, indeed you did, and freely, but only because in eternity God had first decided for you.'

Scripture nowhere dispels the mystery of election, and we should beware of any who try to systematize it too precisely or rigidly. It is not likely that we shall discover a simple solution to a problem which has baffled the best brains of Christendom for centuries. But here at least in our text are three important truths to grasp and remember:

a. The doctrine of election is a divine revelation, not a human speculation

It was not invented by Augustine of Hippo or Calvin of Geneva. On the contrary, it is without question a biblical doctrine, and no biblical Christian can ignore it. According to the Old Testament, God chose Israel out of all the nations of the world to be his special people.[4] According to the New Testament he is choosing an international community to be his 'saints' (verse 1), his holy or special people.[5] So we must not reject the notion of election as if it were a weird fantasy of men, but rather humbly accept it (even though we do not fully understand it) as a truth which God himself has revealed. It seems natural that at this point we should seek help from Calvin. He preached through Ephesians, from the pulpit of St Peter's church, Geneva, in forty-eight sermons beginning on 1

---

of love. This may well be the correct translation, since the words 'in love' occur in five more contexts of Ephesians and in each case describe Christian people (3:17; 4:2,15,16; 5:2). RSV, however, attaches the words to the verb 'destined us' because it understands them as referring to God's love, not ours. I myself favour this interpretation because the context appears to be emphasizing love as the source rather than the result of our election.

[4] *E.g.* 'you shall be my own possession among all peoples' (Ex. 19:4–6; *cf.* Dt. 7:6 ff; Is. 42:1 and 43:1).

[5] *Cf.* 1 Pet. 2:9–10.

May 1558. Here is one of his comments: 'Although we cannot conceive either by argument or reason how God has elected us before the creation of the world, yet we know it by his declaring it to us; and experience itself vouches for it sufficiently, when we are enlightened in the faith.'[6]

b. The doctrine of election is an incentive to holiness, not an excuse for sin

True, the doctrine gives us a strong assurance of eternal security, since he who chose and called us will surely keep us to the end. But our security cannot be used to condone, still less to encourage, sin. Some people seem to imagine a Christian talking to himself in such terms as these: 'I'm one of God's chosen people, safe and secure. So there's no need for me to bother about holiness. I can behave as I please.' Such appalling presumption finds no support in the true doctrine of election, however. Rather the reverse. For Paul here writes that God chose us in Christ in order *that we should be holy and blameless before him* (verse 4). 'Blameless' (*amōmos*) is the Old Testament word for an 'unblemished' sacrifice. 'Holy and blameless' as a couplet recurs in 5:27 and Colossians 1:22, where it points to our final state of perfection. But the process of sanctification begins in the here and now. So, far from encouraging sin, the doctrine of election forbids it and lays upon us instead the necessity of holiness. For holiness is the very purpose of our election. So ultimately the only evidence of election is a holy life. F. F. Bruce wisely comments: 'The predestinating love of God is commended more by those who lead holy and Christlike lives than by those whose attempts to unravel the mystery partake of the nature of logic-chopping.'[7]

c. The doctrine of election is a stimulus to humility, not a ground for boasting

Some people think that to believe oneself one of God's chosen people is about the most arrogant thought anybody

---

[6] Calvin, p. 69.   [7] Bruce, p. 28.

could entertain. And so it would be if we imagined that God had chosen us because of some merit of ours. But there is no room at all for merit in the biblical doctrine of election. The opposite is the case. God specifically explained to Israel that he had not chosen them because they out-matched the other nations in numbers or in any other way, for they did not. Why then? Simply because he loved them.[8] The reason why he chose them was in himself (love), not in them (merit). The same truth is hammered home in Ephesians. The emphasis of the whole first paragraph is on God's grace, God's love, God's will, God's purpose and God's choice. For he chose us in Christ, Paul declares, *before the foundation of the world*, which was before we existed, let alone could lay claim to any merit. So 'God's election is free and beats down and annihilates all the worthiness, works and virtues of men.'[9]

Therefore the truth of God's election, however many its unresolved problems, should lead us to righteousness, not to sin; and to humble adoring gratitude, not to boasting. Its practical consequences should always be that we live on the one hand *holy and blameless before him* (verse 4) and on the other *to the praise of his glorious grace* (verse 6).

2. The present blessing of adoption (verses 5–8)

God *destined us in love to be his sons*. This expression seems to be the key to our understanding of the present consequences of our election. Election is with a view to adoption. Indeed, when people ask us the speculative question why God went ahead with the creation when he knew that it would be followed by the fall, one answer we can tentatively give is that he destined us for a higher dignity than even creation would bestow on us. He intended to 'adopt' us, to make us the sons and daughters of his family. And in Roman law (part of the background to Paul's writing) adopted children enjoyed the same rights as natural children. The New Testament has much to say about this status of 'sonship', its rich privileges and

[8] Dt. 7:7–8.   [9] Calvin, p. 33.

demanding responsibilities. Both are touched upon in these verses.

Take our privilege first. It is only those who have been adopted into God's family who can say: *In him we have redemption through his blood, the forgiveness of our trespasses, according to the riches of his grace which he lavished upon us* (verses 7–8). For God's children enjoy a free access to their heavenly Father, and their confidence before him is due to the knowledge that they have been redeemed and forgiven. *Redemption* (*apolutrōsis*) means 'deliverance by payment of a price'; it was specially applied to the ransoming of slaves. Here it is equated with *forgiveness*, for the deliverance in question is a rescue from the just judgment of God upon our sins, and the price paid was the shedding of Christ's blood when he died for our sins on the cross. So redemption, forgiveness and adoption all go together;[1] redemption or forgiveness is a present privilege which *we have* and enjoy now. It makes possible a filial relation to God. It comes from the lavish outpouring of his grace upon us.

But sonship implies responsibility too. For the heavenly Father does not spoil his children. On the contrary, 'he disciplines us for our good, that we may share his holiness'.[2] So Paul's two statements are parallel, that 'he destined us . . . to be his sons' (verse 5) and 'he chose us . . . that we should be holy'. The apostle will return to this vital theme later: 'Be imitators of God, as his beloved children' (5:1). It is inconceivable that we should enjoy a relationship with God as his children without accepting the obligation to imitate our Father and cultivate the family likeness.

So then adoption as God's sons and daughters brings both a plus and a minus, an immense gain and a necessary loss. We gain access to him as our Father through redemption or forgiveness. But we lose our blemishes, beginning at once by the sanctifying work of the Holy Spirit, until we are finally made perfect in heaven. The words which seem to unite the privilege and the responsibility of our adoption are the expression *before him* (verse

---

[1] *Cf.* Gal. 4:5. [2] Heb. 12:10.

4), meaning 'in his sight' or 'in his presence'. For to live our life in the conscious presence of our Father is both an immeasurable privilege and a constant challenge to please him.

3. The future blessing of unification (verses 9–10)

God has done more than 'choose' us in Christ in a past eternity and give us 'sonship' now as a present possession, with all its attendant joys and duties. He has also *made known to us in all wisdom and insight the mystery of his will* for the future. It concerns *his purpose which he set forth in Christ as a plan for the fullness of time* (verses 9–10). For history is neither meaningless nor purposeless. It is moving towards a glorious goal. What, then, is this 'mystery' which God has 'made known', this revealed secret, this 'will' or 'purpose' or 'plan' of his? In chapter 3 the 'mystery' is the inclusion of Gentiles in God's new society on equal terms with Jews. But this present ethnic unity is a symbol or foretaste of a future unity that will be greater and more wonderful still.

God's plan 'for the fullness of the times', when time merges into eternity again, is *to unite all things in him* (Christ), *things in heaven and things on earth* (verse 10). The Greek verb translated 'unite' (*anakephalaioō*) 'is rich in allusion and significance'.[3] It was rare in secular Greek. According to Moulton and Milligan, although unknown in non-literary documents because too sophisticated for them, yet 'the commonness of *kephalaion* ("sum", "total") would make the meaning obvious even to ordinary readers'. Thus the verb *anakephalaioō* meant 'to bring something to a *kephalaion*' 'to sum up', either in the sense of 'summing up in reflection or speech' ('to condense into a summary'—Thayer) or in the sense of 'the gathering together of things'. The only other New Testament occurrence of the verb is in Romans 13:9, where all the commandments of the law's second table 'are summed up in this sentence, "You shall love your neighbour as yourself." '

The context of Ephesians 1 certainly seems to suit the notion of 'gathering together' better than that of 'con-

[3] *TDNT* I, p. 681.

41

densing'. For a little later, in verse 22, Paul will be affirming that God has made Jesus Christ 'the head (*kephalē*) over all things for the church'. So here he seems to be saying that 'the summing up of the totality takes place in its subjection to the Head'.[4] Already Christ is head of his body, the church, but one day 'all things' will acknowledge his headship. At present there is still discord in the universe, but in the fullness of time the discord will cease, and that unity for which we long will come into being under the headship of Jesus Christ.

This prospect prompts an important question: who and what will be included in this final unity and under this headship? A number of theologians both ancient and modern have seized on the expression 'all things' as a basis on which to build universalistic dreams. That is, they speculate that everybody is going to be saved in the end, that those who die impenitent will one day be brought to penitence, and that even demons will finally be redeemed, since literally 'all things, things in heaven and things on earth' are going to be gathered together into one under Christ's saving rule. One eloquent contemporary advocate of universalism is Markus Barth. True, he seems in one or two places to deny it, saying that we must not forget Christ's teaching about the unforgivable sin.[5] Yet the general impression he gives is plain. 'The Church . . . is Christ's living and growing body. The Church includes by this definition virtually all who are still unbelievers . . . Jesus Christ is not only "head of the Church". He is as much . . . head also of every man, whether that man believes in Christ or not.'[6] It is simply that all people do not yet know and acknowledge Christ, as the Church does. 'Therefore we may call the Church the firstfruit, the beginning, the example, the sign or the manifestation of that dominion and praise which are to be known universally and enjoyed consciously by all men. The Church is but a preliminary, transitory and serving institution. For the time being she is the only community on earth that consciously serves Jesus Christ.'[7] A little later, when commenting on the middle wall of partition which Jesus

[4] *TDNT* I, p. 682.   [5] Barth, *Broken Wall*, p. 255.
[6] *Ibid.*, p. 110.   [7] *Ibid.*, p. 139.

Christ has broken down, he declares: 'There is no wall between the Church and the world!' Yet many Christians meet behind the walls of church buildings and ecclesiastical traditions. 'A church. that secures herself against the world . . . can only learn from Ephesians that the world is right in treating it or bypassing it with the pity or contempt fit for the hypocrite'. Markus Barth rejects such a 'wall-church'. 'In conclusion', he writes, 'there is according to the gospel of peace *no* wall between the near and the far, between the Church and the world!'[8]

On reading his passionate assault on 'wall-churches', one suspects that he is reacting against the smug, withdrawn and loveless attitudes of some Christians today—and rightly so. If he means only that the church must not barricade itself against the world, but rather go out into it in compassionate service and witness, we would wholeheartedly agree with him. But he goes well beyond this to a declaration of 'solidarity' between church and world which refuses to recognize any distinction between them except that the one has come consciously to acknowledge Jesus Christ, while the other has not.

This refusal to accept a radical distinction between church and world, between the new society and the old, really cannot be defended from Ephesians. The dividing wall which Jesus has abolished is not the barrier which separates the world *from* the church; it is the barrier which segregates groups and individuals from one another *within* the church. Besides, the Ephesians' picture of the 'Gentiles' is not just that they are ignorant of salvation. Their condition is described in 4:17 ff. To their 'futility of mind' Paul adds 'hardness of heart'. They are alienated from God's life, live in darkness and are greedy for uncleanness. Twice the apostle calls them 'sons of disobedience' (once referring to their present state, and once to their future destiny) and in both contexts he alludes also to God's terrible but righteous wrath: they are 'children of wrath' now, and 'the wrath of God' will come upon them on the last day (2:3; 5:6).

So, returning to Ephesians 1:10, we cannot legitimately press the 'all things' into an argument for universal

8 *Ibid.*, pp. 144–146.

salvation, unless we are prepared to accuse Paul of theological confusion and self-contradiction. What, then, are the 'all things, things in heaven and things on earth' which will one day be united under Christ's headship? Certainly they include the Christian living and the Christian dead, the church on earth and the church in heaven. That is, those who are 'in Christ' now (verse 1), and who 'in Christ' have received blessing (verse 3), election (verse 4), adoption (verse 5), grace (verse 6), and redemption or forgiveness (verse 7), will one day be perfectly united 'in him' (verse 10). No doubt the angels will be included too (*cf.* 3:10,15). But 'all things' (*ta panta*) normally means the universe, which Christ created and sustains.[9] So Paul seems to be referring again to that cosmic renewal, that regeneration of the universe, that liberation of the groaning creation, of which he has already written to the Romans.[1] God's plan is that 'all things' which were created through Christ and for Christ, and which hold together in Christ,[2] will finally be united under Christ by being subjected to his headship. For the New Testament declares him to be 'the heir of all things'.[3]

So NEB translates verse 10, 'that the universe might be brought into a unity in Christ', and J. B. Lightfoot writes of 'the entire harmony of the universe, which shall no longer contain alien and discordant elements, but of which all the parts shall find their centre and bond of union in Christ.'[4]

In the fullness of time, God's two creations, his whole universe and his whole church, will be unified under the cosmic Christ who is the supreme head of both.

At this point it may be wise to pause a moment and consider how much all of us need to develop Paul's broad perspective. Let me remind you that he was a prisoner in Rome. Not indeed in a cell or dungeon, but still under house arrest and handcuffed to a Roman soldier. Yet, though his wrist was chained and his body was confined, his heart and mind inhabited eternity. He peered back 'before the foundation of the world' (verse 4) and on to

[9] Heb. 1.2–3.   [1] Rom. 8:18 ff; *cf.* Mt. 19:28; 2 Pet. 3:10–13.
[2] Col. 1:16–17.   [3] Heb. 1:2.   [4] Lightfoot, p. 322.

'the fullness of time' (verse 10), and grasped hold of what 'we have' now (verse 7) and ought to 'be' now (verse 4) in the light of those two eternities. As for us, how blinkered is our vision in comparison with his, how small is our mind, how narrow are our horizons! Easily and naturally we slip into a preoccupation with our own petty little affairs. But we need to see time in the light of eternity, and our present privileges and obligations in the light of our past election and future perfection. Then, if we shared the apostle's perspective, we would also share his praise. For doctrine leads to doxology as well as to duty. Life would become worship, and we would bless God constantly for having blessed us so richly in Christ.

4. The scope of these blessings (verses 11–14)

After describing the spiritual blessings which God gives to his people in Christ, Paul adds a further paragraph to emphasize that the blessings belong equally to Jewish and Gentile believers. The structure of the paragraph makes this plain: *in him ... we* (Jews) *who first hoped in Christ have been destined ... to live for the praise of his glory. In him you* (Gentiles) *also, who ... believed in him, were sealed with the promised Holy Spirit which is the guarantee of our inheritance ...* The apostle moves from the pronoun *we* (himself and his fellow Jewish believers) to *you also* (his believing Gentile readers) to *our* inheritance (in which both groups equally share). He is anticipating his theme of the reconciliation of Jews and Gentiles which he will elaborate in the second part of chapter 2. Already, however, by the repetition of the words *in him* (verses 11,13) he emphasizes that Christ is the reconciler, and that it is through union with Christ that the people of God are one. He shares with us three great truths about God's people.

a. God's people are God's possession

One would not guess from RSV that the truth of God's people as God's 'possession' was taught in this paragraph, but it almost certainly is. The apostle employs two Greek

45

expressions whose Old Testament background strongly suggests this meaning. The first is translated by RSV 'destined' (verse 12). It is the verb *klēroō*, which can mean to give or to receive a *klēros*, an inheritance. The question is to what inheritance Paul is referring. It could be ours, a gift which we have received. So NEB: 'In Christ . . . we have been given our share in the heritage.' Alternatively, it could be God's because he has taken us to be his own. RV understands it in this way: 'in whom also we were made a heritage'. So does Armitage Robinson: 'We have been chosen as God's portion.'[5] Linguistically, this translation is more natural. But, more important, the Old Testament background seems almost to demand it. Israel was God's *klēros*, his 'heritage'. Again and again this truth was repeated. For example, 'The Lord's portion is his people, Jacob his allotted heritage,' and 'Blessed is the nation whose God is the Lord, the people whom he has chosen as his heritage.'[6] Paul's use of the verb *klēroō* in this paragraph seems to indicate his conviction that all those who are in Christ, Gentiles as well as Jews, are now God's *klēros*, as only Israel was in Old Testament days.

This is confirmed by the second term he employs, which is also rich in Old Testament associations, and which comes at the end of the paragraph (verse 14). The AV translation is literal but unintelligible, namely 'until the redemption of the purchased possession' (*eis apolutrōsin tēs peripoiēseōs*). The question we have to ask about this 'possession' is the same question we asked above about the 'inheritance': is it ours or God's? RSV assumes it is ours: 'until *we* acquire possession of it'. But J. H. Houlden goes so far as to call this 'a loose and tendentious translation'.[7] It seems more probable that the possession (like the inheritance) is God's and that it again refers to his people. So NIV: 'until the redemption of those who are God's possession'. The main argument for interpreting it this way is once more the Old Testament background. For the noun *peripoiēsis* ('possession'), or its cognate adjective, occurs quite frequently

[5] Armitage Robinson, pp. 34, 146.
[6] *Cf.* the LXX version of Dt. 32:9; Ps. 33:12. *Cf.* Dt. 4:20; 9:29, 1 Kgs. 8:51; Ps. 106:40, 135:4; Je. 10:16; Zc. 2:12; *etc.*
[7] Houlden, p. 271.

in LXX as a description of Israel, *e.g.* 'You shall be my own possession among all peoples,' and 'The Lord your God has chosen you to be a people for his own possession.'[8] Certainly this phraseology is taken up in the New Testament in relation to the church which Christ has purchased for himself.[9]

Putting these two Greek expressions together, with their clear Old Testament background, it is difficult to resist the conclusion that Paul is alluding to the church as God's 'inheritance' and 'possession'. These words used to be applied exclusively to the one nation of Israel, but are now reapplied to an international people whose common factor is that they are all 'in Christ'. The fact that the same vocabulary is used of both peoples indicates the spiritual continuity between them.

This teaching, though entirely hidden by RSV and obscured by most of the English versions, is nevertheless basic to what Paul is writing in this paragraph. God's people are God's 'saints' (verse 1), God's heritage (verse 12), God's possession (verse 14). Only when that has been grasped, are we ready to ask two further questions. First, *how* did we become God's people? Secondly, *why* did he make us his people? Paul answers the first question by reference to God's will and the second by reference to his glory. And he states each truth three times.

b. God's people depend on God's will

How did we become God's people or possession? There can be no doubt about Paul's reply. It was by the will of God. He destined us to be his sons *according to the purpose of his will* (verse 5); he has made known to us *the mystery of his will according to his purpose* (verse 9); and we have become God's heritage *according to the purpose of him who accomplishes all things according to the counsel of his will* (verses 11–12). The whole passage is full of references to God's will (*thelēma*), good pleasure (*eudokia*) or purpose (*prothesis*), and to the plan or programme in

[8] See the LXX version of Ex. 19:5; Dt. 7:6. *Cf.* Dt. 14:2; 26:18; Is. 43:21; Mal. 3:17; *etc.*
[9] See Acts 20:28; Tit. 2.14 and 1 Pet. 2:9.

which these have been expressed. Paul could hardly have insisted more forcefully that our becoming members of God's new community was due neither to chance nor to choice (if by that is meant our choice), but to God's own sovereign will and pleasure. This was the decisive factor, as it is in every conversion.

Not that we were ourselves inactive, however. Far from it. In this very context, in which our salvation is attributed entirely to the will of God, our own responsibility is also described. For (verse 13) first *we heard the word of truth*, which is also called *the gospel of your salvation*; then we *believed in him* (Christ), and so *were sealed with the promised Holy Spirit*. Let no one say, therefore, that the doctrine of election by the sovereign will and mercy of God, mysterious as it is, makes either evangelism or faith unnecessary. The opposite is the case. It is only because of God's gracious will to save that evangelism has any hope of success and faith becomes possible. The preaching of the gospel is the very means that God has appointed by which he delivers from blindness and bondage those whom he chose in Christ before the foundation of the world, sets them free to believe in Jesus, and so causes his will to be done.[1]

And the assurance that God is thus active in the lives of his people is given through the Holy Spirit, who in verses 13 and 14 is given three designations—a 'promise', a 'seal' and a 'guarantee'. First he is (literally) 'the Spirit of the promise' because God promised through the Old Testament prophets and through Jesus to send him (which he did on the Day of Pentecost) and God promises to give him today to everyone who repents and believes (which he does).[2]

Secondly, the Holy Spirit is not only God's 'promise', but also God's 'seal'. A seal is a mark of ownership and of authenticity. Cattle, and even slaves, were branded with a seal by their masters, in order to indicate to whom they

[1] For a fuller exposition of this important theme see *Evangelism and the Sovereignty of God* by J. I. Packer (Inter-Varsity Press, 1961).

[2] See *e.g.* Ezk. 36:27; Joel 2:28; Jn. 14 – 16; Lk 24:49; Acts 1:4–5; 2:33,38–39; Gal. 3:14,16.

belonged. But such seals were external, while God's is in the heart. He puts his Spirit within his people in order to mark them as his own.[3]

Thirdly, the Holy Spirit is God's 'guarantee' or pledge, by which he undertakes to bring his people safely to their final inheritance. 'Guarantee' here is *arrabōn*, originally a Hebrew word which seems to have come into Greek usage through Phoenician traders. It is used in modern Greek for an engagement ring. But in ancient commercial transactions it signified a *'first instalment, deposit, down payment, pledge*, that pays a part of the purchase price in advance, and so secures a legal claim to the article in question, or makes a contract valid' (AG). In this case the guarantee is not something separate from what it guarantees, but actually the first portion of it. An engagement ring promises marriage but is not itself a part of the marriage. A deposit on a house or in a hire-purchase agreement, however, is more than a guarantee of payment; it is itself the first instalment of the purchase price. So it is with the Holy Spirit. In giving him to us, God is not just promising us our final inheritance but actually giving us a foretaste of it, which, however, 'is only a *small fraction* of the future endowment'.[4]

c. God's people live for God's glory

From the question *how* we became God's people, we now turn to the question *why* God made us his people, and so from his will to his glory. We saw earlier how three times Paul alluded to 'the purpose of his will' or something similar. Now we have to see that three times he alludes also to God's glory. He writes that God destined us to be his children *to the praise of his glorious grace* (5–6); that

[3] For the concept of 'sealing' see Ezk. 9:4 ff. and Rev. 7:4 ff.; 9:4. For the Holy Spirit as the Christian's distinguishing mark see 2 Cor. 1:21–22; Eph. 4:30. From the second century onwards some authors have identified the seal of the Spirit with baptism, partly because baptism and the gift of the Spirit are linked in the New Testament and partly by analogy with circumcision which Paul calls a seal (Rom. 4:11). But baptism is an outward and visible sign or seal, whereas the inward and invisible seal God gives to mark his people as his own is the presence of his Spirit in their hearts. See Rom. 8:16.

[4] Lightfoot, p. 324. *Cf.* 2 Cor. 1:22; 5:5; Rom. 8:23.

49

he made us his heritage and appointed us to live *for the praise of his glory* (verse 12); and that one day he will finally redeem his people who are his possession, *to the praise of his glory* (verse 14).

This beautiful phrase needs to be unpacked. The glory of God is the revelation of God, and the glory of his grace is his self-disclosure as a gracious God. To live to the praise of the glory of his grace is both to worship him ourselves by our words and deeds as the gracious God he is, and to cause others to see and to praise him too. This was God's will for Israel in Old Testament days,[5] and it is also his purpose for his people today. I myself shall always be grateful to one of my former colleagues at All Souls Church, who when he left our staff team for other work gave me a paperknife for my desk, having first had engraved upon it the words 'To the praise of his glory'. It lies before me as I write, and is a permanent reminder and challenge.

Here then are the 'how' and the 'why' of God's people, who are also his 'heritage' and his 'possession'. *How* did we become his people? Answer: 'According to the good pleasure of his will.' *Why* did he make us his people? Answer: 'For the praise of the glory of his grace.' Thus everything we have and are in Christ both comes from God and returns to God. It begins in his will and ends in his glory. For this is where everything begins and ends.

Yet such Christian talk comes into violent collision with the man-centredness and self-centredness of the world. Fallen man, imprisoned in his own little ego, has an almost boundless confidence in the power of his own will, and an almost insatiable appetite for the praise of his own glory. But the people of God have at least begun to be turned inside out. The new society has new values and new ideals. For God's people are God's possession who live by God's will and for God's glory.

[5] *E.g.* Is. 43:21; Je. 13:11.

2. A prayer for knowledge

For this reason, because I have heard of your faith in the Lord Jesus and your love toward all the saints, [16]I do not cease to give thanks for you, remembering you in my prayers, [17]that the God of our Lord Jesus Christ, the Father of glory, may give you a spirit of wisdom and of revelation in the knowledge of him, [18]having the eyes of your hearts enlightened, that you may know what is the hope to which he has called you, what are the riches of his glorious inheritance in the saints, [19]and what is the immeasurable greatness of his power in us who believe, according to the working of his great might [20]which he accomplished in Christ when he raised him from the dead and made him sit at his right hand in the heavenly places, [21]far above all rule and authority and power and dominion, and above every name that is named, not only in this age but also in that which is to come; [22]and he has put all things under his feet and has made him the head over all things for the church, [23]which is his body, the fullness of him who fills all in all.

Although Paul is naturally thinking of his Asian readers to whom he is writing, yet throughout the first chapter of his letter he addresses himself rather to God than to them. He begins with a great benediction (1:3–14) and continues with a great intercession (1:15–23). Ephesians 1 is, in fact, divided into these two sections. First, he blesses God for having blessed us in Christ; then he prays that

51

God will open our eyes to grasp the fullness of this blessing.

For a healthy Christian life today it is of the utmost importance to follow Paul's example and keep Christian praise and Christian prayer together. Yet many do not manage to preserve this balance. Some Christians seem to do little but pray for new spiritual blessings, apparently oblivious of the fact that God has already blessed them in Christ with every spiritual blessing. Others lay such emphasis on the undoubted truth that everything is already theirs in Christ, that they become complacent and appear to have no appetite to know or experience their Christian privileges more deeply. Both these groups must be declared unbalanced. They have created a polarization which Scripture will not tolerate. What Paul does in Ephesians 1, and therefore encourages us to copy, is both to keep praising God that in Christ all spiritual blessings are ours and to keep praying that we may know the fullness of what he has given us. If we keep together praise and prayer, benediction and petition, we are unlikely to lose our spiritual equilibrium.

As we continue to compare the two halves of Ephesians 1, another feature of them strikes us: both are essentially trinitarian. For both are addressed to God the Father, the benediction to 'the God and Father of our Lord Jesus Christ' (verse 3) and the intercession to 'the God of our Lord Jesus Christ' (verse 17), who is also called 'the Father of glory' or (NEB) 'the all-glorious Father'. Next, both refer specifically to God's work in and through Christ, for on the one hand he 'has blessed us in Christ' (verse 3) and on the other he 'accomplished in Christ' a mighty act of power when he resurrected and enthroned him (verse 20). And thirdly both sections of the chapter allude—even if obliquely—to the work of the Holy Spirit, since the blessings God bestows on us in Christ are 'spiritual' blessings (verse 3), and it is only 'by a spirit (or Spirit) of wisdom and of revelation' that we can come to know them (verse 17). I do not think it is far-fetched to discern this trinitarian structure. Christian faith and Christian life are both fundamentally trinitarian. And the one is a response to the other. It is because the Father has approached us in blessing through the Son and by the Spirit that we approach him in prayer through the Son and by the Spirit also (*cf.* 2:18).

What prompts Paul to launch into prayer for his readers is something he had heard about them. In the previous paragraph he has written in fairly general terms how he and his fellow Jewish Christians had 'first hoped in Christ' (verse 12) and how his readers as Gentile believers had 'heard the word of truth . . . and believed in' Christ (verse 13). Now he becomes more personal : *I have heard of your faith in the Lord Jesus and your love toward all the saints.* Strangely, the best manuscripts omit the words 'your love'. Without them 'the Lord Jesus' and 'all the saints' become bracketed as the object of the Ephesians' faith. So unusual is this notion of faith in Christians as well as in Christ, and so unlike anything Paul writes elsewhere, that we are faced with a choice. Either we must follow Markus Barth in translating 'faith' as 'faithfulness' or 'loyalty', which is 'something similar to love'[1] and could conceivably be directed to both Christ and Christians, or we must conclude, even against the strong manuscript evidence, that the words 'your love' were indeed dictated by Paul but somehow got dropped out by an early copyist. In the latter case we have the familiar couplet of faith in Christ and love for his people, which is exactly paralleled in Colossians 1:4. Every Christian both believes and loves. Faith and love are basic Christian graces, as also is hope, the third member of the triad, which has already been mentioned in verse 12 and occurs again in verse 18. It is impossible to be in Christ and not to find oneself drawn both to him in trust and to his people in love (to *all* of them too, in this case Jews and Gentiles without distinction).

Having heard of their Christian faith and love, Paul says he continuously thanks God for them (acknowledging him as the author of both qualities), and then encompasses them with his prayers. For despite his unceasing gratitude to God for them, he is still not satisfied with them. So what is his request? It is not that they may receive a 'second blessing', but rather that they may appreciate to

[1] Barth, *Ephesians*, I, p. 146.

the fullest possible extent the implications of the blessing they have already received. So the essence of his prayer for them is *that you may know* (verse 18). Although his other recorded prayers range more widely than this, they all include a similar petition either for 'power to comprehend' (3:18) or for 'the knowledge of his will in all wisdom and understanding'[2] or for 'knowledge and all discernment'.[3] We must not overlook this emphasis. Growth in knowledge is indispensable to growth in holiness. Indeed, knowledge and holiness are even more intimately linked than as means and end. For the 'knowledge' for which Paul prays is more Hebrew than Greek in concept; it adds the knowledge of experience to the knowledge of understanding. More than this, it emphasizes *the knowledge of him* (verse 17), of God himself personally, as the context within which we *may know what is* . . . (verse 18), that is, may come to know truths about him. There is no higher knowledge than the knowledge of God himself. As Adolphe Monod expressed it: 'Philosophy taking man for its centre says *know thyself*; only the inspired word which proceeds from God has been able to say *know God*.'[4]

Such knowledge is impossible without revelation. So Paul prays that God *may give you a spirit of wisdom and of revelation in the knowledge of him* (verse 17). Although RSV writes 'spirit' with a small 's', the reference is likely to be to the Holy Spirit, since Scripture speaks of him as 'the Spirit of truth', the agent of revelation, and the teacher of the people of God. Not that we can ask God to 'give' the Holy Spirit himself to those who have already received him and been 'sealed' with him (verse 13), but rather that we may and should pray for his ministry of illumination. It is because of his confidence in this ministry of the Spirit that Paul can continue his prayer: *having the eyes of your hearts enlightened, that you may know* . . . In biblical usage the heart is the whole inward self, comprising mind as well as emotion. So 'the eyes of the heart' are simply our 'inner eyes', which need to be opened or 'enlightened' before we can grasp God's truth.

The apostle now brings together three great truths which

[2] Col. 1:9.   [3] Phil. 1:9.   [4] Quoted by Findlay, p. 68.

he wants his readers (though the enlightenment of the Holy Spirit) to know in mind and experience. They concern God's call, inheritance and power. More particularly, he prays that they may know the 'hope' of God's call, the 'glory' (indeed 'the riches of the glory') of his inheritance, and the 'greatness' (indeed 'the immeasurable greatness') of his power.

1. The hope of God's call

The call of God takes us back to the very beginning of our Christian lives. 'Those whom he predestined he also called; and those whom he called he also justified.'[5] True, we called on him to save us,[6] but our call was a response to his.

The question now is: what did God call us for? His call was not a random or purposeless thing. He had some object in view when he called us. He called us to something and for something. And it is this that is meant by 'the hope of his call' (verse 18, literally) which in 4:4 is referred to as the 'hope of *your* call'. It is the expectation which we enjoy as a result of the fact that God has called us.

What this is the rest of the New Testament tells us. It is a rich and varied expectation. For God has called us 'to belong to Jesus Christ' and 'into the fellowship of . . . Jesus Christ.'[7] He has called us 'to be saints' or 'called us with a holy calling', since he who has called us is holy himself and says to us 'you shall be holy, for I am holy'.[8] One of the characteristics of the 'holy' or special people of God is liberation from the judgment of God's law. So we are not to lapse into slavery again, for we were 'called to freedom'.[9] Another characteristic is harmonious fellowship across the barriers of race and class, for we 'were called in the one body' to enjoy 'the peace of Christ', and must live a life that is 'worthy of the calling to which we have been called . . . forbearing one another in love.'[1] At the same time, though we may enjoy peace within the Christian community, we are bound to experience opposition from

[5] Rom. 8:30.   [6] Rom. 10:12–13.   [7] Rom. 1:6; 1 Cor. 1:9.
[8] Rom. 1:7; 1 Cor. 1:2; 2 Tim. 1:9; 1 Pet. 1:15; *cf.* 1 Thes. 4:7.
[9] Gal. 5:1,13.   [1] Col. 3:15; Eph. 4:1–2.

the unbelieving world. Yet we must not retaliate: 'For to this (this unjust suffering and this patient endurance) you have been called, because Christ also suffered for you, leaving you an example, that you should follow in his steps.'[2] Besides, we know that beyond the suffering lies the glory. For God has also called us 'into his own kingdom and glory' or 'to his eternal glory in Christ'. This is what Paul calls 'the upward call of God in Christ Jesus', for the sake of which he presses on in the Christian race towards the goal.[3]

All this was in God's mind when he called us. He called us to Christ and holiness, to freedom and peace, to suffering and glory. More simply, it was a call to an altogether new life in which we know, love, obey and serve Christ, enjoy fellowship with him and with each other, and look beyond our present suffering to the glory which will one day be revealed. This is *the hope to which he has called you*. Paul prays that our eyes may be opened to know it.

2. The glory of God's inheritance

The apostle's second prayer to God is that we may know *what are the riches of his glorious inheritance in the saints* (verse 18b). The Greek expression, like the English, could mean either God's inheritance or ours, that is, either the inheritance he receives or the inheritance he bestows. Some commentators take it in the former sense and understand it to refer to the inheritance which God possesses among his people. Certainly the Old Testament authors taught consistently that God's people were his 'inheritance' or 'possession', and in the last chapter we found a reference to this truth in verses 12 and 14. But the parallel passage in Colossians 1:12 strongly suggests the other interpretation here, namely that 'God's inheritance' refers to what he will give us, for we are to give thanks to the Father, 'who has qualified us to share in the inheritance of the saints in light'.

In this case, if God's 'call' points back to the beginning

of our Christian life, God's 'inheritance' points on to its end, to that final inheritance of which the Holy Spirit is the guarantee (verse 14) and which Peter describes as 'imperishable, undefiled and unfading, kept in heaven for you'.[4] For God's children are God's heirs, in fact 'fellow heirs with Christ',[5] and one day by his grace the inheritance will be ours. Exactly what it will be like is beyond our capacity to imagine. So we shall be wise not to be too dogmatic about it. Nevertheless certain aspects of it have been revealed in the New Testament, and we shall not go wrong if we hold fast to these. We are told that we shall 'see' God and his Christ, and worship him; that this 'beatific' vision will be a transforming vision, for 'when he appears we shall be like him', not only in body but in character; and that we shall enjoy perfect fellowship with each other. For God's inheritance (the inheritance he gives us) will not be a little private party for each individual but rather 'among the saints' as we join that 'great multitude which no man could number, from every nation, from all tribes and peoples and tongues, standing before the throne and before the Lamb'.[6]

Paul does not regard it as presumptuous that we should think about our heavenly inheritance or even anticipate it with joy and gratitude. On the contrary, he prays that we may 'know it', the 'glory' of it, indeed, 'the riches of the glory' of it.

3. The greatness of God's power

If God's 'call' looks back to the beginning, and God's 'inheritance' looks on to the end, then surely God's 'power' spans the interim period in between. It is on this that the apostle concentrates, for only God's power can fulfil the expectation which belongs to his call and bring us safely to the riches of the glory of the final inheritance he will give us in heaven. Paul is convinced that God's power is sufficient, and he accumulates words to convince us. He

---

[4] 1 Pet. 1:4.   [5] Rom. 8:17.

[6] For the New Testament's teaching about our heavenly inheritance, alluded to here, see Rev. 22:3–4; 1 Jn. 3:2; Phil. 3:21; Rev. 7:9; *cf.* Acts 20:32.

writes not only of God's 'power', but also of 'the energy of the might of his strength' (a literal rendering of *the working of his great might*, verse 19), and he prays that we may know *the greatness* of it, indeed the *immeasurable* greatness of it *in* (better 'for' or 'towards') *us who believe*.

How shall we come to know the surpassing greatness of the power of God? Because he has given a public demonstration of it in the resurrection and exaltation of Christ (verses 20–23). Paul actually refers to three successive events: first, *he raised him from the dead* (verse 20a); secondly, he *made him sit at his right hand in the heavenly places*, far above all competitors (verses 20b, 21), and *has put all things under his feet* (verse 22a); and thirdly, *he has made him the head over all things for the church, which is his body . . .* (verses 22b, 23). These three belong together. It is because of Christ's resurrection from the dead and enthronement over the powers of evil that he has been given headship over the church. The resurrection and ascension were a decisive demonstration of divine power. For if there are two powers which man cannot control, but which hold him in bondage, they are death and evil. Man is mortal; he cannot avoid death. Man is fallen; he cannot overcome evil. But God in Christ has conquered both, and therefore can rescue us from both.

a. Jesus Christ's resurrection from the dead

Death is a bitter and relentless enemy. It will come to all of us one day. A few years ago I was summoned to a London hospital to visit a parishioner who had been admitted as an emergency. I expected to find her at death's door, but instead she was sitting up in bed and smiling. 'When I was brought in', she said, 'the doctors and nurses all gathered round me as if I was going to die. But I decided I wasn't going to die!' It was a spirited remark, but not an entirely accurate one. That lady has, in fact, since died. For we may succeed in postponing death; we cannot escape it. And after death nothing can stop the process of decay and decomposition. Even the most sophisticated embalming techniques of modern American morticians cannot preserve the body for ever. No. We are dust, and to dust we shall inevitably return.[7] No human power can prevent this, let alone bring a dead person back to life.

But God has done what man cannot do. He raised Jesus Christ from the dead. First, he arrested the natural process of decay, refusing to allow his Holy One to see corruption.[8] Then he did not just reverse the process, restoring the dead Jesus to this life, but transcended it. He raised Jesus to an altogether new life (immortal, glorious and free), which nobody had ever experienced before, and which nobody has experienced since—or not yet.

This was the first part of the public display of God's power. He raised Jesus from the dead to a new dimension of human experience. The empty tomb and the resurrection appearances were the evidence. It would be quite impossible, therefore, to square Paul's teaching in this passage with the attempted reconstructions of the demythologizers. Rudolph Bultmann will always be remembered for his thesis that 'Christ has risen into the *kerygma*'. That is, he did not rise in any objective historical or physical sense, but only in the recovered faith and in the triumphant proclamation (*kerygma*) of his disciples. But what Paul sets forth here as a demonstration of divine power is what *he accomplished in Christ*, not in his followers.

b. Jesus Christ's enthronement over evil

Having raised Jesus from among the dead and out of the domain of death, God *made him sit at his right hand in the heavenly places* (verse 20). That is, he promoted him to the place of supreme honour and executive authority. In doing so, he fulfilled the messianic promise of Psalm 110:1: 'The Lord says to my Lord: "Sit at my right hand, till I make your enemies your footstool." ' Reminiscences of this verse are to be found not only in the references to God's 'right hand' and to Christ's being made to 'sit' there, but also in the later statement that God has put all things 'under his feet', thus making them his 'footstool'. In Psalm 110 his footstool consists of his 'enemies'. It seems safe to assume, therefore, that the 'principalities and

[7] Gn. 3:19.   [8] Acts 2:27.

powers' above which he has been exalted (*all rule and authority and power and dominion*) are here not angels but demons, those 'world rulers of this present darkness' or 'spiritual hosts of wickedness' against which Paul later summons us to fight,[9] although, to be sure, they have not yet finally conceded Christ's victory.[1] The more general expression which follows, *every name that is named, not only in this age but also in that which is to come* (verse 21b), may be added in order to include angels as well, indeed every conceivable intelligent being, over whom Christ reigns in absolute supremacy.

That all things are now under the feet of Jesus is probably also an allusion to another strand of biblical teaching. Adam made in God's likeness was given dominion over the earth and its creatures, and did not altogether forfeit it when he fell into disobedience. On the contrary, the Psalmist in his meditation on the record of man's creation in Genesis 1 addresses God in these words: 'Thou hast given him dominion over the works of thy hands; thou hast put all things under his feet, all sheep and oxen, and also the beasts of the field, the birds of the air, and the fish of the sea . . .'[2] Yet man's dominion has been limited by the fall, and is distorted whenever he exploits or pollutes the environment, whose responsible steward he was originally appointed to be. So the full dominion which God intended man to enjoy is now exercised only by the man Christ Jesus: 'We do not yet see everything in subjection to him (*sc.* man). But we see Jesus . . . crowned with glory and honour . . .'[3] Already Jesus has dethroned death, and one day this 'last enemy' will be finally destroyed .[4]

c. Jesus Christ's headship of the church

Still Paul has not finished his account of the sovereign exaltation of Jesus. He has written of his resurrection *from the dead* (verse 20) and of his enthronement *far above all rule* (verse 21); but now he goes on to relate the meaning

[9] 6:12; see discussion there of the identity of these 'powers'.
[1] 1 Cor. 15:25; Heb. 10:13   [2] Gn. 1:27–28; Ps. 8:6–8.
[3] Heb. 2:5–9.   [4] Heb. 2:14,15; 1 Cor. 15:25–27.

of this double triumph *for the church* (verse 22). This further truth he outlines in two pregnant expressions, both of which have caused much trouble to commentators. The first is that God *made* Jesus *the head over all things for the church which is his body* (verses 22–23a), and the second is the phrase *the fullness of him who fills all in all* (23b). Difficult as these clauses are, they are so important that we must spend a little time seeking to fathom them.

The first speaks of Jesus as 'head', and assigns him a headship which extends over 'all things'. 'All things' are mentioned twice in verse 22, and in the context embrace not only the material universe but also and especially all intelligent beings good and evil, angelic and demonic, who people it. This universe and these beings Christ rules. Since 'all things' have been put under his feet by God, he is thereby 'the head over all things'. The 'head' and the 'feet', the 'over' and the 'under', are obviously complementary.

But Paul goes further than this. His point is not just that God made Jesus head over all things but that he 'gave' (*edōke*) him as head-over-all-things *to the church which is his body*. For he whom God gave to the church to be its head was already head of the universe. Thus both universe and church have in Jesus Christ the same head.

The other puzzling expression, on the elucidation of which gallons of printer's ink have been expended, is the final one, *the fullness of him who fills all in all*. All readers of Ephesians ought to be aware of the three main alternative explanations of these words. As far as grammar and language are concerned all three are possible, and all three have had distinguished advocates. If I tentatively opt for the third, it is on consideration of context and the analogy of Scripture, rather than of grammar and vocabulary. But the reader must make up his own mind.

The first explanation takes the phrase as a description not of the church (the body) but of Christ (the head), *i.e.* '. . . the church, which is the body of him who is the fullness of him who fills all in all'. In this case Paul is saying not that the church is the fullness of Christ, but that Christ is the fullness of God, who fills Christ as indeed he fills all things. At first sight this is an attractive

61

interpretation. It fits the context of Christ's supremacy. It also has parallels in Scripture, for God is said elsewhere to 'fill heaven and earth',[5] and in Colossians the fullness of the Godhead is said to dwell in Christ.[6] Also this interpretation has had learned proponents, including among the fathers Theodoret, and in modern times C. F. D. Moule of Cambridge[7] and G. B. Caird of Oxford.[8] Yet the difficulties are considerable. For one thing the syntax is awkward, requiring God to be both subject and object of the same sentence ('God . . . gave as head to the church Christ who is the fullness of God'). For another the parallels are not exact. Colossians indeed says that God's fullness dwells 'in Christ', but stops short of identifying Christ with God's fullness. Hodge goes so far as to say that the latter identification is 'unscriptural': 'The fullness of the Godhead is said to be in Christ; but Christ is never said to be the fullness of God.'[9] And there is another inexact parallel. In both Ephesians and Colossians it is Christ, not God, who 'fills all things'.[1]

If, then, we hesitatingly reject this first explanation, we move on to two more, both of which take 'the fullness' as being a description of the church rather than of Christ. These verses do in fact contain the first use of the word 'church' in Ephesians. It is first identified as Christ's 'body', and then as his 'fullness', *the fullness of him who fills all in all.* The difficulty here is that the noun 'fullness' (*plērōma*) can have either an active or a passive meaning. Actively, it means 'that which fills' or the 'contents' of something; passively it means 'that which is filled or full', not the contents but the container. Both senses have been applied to the text we are considering.

Take the active sense first: 'that which fills or completes'. Scholars are agreed that this is the commoner use of *plērōma*. In classical Greek it was used of the contents of a bowl or basin, and of either a ship's cargo or a ship's crew. And this active meaning is frequent in the New Testament. Thus, the fragments of loaves and fishes which

---

[5] Je. 23:24; *cf.* 1 Kgs. 8:27; Ps. 139:7. [6] 1:19; 2:9.
[7] *Colossians and Philemon* (Cambridge University Press, 1957), p. 168.
[8] Caird, p. 48. [9] Hodge, p. 88. [1] Eph. 4:10; Col. 1:16–17.

filled the baskets are *plērōmata*.[2] *Plērōma* is the word used
for a 'patch' of new, unshrunk cloth which when sewn on
to an old garment fills up the hole or tear.[3] Again, in the
quotation from Psalm 24:1, 'the earth is the Lord's', the
Greek for 'and everything in it' is 'and its fullness', *i.e.*
its contents.[4] And we have already seen that God's fullness
dwells in Christ, meaning that whatever fills the Father
also fills the Son.[5]

If this is the sense of *plērōma* in Ephesians 1:23, then
the church is said to 'fill' or to 'complete' Christ, and
Christ is represented as incomplete without it. One cannot
deny that this sense is compatible with the head-body
metaphor which Paul has just employed. Thus, the church
is 'the complement of Christ who is the head' (AG), 'just
as the body is the necessary complement of the head in
order to make up a complete man'.[6] Startling as this
thought is, notable commentators of the past and the
present have embraced it. Calvin took this view: 'By this
word "fullness" he means that our Lord Jesus Christ and
even God his Father account themselves imperfect, unless
we are joined to him . . . as if a father should say, My
house seems empty to me when I do not see my child in
it. A husband will say, I seem to be only half a man when
my wife is not with me. After the same manner God says
that he does not consider himself full and perfect, except
by gathering us to himself and by making us all one with
himself.'[7] Rather similarly William Hendriksen writes of
Christ: 'As bridegroom he is incomplete without the bride;
as vine he cannot be thought of without the branches; as
shepherd he is not seen without his sheep; and so also as
head he finds his full expression in his body, the church.'[8]
In the same reformed tradition Charles Hodge leans to this
interpretation, and bases his decision on the linguistic
evidence: 'In every other case in which it occurs in the
New Testament it (sc. *plērōma*) is used actively—*that which
doth fill* . . . The common usage of the word in the New
Testament is . . . clearly in favour of its being taken in

[2] Mk. 6:43; *cf.* 8:20.   [3] Mk. 2:21; Mt. 9:16.   [4] 1 Cor.10:26.
[5] Col. 1:19; 2:9.   [6] Bruce, p. 45.
[7] Calvin, pp. 122–3.   [8] Hendriksen, p. 104.

63

an active sense here.'[9]

Further, the following participle can be translated in such a way as to support this explanation. True, *plēroumenou* could be in the middle voice and so have an active sense. It is so taken by AV and RSV, 'him who fills'. But it could equally be passive ('who is being filled'). So the ancient versions (*e.g.* Latin, Syriac and Egyptian) took it, and the great Greek commentators Origen and Chrysostom. Then the active noun and the passive verb fit neatly into each other, and the church is 'that which fills Christ who is being filled by it'. Of the more modern commentators it is Armitage Robinson who has been the most successful in popularizing this interpretation. Affirming that this is 'perhaps the most remarkable expression in the whole epistle',[1] he goes on to explain it: 'In some mysterious sense the church is that without which the Christ is not complete, but with which he is or will be complete. That is to say, he (*sc.* Paul) looks upon the Christ as in a sense waiting for completeness, and destined in the purpose of God to find completeness in the church.'[2] So he paraphrases: 'The Head finds completeness in the Body: the Church is the completion of the Christ: for the Christ is being *all in all fulfilled*, is moving towards a completeness absolute and all-inclusive.'[3]

Now we come to the third alternative, which takes *plērōma* in its passive sense, not as 'that which fills' but as 'that which is filled', not the contents but the filled container. According to AG this is 'much more probably the meaning here'. If so, then the church is the fullness of Christ not because it fills him, but because he fills it. And he who fills it is described either as filling 'all things', 'the whole creation' (JB), which is precisely what he is said to do in 4:9,10, or as himself being filled, *i.e.* by God as in Colossians 1:19 and 2:9. Putting the two parts of the clause together, it will then mean either that Christ who fills the church fills the universe also, or that Christ who fills the church is himself filled by God. The former is the more natural because God is not mentioned by name. But

[9] Hodge, pp. 89–90.   [1] Armitage Robinson, p. 42.
[2] *Ibid*, pp. 42, 43, *cf. ibid*., p. 259.   [3] *Ibid*., p. 45.

in either case the church is Christ's 'fullness' in the sense that it fills it.

After considerable reflection on the whole passage and on the expositions of ·many commentators, I have come to think that this last alternative is the most likely to be the correct interpretation, for three reasons. First, because of the analogy of Scripture. The safest of all principles of biblical interpretation is to allow Scripture to explain Scripture. Certainly nowhere else in Scripture is the church explicitly said to 'fill' or 'complete' Christ,[4] whereas constantly Christ is said to indwell and fill his church. For the church is God's temple (2:21–22). As his glory filled the Jerusalem temple, so today Jesus Christ who is the glory of God fills the church by his Spirit.

Next, the context confirms this. In the latter part of Ephesians 1 Paul refers to the resurrection and enthronement of Jesus as the outstanding historical display of God's power. His emphasis throughout is on the lordship and the sovereignty of Jesus over all things. For him to go on to say that the church somehow 'completes' this supreme Christ would seem very incongruous. A more appropriate conclusion would surely be to stress how this supreme Christ fills his church, as he also fills the universe.

The third argument concerns the bracketing in verse 23 of his 'body' and his 'fullness' as successive descriptions of the church. Being in apposition to one another it would be natural to expect both pictures to illustrate at least a similar truth, namely Christ's rule over his church. The church is his 'body' (he directs it); the church is his 'fullness' (he fills it). Further, both teach Christ's double rule over universe and church. For on the one hand God gave Christ to the church as head-over-all-things (verse 22), and on the other the church is filled by Christ who also fills all things (verse 23). It is this which leads Markus Barth to go further and propose an actual fusion of the metaphors. Pointing out that the 'body' and the 'fullness' images come together in Ephesians 4:13–16 and Colossians 1:18–19 as

---

[4] It is true that in Col. 1:24 Paul claims that his sufferings 'complete' Christ's, but the reference is specifically to suffering, and indeed to his own sufferings, not to the church's.

well as here, and that medical writers of approximately Paul's time, like Hippocrates and Galen, thought of the head or brain as controlling and coordinating the functions of the body, Dr Barth summarizes Paul's understanding that 'the head fills the body with powers of movement and perception, and thereby inspires the whole body with life and direction'.[5]

Conclusion

It is time now to step back from the detailed questions which have necessarily been occupying us and survey the sweep of Paul's prayer for his readers. To me one of its most impressive features is his emphasis on the importance for Christian maturity of 'knowledge' (*that you may know*), together with his teaching on how knowledge is attained and how it is related to faith. For in this apostolic instruction he unites what we moderns, with disastrous consequences, too often separate.

a. Enlightenment and thought

The whole thrust of Paul's prayer is that his readers may have a thorough knowledge of God's call, inheritance and power, especially the latter. But how did he expect his prayer to be answered? How do Christians grow in understanding? Some will reply that knowledge depends on the enlightenment of the Holy Spirit. And they are right, at least in part. For Paul prays that 'the Spirit of wisdom and revelation' may increase their knowledge of God and enlighten the eyes of their hearts. We have no liberty to infer from this, however, that our responsibility is solely to pray and to wait for illumination, and not at all to think. Others make the opposite mistake: they use their minds and think, but leave little room for the enlightenment of the Holy Spirit.

The apostle Paul brings the two together. First he prays that the eyes of his readers' hearts may be enlightened to know God's power. Then he teaches that God has already

[5] Barth, *Ephesians*, I, p. 208. See his lengthy excursus on 'Head, Body and Fullness', pp. 183–210.

supplied historical evidence of his power by raising and exalting Jesus. Thus, God has revealed his power objectively in Jesus Christ, and now illumines our minds by his Spirit to grasp this revelation. Divine illumination and human thought belong together. All our thinking is unproductive without the Spirit of truth; yet his enlightenment is not intended to save us the trouble of using our minds. It is precisely as we ponder what God has done in Christ that the Spirit will open our eyes to grasp its implications.

b. Knowledge and faith

It is commonly assumed that faith and reason are incompatible. This is not so. The two are never contrasted in Scripture, as if we had to choose between them. Faith goes beyond reason, but rests on it. Knowledge is the ladder by which faith climbs higher, the springboard from which it leaps further.

So Paul prayed: 'that you may know . . . what is the immeasurable greatness of his power in (better, 'for' or 'towards') us who *believe* . . . which he accomplished in Christ . . .' It is vital to see how Paul brings together the verbs 'to know' and 'to believe'. The very same resurrection power which God exhibited in Christ is now available for us. First we are to know its surpassing greatness as demonstrated in Christ's resurrection and enthronement, and then we are to lay hold of it experimentally for ourselves by faith. Of course we are already believers. Our faith has already been mentioned in verses 1, 13 and 15. But now the present participle *pisteuontas* (verse 19) emphasizes the need for the continuing exercise of faith in the apprehension of God's power. Thus knowledge and faith need each other. Faith cannot grow without a firm basis of knowledge; knowledge is sterile if it does not bring forth faith.

How much do we know of the power of God, which raised Jesus from death and enthroned him over evil? True, the very same power of God has raised us with Jesus from spiritual death, and enthroned us with Jesus in heavenly places, as Paul will go on to show in 2:1–10. But how much of this is theory, and how much is experience? It is not difficult to think of our human weakness: our tongue or our temper, malice, greed, lust, jealousy or pride. These things are certainly beyond our power to control. And we have to humble ourselves to admit it. 'The words the apostle uses here are so many thunderclaps and lightnings, to beat down and subdue all the pride of man.'[6] But are our weaknesses beyond the power of God? Paul will soon assure us that God is able far to surpass our thoughts and prayers 'by the power at work within us' (3:20), and he will go on to exhort us to 'be strong in the Lord and in the strength of his might' (6:10). This is the power of God which raised Jesus from the dead, and raised us with him. It has put all things under his feet; it can put all evil under ours.

[6] Calvin, p. 109.

2:1–10

3. Resurrected with Christ

I sometimes wonder if good and thoughtful people have ever been more depressed about the human predicament than they are today. Of course every age is bound to have a blurred vision of its own problems, because it is too close to them to get them into focus. And every generation breeds new prophets of doom. Nevertheless, the media enable us to grasp the worldwide extent of contemporary evil, and it is this which makes the modern scene look so dark. It is partly the escalating economic problem (population growth, the spoliation of natural resources, inflation, unemployment, hunger), partly the spread of social conflict (racism, tribalism, the class struggle, disintegrating family life) and partly the absence of accepted moral guidelines (leading to violence, dishonesty and sexual promiscuity). Man seems incapable of managing his own affairs or of creating a just, free, humane and tranquil society. For man himself is askew.

Against the sombre background of our world today Ephesians 2:1–10 stands out in striking relevance. Paul first plumbs the depths of pessimism about man, and then rises to the heights of optimism about God. It is this combination of pessimism and optimism, of despair and faith, which constitutes the refreshing realism of the Bible. For what Paul does in this passage is to paint a vivid contrast between what man is by nature and what he can become by grace.

And you he made alive, when you were dead through the trespasses and sins ²in which you once walked, following

*the course of this world, following the prince of the power
of the air, the spirit that is now at work in the sons of
disobedience. ³Among these we all once lived in the passions
of our flesh, following the desires of body and mind, and
so we were by nature children of wrath, like the rest of
mankind. ⁴But God, who is rich in mercy, out of the great
love with which he loved us, ⁵even when we were dead
through our trespasses, made us alive together with Christ
(by grace you have been saved), ⁶and raised us up with
him, and made us sit with him in the heavenly places in
Christ Jesus, ⁷that in the coming ages he might show the
immeasurable riches of his grace in kindness toward us in
Christ Jesus. ⁸For by grace you have been saved through
faith; and this is not your own doing, it is the gift of
God—⁹not because of works, lest any man should boast.
¹⁰For we are his workmanship, created in Christ Jesus for
good works, which God prepared beforehand, that we
should walk in them.*

It is important to set this paragraph in its context. We
have been considering Paul's prayer (1:15–23) that his
readers' inward eyes might be enlightened by the Holy
Spirit to know the implications of God's call to them, the
wealth of his inheritance which awaits them in heaven and
above all the surpassing greatness of his power which is
available for them meanwhile. Of this power God has
given a supreme historical demonstration by raising Christ
from the dead and exalting him over all the powers of evil.
But he has given a further demonstration of it by raising
and exalting us with Christ, and so delivering us from the
bondage of death and evil. This paragraph, then, is really
a part of Paul's prayer that they (and we) might know how
powerful God is. Its first few words emphasize this: 'And
you being dead . . .' In the Greek sentence there is no
main verb portraying God's action until verse 5 ('He made
us alive with Christ'); the English versions bring it forward
to verse 1 simply in order to ease the awkward suspense
of waiting for it so long. In any case the sequence of
thought is clear: 'Jesus Christ was dead, but God raised
and exalted him. And you also were dead, but God raised
and exalted you with Christ.'

1. Man by nature, or the human condition (verses 1-3)

Before we look in detail at this devastating description of
the human condition apart from God, we need to be clear
that it is a description of everybody. Paul is not giving
us a portrait of some particularly decadent tribe or degraded
segment of society, or even of the extremely corrupt
paganism of his own day. No, this is the biblical diagnosis
of fallen man in fallen society everywhere. True, Paul
begins with an emphatic *you*, indicating in the first place
his Gentile readers in Asia Minor, but he quickly goes on
to write (verse 3a) that *we all once lived* in the same way
(thus adding himself and his fellow Jews), and he concludes
with a reference to *the rest of mankind* (verse 3b). Here
then is the apostle's estimate of everyman without God,
of the universal human condition. It is a condensation into
three verses of the first three chapters of Romans, in which
he argues his case for the sin and guilt first of pagans, then
of Jews, and so of all mankind. Here he singles out three
appalling truths about unredeemed human beings, which
includes ourselves until God had mercy on us.

a. We were dead

*And you he made alive, when you were dead through the
trespasses and sins in which you once walked* (verses 1-2a).
The death to which Paul refers is not a figure of speech,
as in the parable of the Prodigal Son, 'This my son was
dead'; it is a factual statement of everybody's spiritual
condition outside Christ. And it is traced to their *trespasses
and sins*. These two words seem to have been carefully
chosen to give a comprehensive account of human evil. A
'trespass' (*paraptōma*) is a false step, involving either the
crossing of a known boundary or a deviation from the
right path. A 'sin' (*hamartia*), however, means rather a
missing of the mark, a falling short of a standard. Together
the two words cover the positive and negative, or active
and passive, aspects of human wrongdoing, that is to say,
our sins of commission and of omission. Before God we
are both rebels and failures. As a result, we are 'dead' or
'alienated from the life of God' (4:18). For true life, 'eternal

71

life', is fellowship with the living God, and spiritual death is the separation from him which sin inevitably brings: 'Your iniquities have made a separation between you and your God, and your sins have hid his face from you so that he does not hear.'[1]

This biblical statement about the 'deadness' of non-Christian people raises problems for many because it does not seem to square with the facts of everyday experience. Lots of people who make no Christian profession whatever, who even openly repudiate Jesus Christ, appear to be very much alive. One has the vigorous body of an athlete, another the lively mind of a scholar, a third the vivacious personality of a filmstar. Are we to say that such people, if Christ has not saved them, are dead? Yes, indeed, we must and do say this very thing. For in the sphere which matters supremely (which is neither the body, nor the mind, nor the personality, but the soul) they have no life. And you can tell it. They are blind to the glory of Jesus Christ, and deaf to the voice of the Holy Spirit. They have no love for God, no sensitive awareness of his personal reality, no leaping of their spirit towards him in the cry, 'Abba, Father', no longing for fellowship with his people. They are as unresponsive to him as a corpse. So we should not hesitate to affirm that a life without God (however physically fit and mentally alert the person may be) is a living death, and that those who live it are dead even while they are living.[2] To affirm this paradox is to become aware of the basic tragedy of fallen human existence. It is that people who were created by God and for God should now be living without God. Indeed, that was our condition until the Good Shepherd found us.

b. We were enslaved

Paul is not content to say simply that we *once walked* in *trespasses and sins*. The expression is a Hebraism, indicating our former behaviour or lifestyle. But a 'walk' suggests (at least to western minds) a pleasant promenade in the countryside, with leisured freedom to enjoy the beauties of our surroundings. Very different, however, was our

---

[1] Is. 59:2.   [2] *Cf.* 1 Tim. 5:6.

former 'walk in trespasses and sins'. There was no true freedom there, but rather a fearful bondage to forces over which we had no control. What were they? If behind death lies sin, what lies behind sin that we are held in such captivity? Paul's answer, when put into later ecclesiastical terminology, is 'the world, the flesh and the devil'. For he refers to these three influences as controlling and directing our former pre-Christian existence.

First, he describes us as *following the course of this world*. The Greek phrase is 'according the age of this world'. It brings together the two concepts of 'this age' of evil and darkness (in contrast to 'the age to come' which Jesus introduced) and of 'this world', society organized without reference to God or—as we might say—'secularism' (in contrast to God's kingdom, which is his new society under his rule). So both words 'age' and 'world' express a whole social value-system which is alien to God. It permeates, indeed dominates, non-Christian society and holds people in captivity. Wherever human beings are being dehumanized—by political oppression or bureaucratic tyranny, by an outlook that is secular (repudiating God), amoral (repudiating absolutes) or materialistic (glorifying the consumer market), by poverty, hunger or unemployment, by racial discrimination, or by any form of injustice—there we can detect the sub-human values of 'this age' and 'this world'. Their influence is pervasive. People tend not to have a mind of their own, but to surrender to the pop-culture of television and the glossy magazines. It is a cultural bondage. We were all the same until Jesus liberated us. We 'drifted along the stream of this world's ideas of living' (JBP).

Our second captivity was to the devil, who is here named *the prince of the power of the air* or (AG) 'the ruler of the kingdom of the air'. The word for 'air' could be translated 'foggy atmosphere', indicating the darkness which the devil prefers to light. But the whole phrase need mean no more than that he has command of those 'principalities and powers' already mentioned, who operate in the unseen world. It is unfashionable nowadays in the church (even while satanism flourishes outside it) to believe either in a personal devil or in personal demonic intelligences under

73

his command. But there is no obvious reason why church fashion should be the director of theology, whereas the plain teaching of Jesus and his apostles (not to mention the church of the subsequent centuries) endorsed their malevolent existence.

A further phrase is *the spirit that is now at work in the sons of disobedience*. Since the words *the spirit* are in the genitive, they are not in apposition to *the prince* (accusative). We must rather understand that 'the ruler of the kingdom of the air' is also 'the ruler of the spirit which works in disobedient people'. 'Spirit' then becomes an impersonal force or mood which is actively at work in non-Christian people. Since Scripture identifies the devil not only as the source of temptations to sin, but also as a 'lion' and a 'murderer', we may safely trace all evil, error and violence back to him in the end. When he and the mood he inspires are said to be at work in human beings, the verb (*energeō*) is the same as that used of God's power (1:20) which raised Jesus from the dead. Only that divine energy or action could have rescued us from the devil.

The third influence which holds us in bondage is *the passions of the flesh* (verse 3a), where 'flesh' means not the living fabric which covers our bony skeleton but our fallen, self-centred human nature. Its 'passions' are further defined as *the desires of body and mind*. This addition is particularly important because it shows the error of equating 'the passions of the flesh' with what are popularly called 'the sins of the flesh'. Two clarifications are needed. First, there is nothing wrong with natural bodily desires, whether for food, sleep or sex. For God has made the human body that way. It is only when the appetite for food becomes gluttony, for sleep sloth and for sex lust, that natural desires have been perverted into sinful desires. Secondly, 'the passions of the flesh' include the wrong desires of the *mind* as well as of the *body*, namely such sins as intellectual pride, false ambition, rejection of known truth, and malicious or vengeful thoughts. Indeed, according to Paul's exposition in Philippians 3:3–6, 'the flesh' covers all forms of self-confidence, even pride of ancestry, parentage, race, religion and righteousness. Wherever 'self' rears its ugly head against God or man, there is 'the flesh'. As F. F.

Bruce justly comments, it 'can manifest itself in respectable forms as well as in the disreputable pursuits of first-century paganism'.[3] And, however respectable the public guise (or disguise) it adopts, our ingrained self-centredness is a horrible bondage.

So then, before Jesus Christ set us free, we were subject to oppressive influences from both within and without. Outside was 'the world' (the prevailing secular culture); inside was 'the flesh' (our fallen nature twisted with self-centredness); and beyond both, actively working through both, was that evil spirit, the devil, 'the ruler of the kingdom of darkness', who held us in captivity. Not that we can now conveniently shift all the blame for our slavery on to 'the world, the flesh and the devil', and accept no responsibility for it ourselves. On the contrary, it is significant that in these verses 'you' and 'we' are not identified with these forces but distinguished from them, although enslaved by them. We ourselves, however, are termed *sons of disobedience* (verse 2b), that is, 'God's rebel subjects' (NEB). We had rebelled, knowingly and voluntarily, against the loving authority of God and so had fallen under the dominion of Satan.

c. We were condemned

Paul has not yet completed his description of our pre-Christian state. He has one more unpleasant truth to tell us about ourselves. Not only were we dead and enslaved, he says, but we were also condemned: *we were by nature children of wrath, like the rest of mankind* (verse 3b). I doubt if there is an expression in Ephesians which has provoked more hostility than this. Some commentators make little or no attempt to understand, let alone defend, it; they dismiss it as untenable today. The causes of their hostility are three. They concern the words 'wrath', 'children' and 'by nature'. We must now consider carefully what Paul means by them, and try to clear them from misconception.

First, the wrath of God. God's wrath is not like man's. It is not bad temper, so that he may fly off the handle

[3] Bruce, p. 49.

at any moment. It is neither spite, nor malice, nor animosity, nor revenge. It is never arbitrary, since it is the divine reaction to only one situation, namely evil. Therefore it is entirely predictable, and it is never subject to mood, whim, or caprice. Further, it is not the impersonal outworking of retribution in society, 'an inevitable process of cause and effect in a moral universe', whether through social disintegration or through the administration of justice by the law courts or in some other way, as C. H. Dodd argued in his famous Moffatt commentary on the letter to the Romans.[4] The fact that 'wrath' (*orgē*) or 'the wrath' (*hē orgē*) occurs without the addition of the words 'of God', does not make his wrath impersonal any more than his grace becomes impersonal when the words 'of God' are omitted as in verses 5 and 8 of this chapter ('by grace you have been saved'). No, the wrath that judges and the grace that saves are both personal. They are the wrath and the grace of God.

So what is his wrath if it is neither an arbitrary reaction nor an impersonal process? It is God's personal, righteous, constant hostility to evil, his settled refusal to compromise with it, and his resolve instead to condemn it. Further, his wrath is not incompatible with his love. The contrast between verses 3 and 4 is notable: *we were by nature children of wrath . . . But God, who is rich in mercy, out of the great love with which he loved us. . .* Thus Paul moves from the wrath of God to the mercy and love of God without any sense of embarrassment or anomaly. He is able to hold them together in his mind because he believed that they were held together in God's character. We need, I think, to be more grateful to God for his wrath, and to worship him that because his righteousness is perfect he always reacts to evil in the same unchanging, predictable, uncompromising way. Without his moral constancy we could enjoy no peace.

The second problem people find is in the phrase *children of wrath*. For the words conjure up a picture of little children, even newborn babies, as under God's wrath, and understandably people do not like what they see in their minds. But it is safe to say that there is no allusion here to little children. The expression is another Hebraism, like 'sons of disobedience' in verse 2, and refers to people of all ages. NEB helpfully substitutes the statement: 'we lay under the dreadful judgment of God'.

The third problem is in the adverbial clause *by nature*. In what sense is it 'by nature' that we were the objects of God's wrath and judgment? To begin with, we can surely all agree that Paul draws a deliberate contrast between what we were 'by nature' (*phusei*, verse 3) and what we have become 'by grace' (*chariti*, verse 5). It is a contrast between the past and the present, between what we were when left to ourselves and what we have become because God intervened on our behalf, and so between judgment and salvation: 'By nature we were under God's wrath, by grace we have been saved.' That much is clear, and uncontroversial.

But *phusei*, 'by nature', seems to describe more than our 'natural' condition, when left to ourselves. It seems also to point to the origin of our condition 'as members of a fallen race',[5] and so to raise difficult questions about our genetic inheritance, and therefore about our moral responsibility. Is Paul's phrase shorthand for something longer such as that by birth we have a tendency to sin, that we therefore do sin, and that our sin brings us under the judgment of God? Or is he saying that our very being as humans is from birth under God's judgment? I have not found a stronger repudiation of the latter notion than the following words of R. W. Dale. Without doubt he speaks for many: 'This phrase is sometimes quoted as though it were intended to affirm the dreadful doctrine that by our mere birth we incur the divine anger and that apart from any voluntary wrongdoing we are under the divine curse. This appalling theory receives no sanction from either Old Testament or New.'[6] Yet R. W. Dale knew that the very doctrine he so vigorously repudiated is taught by the great reformed confessions like the Thirty-Nine Articles and the Westminster Confession. Here is Anglican Article 9:

[5] F. F. Bruce in a footnote, Simpson, p. 46.
[6] Dale, p. 162.

77

'Original sin standeth not in the following of Adam (that is, in imitating him) . . . but it is the fault or corruption of the nature of every man that naturally is ingendered of the offspring of Adam; whereby man is very far gone from original righteousness, and is of his own nature inclined to evil, so that the flesh lusteth always contrary to the spirit; and therefore in every person born into this world, it deserveth God's wrath and damnation. . .' In other words, our inherited human nature itself deserves God's wrath and judgment. This is what Paul seems to be teaching here; how can we understand him?

Probably the best commentary is his own as it is found in Romans. Just as these verses are a condensed version of Romans 1–3, so the expression 'by nature children of wrath' is a summary of Romans 5:12–14. His argument there that 'death spread to all men because all men sinned' is not that all inherited a sinful nature which led them to sin and so to die, but that 'all men sinned' in and with Adam. The Old Testament has a strong sense of the solidarity of the human race. It speaks of the next generation as being already 'in the loins' of the present generation, a truth which modern genetics may be said to underline. Paul is saying, then, that we cannot make Adam our scapegoat and blame him for our sin, guilt and condemnation. For we were ourselves in Adam. It may truly be said that we sinned in Adam, and that in and with him we incurred guilt and died. Is it not in this sense that we may be described as 'by nature' sinners and subject to God's just judgment? The great majority of Protestant theologians have always wanted to add (even if tentatively) that they believe God's grace and Christ's atonement cover the years of childhood before the age of responsibility, and those in the reformed tradition have drawn attention to the biblical evidence that children with Christian parents are born within the covenant.[7] Yet even these important qualifications do not alter the facts of our inherited sin and guilt, or of the judgment we deserve.

Death, slavery and condemnation: these are the three concepts which Paul brings together in order to portray

[7] *Cf.* 1 Cor. 7:14.

EPHESIANS 2:1-10

our lost human condition. Is it too pessimistic? Well, we
must agree (as he would have done) that this is not the
whole truth about mankind. He says nothing here about
'the image of God', in which human beings were originally
created and which—now grievously damaged—they retain,
although he certainly believes it and speaks of our
redemption in terms of a re-creation in God's image (verse
10 and 4:24). He says nothing either about different degrees
of human depravity, although again he would have accepted
this. For the biblical doctrine of 'total depravity' means
neither that all humans are equally depraved, nor that
nobody is capable of any good, but rather that no part
of any human person (mind, emotions, conscience, will,
etc.) has remained untainted by the fall. Nevertheless,
despite this necessary qualification which affirms the
continuing dignity of man on account of the divine image
which he has not altogether lost, Paul's diagnosis remains.
Outside Christ man is dead because of trespasses and sins,
enslaved by the world, the flesh and the devil, and
condemned under the wrath of God.

It is a failure to recognize this gravity of the human
condition which explains people's naive faith in superficial
remedies. Universal education is highly desirable. So are
just laws administered with justice. Both are pleasing to
God who is the Creator and righteous Judge of all
mankind. But neither education nor legislation can rescue
human beings from spiritual death, captivity or condemnation. A radical disease requires a radical remedy. We
shall not on that account give up the quest either for better
education or for a more just society. But we shall add to
these things a new dimension to which non-Christians are
strangers, namely that of evangelism. For God has entrusted
to us a message of good news which offers life to the
dead, release to the captives and forgiveness to the
condemned.

2. Man by grace, or the divine compassion (4–10)

Verse 4 begins with a mighty adversative: *But God* . . .
These two monosyllables set against the desperate condition
of fallen mankind the gracious initiative and sovereign

79

action of God. We were the objects of his wrath, *but God, out of the great love with which he loved us* had mercy upon us. We were dead, and dead men do not rise, *but God* made us alive with Christ. We were slaves, in a situation of dishonour and powerlessness, *but God* has raised us with Christ and set us at his own right hand, in a position of honour and power. Thus God has taken action to reverse our condition in sin. It is essential to hold both parts of this contrast together, namely what we are by nature and what we are by grace, the human condition and the divine compassion, God's wrath and God's love. Christians are sometimes criticized for being morbidly preoccupied with their sin and guilt. The criticism is not fair when we are facing the facts about ourselves (for it is never unhealthy to look reality in the face), but only when we fail to go on to glory in God's mercy and grace.

We need now to enquire exactly what God has done, and also why he has done it.

a. What God has done

In one word he has *saved* us. In both verse 5 and verse 8 the same assertion is made: *By grace you have been saved*. Some commentators have even suggested that verses 4–10 are a kind of hymn celebrating the glories of salvation and of *sola gratia*, which is twice interrupted by the liturgical acclamation 'By grace you have been saved'. 'Saved' is a perfect participle (*sesōsmenoi*). It emphasizes the abiding consequences of God's saving action in the past, as if Paul should say, 'You are people who have been saved and remain for ever saved.' Many today, however, are saying that they find traditional salvation language meaningless. So we need to probe into what Paul writes.

In fact he coins three verbs, which take up what God did to Christ and then (by the addition of the prefix *syn*, 'together with') link us to Christ in these events. Thus first, God *made us alive together with Christ* (verse 5), next he *raised us up with him* (verse 6a), and thirdly he *made us sit with him in the heavenly places in Christ Jesus* (verse 6b). These verbs ('made alive', 'raised' and 'made to sit') refer to the three successive historical events in the saving career of Jesus, which are normally called the resurrection, the ascension and the session. We declare our belief in them when we say the Creed: 'The third day he rose again from the dead, he ascended into heaven, and he sits at the right hand of God the Father.' What excites our amazement, however, is that now Paul is not writing about Christ but about us. He is affirming not that God quickened, raised and seated Christ, but that he quickened, raised and seated us with Christ.

Fundamental to New Testament Christianity is this concept of the union of God's people with Christ. What constitutes the distinctness of the members of God's new society? Not just that they admire and even worship Jesus, not just that they assent to the dogmas of the church, not even that they live by certain moral standards. No, what makes them distinctive is their new solidarity as a people who are 'in Christ'. By virtue of their union with Christ they have actually shared in his resurrection, ascension and session. In the 'heavenly places', the unseen world of spiritual reality, in which the principalities and powers operate (3:10; 6:12) and in which Christ reigns supreme (1:20), there God has blessed his people in Christ (1:3), and there he has seated them with Christ (2:6). For if we are seated with Christ in the heavenlies, there can be no doubt what we are sitting on: thrones! Moreover, this talk about solidarity with Christ in his resurrection and exaltation is not a piece of meaningless Christian mysticism. It bears witness to a living experience, that Christ has given us on the one hand a new life (with a sensitive awareness of the reality of God, and a love for him and for his people) and on the other a new victory (with evil increasingly under our feet). We were dead, but have been made spiritually alive and alert. We were in captivity, but have been enthroned.

b. Why God did it

Paul goes beyond a description of God's saving action; he gives us some understanding of his motivation. Indeed the major emphasis of this whole paragraph is that what prompted God to act on our behalf was not something in us (some supposed merit) but something in himself (his own unmerited favour). Paul assembles four words to express the origins of God's saving initiative. He writes of God's 'mercy' (*God who is rich in mercy*, verse 4a), of God's 'love' (*out of the great love with which he loved us*, verse 4b), of God's 'grace' (*by grace you have been saved*, verses 5 and 8) and of God's 'kindness' (*his ... kindness toward us in Christ Jesus*, verse 7). We were dead, and so helpless to save ourselves: only 'mercy' could reach the helpless, for 'mercy' is love for the down and out. We were under God's wrath: only 'love' could triumph over wrath. We deserved nothing at God's hand but judgment, on account of our trespasses and sins: only 'grace' could rescue us from our deserts, for grace is undeserved favour. Why then did God act? Out of his sheer mercy, love, grace and kindness.

More than that. He saved us in order *that in the coming ages he might show the immeasurable riches of his grace* (verse 7). In raising and exalting Christ he demonstrated 'the immeasurable greatness of his power' (verses 19–20); but in raising and exalting us he displayed also 'the immeasurable riches of his grace', and will continue to do so throughout eternity. For as living evidences of his kindness we shall point people away and beyond ourselves to him to whom we owe our salvation.

Towards the end of my time as a theological student at Ridley Hall, Cambridge, the Rev. Paul Gibson retired as Principal, and a portrait of him was unveiled. In expressing his thanks, he paid a well-deserved compliment to the artist. He said that in future he believed people looking at the picture would ask not 'Who is that man?' but rather 'Who painted that portrait?' Now in our case God has displayed more than skill. A patient after a major operation is a living testimony to his surgeon's skill, and a condemned man after a reprieve to his sovereign's mercy. We are both—exhibits of God's skill and trophies of his grace.

Verses 8–10 elaborate on God's grace, and explain why in the coming ages God will show his grace and kindness towards us in Christ Jesus. It is because of our salvation. God will show his grace towards us because he has saved us by his grace: *For by grace you have been saved through faith*. Here are three foundation words of the Christian good news—salvation, grace and faith. 'Salvation' is more than forgiveness. It is deliverance from the death, slavery and wrath described in verses 1–3. Indeed, it includes the totality of our new life in Christ, together with whom we have been made alive, exalted and seated in the heavenly realm. 'Grace' is God's free and undeserved mercy towards us, and 'faith' is the humble trust with which we receive it for ourselves.

In order to enforce this positive statement that we have been saved only by God's grace through trust in Christ, Paul adds two balancing negatives: first *and this is not your own doing, it is the gift of God* (verse 8b) and secondly *not because of works, lest any man should boast*. Some commentators have taken the word 'this' in the former of these two negatives to refer to faith (*i.e.* 'you were saved . . . through faith, and even this faith by which you were saved is God's gift'). Theologically, this is true. We must never think of salvation as a kind of transaction between God and us in which he contributes grace and we contribute faith. For we were dead, and had to be quickened before we could believe. No, Christ's apostles clearly teach elsewhere that saving faith too is God's gracious gift.[8] Nevertheless, Paul is not directly affirming this here because 'this' (*touto*) is neuter, whereas 'faith' is a feminine noun. We must therefore take 'this' as referring to the whole previous sentence: 'By God's grace you are people who have been saved through faith, and this whole event and experience is . . . God's free gift to you.' It is neither your achievement (*not your own doing*) nor a reward for any of your deeds of religion or philanthropy (*not because of works*). Since, therefore, there is no room for human merit, there is no room for human boasting either. Salvation is God's gift, *lest any man should boast*. Christians are always uncomfortable in the presence of pride, for they sense its incongruity. We shall not be able to strut round heaven like peacocks. Heaven will be filled with the exploits of Christ and the praises of God. There will indeed be display

[8] *E.g.* Acts 18:27; Phil. 1:29.

in heaven. Not self-display, however, but rather a display of the incomparable wealth of God's grace, mercy and kindness through Jesus Christ.

One might imagine that by now Paul has made his point and is ready to pass on to another topic. But no, he is determined not to leave his theme until he has expounded it beyond any possibility of misunderstanding. So he adds one more positive, decisive and glorious affirmation (verse 10): *For we are his workmanship, created in Christ Jesus for good works, which God prepared beforehand, that we should walk in them.* The first and emphatic word of the sentence is *autou*, 'his'. Paul has already declared that salvation is not our achievement. Now he does not just state the opposite, namely that it is God's achievement. He goes further. He leaves behind any thought of salvation as an 'it' or a 'this' outside and apart from ourselves. He is concerned about us, living human beings, who were dead. What are we now? We are God's *workmanship* (*poiēma*, 'his work of art, his masterpiece')[9] *created* (*ktisthentes*) *in Christ Jesus*. Both Greek words speak of creation. So far Paul has described salvation in terms of a resurrection from the dead, a liberation from slavery and a rescue from condemnation. And each declares that the work is God's, for dead people cannot bring themselves to life again, nor can captive and condemned people free themselves. But now he puts the matter beyond even the slightest shadow of doubt. Salvation is creation, re-creation, new creation. And creation language is nonsense unless there is a Creator; self-creation is a patent contradiction in terms. 'You see then', writes Calvin, 'that this word "create" is enough to stop the mouths and put away the cackling of such as boast of having any merit. For when they say so, they presuppose that they were their own creators.'[1]

Not that we remain passive and inert. Some critics have always thought this, and supposed that Paul's doctrine of salvation by grace alone actually encourages us to continue in sin. They are entirely mistaken. Good works are indispensable to salvation—not as its ground or means,

[9] Bruce, p. 52.   [1] Calvin, p. 162.

however, but as its consequence and evidence. We are not saved *because of works* (verses 8–9), but we are created in Christ Jesus *for good works* (verse 10), good works *which God prepared beforehand*, which he designed in a past eternity and for which he has fashioned us, so that we should continuously *walk in them*.

Thus the paragraph ends as it began with our human 'walk', a Hebrew idiom for our manner of life. Formerly we walked in *trespasses and sins* in which the devil had trapped us; now we walk in *good works* which God has eternally planned for us to do. The contrast is complete. It is a contrast between two lifestyles (evil and good), and behind them two masters (the devil and God). What could possibly have effected such a change? Just this: a new creation by the grace and power of God. The key expressions of the paragraph are surely *but God* (verse 4) and *by grace* (verses 5,8).

Paul was under no illusions about the degradation of mankind. He refused to whitewash the situation, for this might have led him to propose superficial solutions. Instead, he began this paragraph with a faithful portrayal of man as subject to three terrible powers, namely 'sin', 'death' and 'wrath'. Yet he refused also to despair, because he believed in God. True, the only hope for dead people lies in a resurrection. But then the living God is the God of resurrection. He is even more than that: he is the God of creation. Both metaphors indicate the indispensable necessity of divine grace. For resurrection is out of death, and creation is out of nothing. That is the true meaning of 'salvation'.

II New Society

Ephesians 2:11 – 3:21

2:11-22

4. A single new humanity

'Alienation' is a popular word in contemporary society. There are many people, especially young people in the so-called 'developed' world, who are disillusioned with 'the system', critical of 'the technocracy' and hostile to 'the establishment', who describe themselves as 'alienated'. Some work for reform, others plot revolution, others drop out. In no case can they accommodate themselves to the *status quo*.

It was Karl Marx who popularized the word, having himself taken it from the German theologian, Ludwig Feuerbach. Marx understood the plight of the proletariat in terms of economic alienation. Every worker puts into his craftsmanship a part of himself. When his employer then sells his product, he is guilty, at least in part, of alienating the worker from himself. This according to Marx was the basis of the class struggle.

Nowadays the word is used more generally of the working man's alienation not only from his achievement and its due reward, but also from the exercise of power, especially in decision-making. In other words, the term has become more political than economic. 'Alienation' is partly a sense of disaffection with what is, and partly a sense of powerlessness to change it. This is a widespread feeling in the democratic countries of the West, and Christians would be foolish to ignore it.

But long before Feuerbach and Marx the Bible spoke of human alienation. It describes two other and even more radical alienations than the economic and the political. One is alienation from God our Creator, and the other alienation from one another, our fellow creatures. Nothing is more dehumanizing than this breakdown of fundamental human relationships. It is then that we become strangers in a world in which we should feel at home, and aliens instead of citizens.

The letter to the Ephesians alludes to both these forms of alienation. Indeed, Paul uses the word in relation to both conditions. The Greek verb is *apallotrioō* and means to estrange, exclude or alienate. In the New Testament it occurs only in these two Ephesians verses, together with the Colossians parallel to one of them:

4:18 'alienated from the life of God' (*cf*.Col. 1:20,21)
2:12 'alienated from the commonwealth of Israel'

Now this double alienation, or rather its replacement by reconciliation, is the theme of Ephesians 2. In the first half of the chapter (verses 1–10) human beings are depicted as alienated from God. The verb is not actually used there, as it is in 4:18, but this is without doubt what is meant when they are portrayed as 'dead through . . . trespasses and sins' and 'by nature children of wrath' (verses 1,3). We considered in the last chapter the meaning of these phrases.

In the second half of Ephesians 2 (verses 11–22), which is our text in this chapter, human beings are depicted as alienated also from each other. In particular, Gentiles are described as 'alienated from the commonwealth of Israel' (verse 12). It is almost impossible for us towards the close of the twentieth century AD to think ourselves back to those days when humanity was deeply divided between Jews and Gentiles. The Bible opens with a clear declaration of the unity of mankind. But after the fall and then the flood it traces the origins of human division and separation. It may seem that God himself contributed to the process by choosing Israel out of all the nations to be his 'holy' or 'distinct' people. But we need to remember that in calling Abraham he promised through his posterity to bless all the earth's families and that in choosing Israel he intended her to become a light to the nations.[1] The tragedy is that Israel forgot her vocation, twisted her privilege into favourtism and ended by heartily despising—even detesting—the heathen as 'dogs'. William Barclay helps us feel the alienation between the two communities, and the deepseated hostility between them, especially on the Jewish side. He writes:

> The Jew had an immense contempt for the Gentile. The Gentiles, said the Jews, were created by God to be fuel for the fires of hell. God, they said, loves only Israel of all the nations that he had made . . . It was not even lawful to render help to a Gentile mother in her hour of sorest need, for that would simply be to bring another Gentile into the world. Until Christ came, the Gentiles were an object of contempt to the Jews. The barrier between them was absolute. If a Jewish boy married a Gentile girl, or if a Jewish girl married a Gentile boy, the funeral of that Jewish boy or girl was carried out. Such contact with a Gentile was the equivalent of death.[2]

Of this double Gentile alienation—from God and from God's people Israel—the so-called 'middle wall of partition' (verse 14, AV) or 'dividing wall of hostility' (RSV) was the standing symbol. It was a notable feature of the magnificent temple built in Jerusalem by Herod the Great. The temple building itself was constructed on an elevated platform. Round it was the Court of the Priests. East of this was the Court of Israel, and further east the court of the women. These three courts—for the priests, the lay men and the lay women of Israel respectively—were all on the same elevation as the temple itself. From this level one descended five steps to a walled platform, and then on the other side of the wall fourteen more steps to another wall, beyond which was the outer court or Court of the Gentiles. This was a spacious court running right round the temple and its inner courts. From any part of it the Gentiles could look up and view the temple, but were not allowed to approach it. They were cut off from it by the surrounding

---

[1] Cf. Gen. 12:1–3; Is. 42:1–6; 49:6.   [2] Barclay, p. 125.

wall, which was a one-and-a-half metre stone barricade, on which were displayed at intervals warning notices in Greek and Latin. They read, in effect, not 'Trespassers will be prosecuted' but 'Trespassers will be executed.'

The famous Jewish historian Josephus describes this barricade in both his books. In his *Antiquities* he writes that the temple was 'encompassed by a stone wall for a partition, with an inscription which forbade any foreigner to go in under pain of death'.[3] In his *Wars of the Jews* he is a little more explicit. There was, he writes, 'a partition made of stone all round, whose height was three cubits. Its construction was very elegant; upon it stood pillars at equal distance from one another, declaring the law of purity, some in Greek and some in Roman letters, that "no foreigner should go within that sanctuary".'[4]

During the last hundred years or so two of the Greek notices have been discovered, one in 1871 and the other in 1935. The former, exhibited in the museum at Istanbul, is a white limestone slab measuring nearly a metre across. Its exact wording is as follows: 'No foreigner may enter within the barrier and enclosure round the temple. Anyone who is caught doing so will have himself to blame for his ensuing death.' Paul knew all about it from personal experience. Only about three years previously he had nearly been lynched himself by an angry Jewish mob who thought he had taken a Gentile with him into the temple, interestingly enough an Ephesian named Trophimus.[5]

This, then, is the historical, social and religious background to Ephesians 2. Although all human beings are alienated from God because of sin, the Gentiles were also alienated from the people of God. And worse even than this double alienation (of which the temple wall was a symbol) was the active 'enmity' or 'hostility' (*echthra*) into which it continuously erupted—enmity between man and God, and enmity between Gentiles and Jews.

The grand theme of Ephesians 2 is that Jesus Christ has destroyed both enmities. Both are mentioned in the second half of the chapter, although in the opposite order:

---

[3] *Antiquities*, XV. 11.5.   [4] *Wars of the Jews*, V.5.2.
[5] Acts 21:27–31.

verse 14   'He . . . has made both one, and has broken
            down the dividing wall of hostility (*echthra*).'
verse 16   'That he . . . might reconcile us both to
            God in one body through the cross, thereby
            bringing the hostility (*echthra*) to an end.'

Alongside his destruction of these two enmities Jesus has
succeeded in creating a new society, in fact a new humanity,
in which alienation has given way to reconciliation, and
hostility to peace. And this new human unity in Christ
is the pledge and foretaste of that final unity under Christ's
headship to which Paul has already looked forward in
1:10.

After this introduction relating to its background and
theme, we are now ready to study the text itself:

*Therefore remember that at one time you Gentiles in the
flesh, called the uncircumcision by what is called the
circumcision, which is made in the flesh by hands—
[12]remember that you were at that time separated from Christ,
alienated from the commonwealth of Israel, and strangers
to the covenants of promise, having no hope and without
God in the world. [13]But now in Christ Jesus you who once
were far off have been brought near in the blood of Christ.
[14]For he is our peace, who has made us both one, and has
broken down the dividing wall of hostility, [15]by abolishing
in his flesh the law of commandments and ordinances, that
he might create in himself one new man in place of the
two, so making peace, [16]and might reconcile us both to God
in one body through the cross, thereby bringing the hostility
to an end. [17]And he came and preached peace to you who
were far off and peace to those who were near; [18]for
through him we both have access in one Spirit to the
Father. [19]So then you are no longer strangers and sojourners,
but you are fellow citizens with the saints and members
of the household of God, [20]built upon the foundation of
the apostles and prophets, Christ Jesus himself being the
cornerstone, [21]in whom the whole structure is joined together
and grows into a holy temple in the Lord; [22]in whom you
also are built into it for a dwelling place of God in the
Spirit.*

It may be helpful if, before immersing ourselves in a more detailed exposition, we grasp the structure of the passage as a whole. Paul traces his Gentile readers' spiritual biography in three stages. Here is the gist of his message to them: '(1) At one time you were alienated from God and from his people Israel. (2) By his death on the cross Christ Jesus has reconciled Jews and Gentiles both to each other and to God, creating "a single new humanity" (verse 15, NEB). (3) You are no longer alienated but full members with Israel of God's people and family.' The three stages are marked by the expressions 'at one time' (verse 11), 'but now' (verse 13) and 'so then' (verse 19). And the sequence runs: *Remember that at one time you ... were alienated ... but now in Christ Jesus you ... have been brought near ... for he is our peace ... So then you are no longer strangers ... but ... fellow citizens with the saints ...* I shall entitle the three unfolding stages of God's plan as follows:

a. the portrait of an alienated humanity, or what we once were (verses 11–12)
b. the portrait of the peacemaking Christ, or what Jesus Christ has done (verses 13–18)
c. the portrait of God's new society, or what we have now become (verses 19–22)

1. The portrait of an alienated humanity, or what we once were (verses 11–12)

In verses 1–3 Paul has portrayed all mankind (Jews and Gentiles alike) in sin and death. Here in verses 11 and 12 he refers particularly to the Gentile or heathen world before Christ, to those whom the Jews (*the circumcision*) scornfully called *the uncircumcision*. Circumcision had of course been given by God to Abraham as the outward sign of membership of his covenant people. But both the physical rite and the word had come to assume an exaggerated importance. Gentiles and Jews regularly called each other by derogatory names. Paul emphasizes this here. Gentiles were *called* 'the uncircumcision' by what is *called* 'the circumcision which is made in the flesh by hands'. It is as if Paul is declaring the unimportance of names and labels, in comparison with the reality behind them, and hinting that behind 'what is called the circumcision which is made in the flesh by hands' there is another kind, a circumcision of the heart, spiritual not physical, which was needed by and available to both Jews and Gentiles alike.[6]

In verse 12 he drops the business of what Jews and Gentiles called each other, and comes on to the serious reality of Gentile alienation. In Romans he had listed Jewish privileges (9:3–5); here he lists Gentile disabilities. First, they were *separated from Christ*. The expression is the more tragic because in chapter 1 he has unfolded the great spiritual blessings of being 'in Christ', and in the earlier part of chapter 2 he has explained how God has quickened, raised and seated us 'with Christ'. But *at one time*, that is throughout the whole period BC, the Gentiles were neither 'in Christ' nor 'with Christ' but 'separated from Christ'; they even had no expectation of a coming Messiah.

The Gentiles' second and third disabilities were similar to one another. They were both *alienated from the commonwealth of Israel* and *strangers to the covenants of promise* (literally 'of the promise', referring probably to the foundation promise made by God to Abraham). Israel was a 'commonwealth' or nation under God, a theocracy, and a 'covenant people' to whom he had committed himself by a solemn pledge. Thus he had bound himself to them and ruled over them. But the Gentiles were excluded from this covenant and kingdom.

The fourth and fifth Gentile disabilities are starkly stated: *having no hope and without God in the world*. They were 'hopeless' because, although God had planned and promised to include them one day, they did not know it, and therefore had no hope to sustain them. And they were 'godless' (*atheoi*) because, although God had revealed himself to all mankind in nature and therefore had not left himself without witness, yet they suppressed the truth they knew and turned instead to idolatry.[7] It was no exaggeration,

[6] *Cf.* Rom. 2:28–29; Phil. 3:3; Col. 2:11–13.
[7] See Acts 14:15 ff; 17:22 ff; Rom. 1:18 ff.

therefore, to describe the ancient non-Jewish world as 'hopeless' and 'godless'. The golden age of the Greeks was past; they had no promised future to look forward to. Moreover, the gods of Greece and Rome entirely failed to satisfy the hunger of human hearts. The people were *atheoi* not in the sense that they disbelieved (on the contrary, they had a plethora of gods), but in the sense that they had no true knowledge of God such as he had given to Israel,[8] and (because of their rejection of the knowledge they had) no personal fellowship with him.

This, then, was the terrible fivefold deprivation of the ancient Gentile world before Christ. They were cut off from the Messiah, from the theocracy and the covenants, from hope, and from God himself. In William Hendriksen's summary they were 'Christless, stateless, friendless, hopeless and Godless'.[9] In Paul's single phrase they were 'far off' (13), alienated from God and from the people of God.

And we ourselves in our pre-Christian days, it is necessary to add, were in exactly the same plight. We were alienated from God and from his people. Worse, there was in our hearts the 'enmity' to which Paul refers later, so that we rebelled against the authority of God and knew little or nothing of true human community. Is it not the same in today's world without Christ? Men still build walls of partition and division like the terrible Berlin wall, or erect invisible curtains of iron or bamboo, or construct barriers of race, colour, caste, tribe or class. Divisiveness is a constant characteristic of every community without Christ. We ourselves experienced it. Now the apostle says *Therefore remember* (verse 11), and again *remember* (verse 12). There are some things which Scripture tells us to forget (like the injuries which others do to us). But there is one thing in particular which we are commanded to remember and never to forget. This is what we were before God's love reached down and found us. For only if we remember our former alienation (distasteful as some of it may be to us), shall we be able to remember the greatness of the grace which forgave and is transforming us.

---

[8] Ps. 147:20.   [9] Hendriksen, p. 129.

2. The portrait of the peacemaking Christ or what Jesus Christ has done (verses 13–18)

The parallel between the two halves of Ephesians 2 is obvious. First comes in both cases a description of life without Christ: 'dead' (verses 1–3) and 'alienated' (verses 11–12). Then follows, again in both cases, the great adversative: 'But God' (verse 4) and 'But now' (verse 13). The main distinction is that in the second half Paul is stressing the Gentile experience. Twice he uses the emphatic pronoun *you* (*hymeis*): 'Remember that once *you* were alienated . . . But now in Christ Jesus *you* . . . have been brought near.'

This, then, in its essence is the difference which Christ has made: *you who once were far off have been brought near*. Such spatial language ('far' and 'near') was not uncommon in the Old Testament. God and Israel were known to be 'near' one another, since God had promised to be their God and to make them his people. Hence Moses could say: 'What great nation is there that has a God so *near* to it as the Lord our God is to us?'[1] Their uniqueness in this respect is repeated in Psalm 148:14, where they are called 'the people of Israel who are *near* to him'. By contrast, the Gentile nations were 'far off', peoples who had to be summoned 'from afar'.[2] But God promised that one day he would speak 'Peace, peace, to the far and to the near', a promise which was fulfilled in Jesus Christ and which is quoted here by Paul with reference to him.[3] And this 'nearness to God' which all Christians enjoy through Christ is a privilege we take too frequently for granted. Our God does not keep his distance or stand on his dignity, like some oriental potentate, nor does he insist on any complicated ritual or protocol. On the contrary, through Jesus Christ and by the Holy Spirit we have immediate 'access' to him as our Father (verse 18). We need to exhort one another to avail ourselves of this privilege.[4]

Verse 13 is more than a statement that we who were

[1] Dt. 4:7.   [2] Is. 49:1.
[3] Is. 57:19; Eph. 2:17.   [4] Heb. 10:22; Jas. 4:8.

'far off' have now been 'brought near'; it contains in addition two important references to Christ. For it states that our new nearness to God is both *in Christ Jesus* and *in* (or by) *the blood of Christ*. It is essential, if we are to be faithful to the apostle's teaching, to hold onto these two expressions, and not to emphasize one at the expense of the other. For 'the blood of Christ' (as in 1:7) signifies his sacrificial death for our sins on the cross, by which he reconciled us to God and to each other, whereas 'in Christ Jesus' signifies the personal union with Christ today through which the reconciliation he achieved is received and enjoyed. Thus the two expressions witness to the two stages by which those 'far off' are 'brought near'. The first is the historical event of the cross, and the second Christian conversion, or the contemporary experience of union with Christ. What Jesus Christ accomplished by his cross Paul will explain in the next verses. Meanwhile, it will be wise for us to observe well the phrase 'in Christ Jesus' with which he introduces his whole exposition of Christ's reconciling work. It is not a universal reconciliation that Christ achieved or that Paul proclaimed: it is rather a nearness to God and to each other gratefully experienced by those who are near Christ, indeed 'in' him in a vital, personal union. This means, as John Mackay expresses it, when commenting on these verses, that God's integrating principle for uniting human beings is neither intellectual (philosophy) as in Roman Catholicism, nor political (conquest) as in Islam or Marxism, but spiritual (redemption by Christ, involving union between Jews and Gentiles, man and God and ultimately heaven and earth). These are three alternative 'imperialisms', the first of mind, the second of force, the third of the kingdom of God.

The apostle goes on to elaborate the work of Christ, in terms both of what he did and of how he did it. What he did is plain: *For he is our peace, who has made both one, and has broken down the dividing wall of hostility* (verse 14). 'He' (*autos*) is strongly emphatic. It is he, Christ Jesus, who shed his blood on the cross and who offers himself to his people today to be united to them, it is he who by what he did once and now offers *is our peace*, that is to say, is the peacemaker between us and

98

with God. The 'both' whom he has *made . . . one* seems clearly to mean Jews and Gentiles, but the reconciliation was broader than that, for, as we saw earlier, *the dividing wall of hostility* which he *has broken down* symbolized Gentile alienation from God as well as from Israel.

This announcement which Paul makes of the breaking down of the wall by Jesus Christ is extremely remarkable. For literally and historically speaking, the wall was not broken down until the Roman legions entered Jerusalem in AD 70. So it was still standing, still surrounding the temple, and still excluding the Gentiles, while Paul was writing this letter. But though materially it remained, spiritually it had already been destroyed in AD 30 or so, when Jesus died on the cross. As Armitage Robinson put it, 'It still stood: but it was already antiquated, obsolete, out of date, so far as its spiritual meaning went. The sign still stood: but the thing signified was broken down.'[5]

We turn now to the question how Christ did it. What did he do when he died on the cross to get rid of the divisive enmity between Jew and Gentile, between man and God? The answer is given in verses 15 and 16. They are packed tight with theology, and need to be unpacked. Perhaps the best way to clarify the apostle's sequence of thought is to isolate the three successive main verbs which he uses, *viz. by abolishing . . . that he might create . . . and might reconcile. . .* We are told that he abolished the law of commandments in order to create a single new humanity and to reconcile both parts of it to God.

a. The abolition of the law of commandments (verse 15a)

The first assertion Paul makes is that Christ broke down the wall, the hostility, *by abolishing in his flesh the law of commandments and ordinances*. At first sight this is a surprising, not to say a startling statement. How can the apostle declare that Christ abolished the law when Christ himself in the Sermon on the Mount specifically declared the opposite, that he had not come to abolish it but to fulfil it?[6] We shall see that the discrepancy is only verbal;

[5] Armitage Robinson, p. 60. [6] Mt. 5:17.

in substance they were referring to the law in two different senses.

In the Sermon on the Mount the context shows that Jesus was referring to the *moral* law. He was teaching the difference between Pharisaic righteousness and Christian righteousness, and urging that Christian righteousness involves a deep and radical obedience to the law. Paul's primary reference here, however, seems to be to the *ceremonial* law and to what NEB calls 'its rules and regulations', that is, to circumcision (the main physical distinction between Jews and Gentiles, verse 11), the material sacrifices, the dietary regulations and the rules about ritual 'cleanness' and 'uncleanness' which governed social relationships. The parallel passage in Colossians alludes to circumcision, and also to 'questions of food and drink', and regulations regarding 'a festival or a new moon or a sabbath' (2:11,16–21); so it seems probable that these were the *commandments and ordinances* which Paul has in mind here. They erected a serious barrier between Jews and Gentiles, but Jesus set this whole ceremonial aside. And he did it *in his flesh* (surely a reference to his physical death) because in the cross he fulfilled all the types and shadows of the Old Testament ceremonial system.

It seems probable, however, that Paul is making another though secondary reference, this time to the moral, not the ceremonial law. Jesus certainly did not abolish the moral law as a standard of behaviour (it is still in force and binding on his followers); but he did abolish it as a way of salvation. Whenever the law is viewed in this light it is divisive. For we cannot obey it, however hard we try. Therefore it separates us from God and from each other. But Jesus himself perfectly obeyed the law in his life, and in his death bore the consequences of our disobedience. He took upon himself 'the curse of the law' (the judgment it threatens to those who disobey it) in order to free us from it.[7] Or, according to the Colossians parallel, God is able to forgive us all our trespasses because he 'cancelled the bond which stood against us with its legal demands; this he set aside, nailing it to the cross' (2:13–14).

[7] Gal. 3:10,13.

Acceptance with God is now through faith in Christ crucified alone, whether for Jews or for Gentiles. The law was a barrier between us, but faith unites us, since all of us have to come to God through Christ in the same way. This had been one of Paul's major emphases in Galatians, namely that we are all brought to the same level at the foot of Christ's cross.

To sum up, Jesus abolished both the regulations of the ceremonial law and the condemnation of the moral law. Both were divisive. Both were put aside by the cross.

b. The creation of a single new humanity (verse 15b)

It is impossible to miss the way in which Paul moves on from the negative to the positive, from the abolition of something old (the divisiveness of the law) to the creation of something new (a single, undivided humanity). In both senses which we have been considering the law had made a deep rift in humanity. Jews and Gentiles were alienated from one another and at enmity with one another. But once the divisive law had been set aside, there was nothing to keep the two parts of humanity apart. Instead Christ brought them together by a sovereign act of creation. Literally, he 'created the two into one new man, so making peace'. 'The new man here', writes F. F. Bruce, 'like the "full-grown man" of Ephesians 4:13, is the Christian community viewed corporately.'[8] What Paul is referring to, in fact, is not a 'new man' but a 'new human race', united by Jesus Christ *in himself*. For although potentially the single new humanity was created when Jesus abolished the divisive law on the cross, actually it comes into existence and grows only by personal union with himself.

This new unity through and in Christ does more than span the Jew-Gentile divide. In other passages Paul says that it also does away with sexual and social distinctions. 'Here there cannot be Greek and Jew, circumcised and uncircumcised, barbarian, Scythian, slave, free man, but Christ is all, and in all.' Again, 'There is neither Jew nor Greek, there is neither slave nor free, there is neither male nor female; for you are all one in Christ Jesus.'[9] Not that

[8] Bruce, p. 55.   [9] Col. 3:11; Gal. 3:28.

the facts of human differentiation are removed. Men remain men and women women, Jews remain Jews and Gentiles Gentiles. But inequality before God is abolished. There is a new unity in Christ.

c. The reconciliation of Jew and Gentile to God (verse 16)

After the abolition of the divisive law and the creation of the undivided humanity came the reconciliation of both parts of the old humanity to God, *thereby bringing the hostility to an end*. Here the 'hostility' is clearly between God and men, just as in verse 14 it was chiefly between Jew and Gentile. And just as there the 'hostility' was mutual, I think we need to see a certain mutuality also in the hostility between men and God. It is not just that our attitude to him has been one of rebellion; it is also that his 'wrath' has been upon us for our sin (verse 3). And only *through the cross* have both 'hostilities' been brought to an end, for when Christ bore our sin and judgment on the cross God turned away his own wrath, and we, seeing his great love, turned away ours also. Thus Christ (literally) 'killed' or 'slew' the hostility. 'Christ in his death was slain', comments Armitage Robinson, 'but the slain was a slayer too.'[1] And the hostility in both directions having been decisively dealt with, the result is reconciliation.

This, then, was the achievement of Christ's cross. First, he abolished the law (its ceremonial regulations and moral condemnation) as a divisive instrument separating men from God and Jews from Gentiles. Secondly he created a single new humanity out of its two former deep divisions, making peace between them. Thirdly, he reconciled this new united humanity to God, having killed through the cross all the hostility between us. Christ crucified has thus brought into being nothing less than a new, united human race, united in itself and united to its creator.

This does not mean that the whole human race is now united and reconciled. We know from observation and experience that it is not. But then Paul does not claim this either. There is a further stage in the work of Christ which

[1] Armitage Robinson, p. 65.

he goes on to mention. It is that Christ *came and preached peace* (verse 17). Already we have been told that *he is our peace* (verse 14) and that he created a new humanity, *so making peace* (verse 15). But now he *preached peace*, publishing abroad the good news of the peace he had made through the cross.[2] First he achieved it; then he announced it. And since the achievement was at the cross, and logically the announcement must follow the achievement, this preaching cannot refer to his public ministry. It must refer rather to his post-resurrection appearances, in which the very first word he spoke to the apostles was 'Peace be with you',[3] and to his proclamation of the gospel of peace to the world through the apostles and through subsequent generations of Christians.[4] Jesus Christ is still preaching peace in the world today, through the lips of his followers. For it is truly a wonderful fact that whenever we proclaim peace, it is Christ who proclaims it through us.

Moreover this good news was addressed from the start to the 'far' and 'near', that is, to Gentiles and Jews equally: *peace to you who were far off and peace to those who were near*. And many of each community embraced it, and thereby found themselves united to God and to each other. For *through him we both have access in one Spirit to the Father* (verse 18). Although 'reconciliation' is an event; 'access' is the continuing relationship to which it leads. 'Since we are justified by faith, we have peace with God through our Lord Jesus Christ. Through him we have obtained access . . .'[5] *Prosagōgē* (*access*) conjures up the scene in an oriental court, when subjects are granted an audience with the king or emperor, and are presented to him. The flavour of the word remains, but the emphasis changes because our access is not to a king but to a Father, before whom we have 'boldness and confidence of access' (3:12). And in the enjoyment of this ready access to God, we find we have no practical difficulty with the mystery of the eternal Trinity. For our access is *to the Father*, *through him* (the Son who made peace and preached it), and *in* or by *one Spirit*, the Spirit who regenerates,

---

[2] *Cf.* Is. 52:7. [3] Jn. 20:19–21.
[4] *Cf.* Acts 10:36; Eph. 6:15. [5] Rom. 5:1–2.

seals and indwells his people, who witnesses with our spirits that we are God's children, who helps us in our weaknesses and teaches us to pray, and who unites us as we pray. For it is *we both*, Jews and Gentiles, who as members of God's new society now approach our Father together. Thus the highest and fullest achievement of the peacemaking Christ is this trinitarian access of the people of God, as through him and by one Spirit we come boldly to our Father.

3. The portrait of God's new society or what we have now become (verses 19–22)

So then, Paul begins his summing up. He has explained step by step what Christ has done to 'bring near', to God and to his people those in the Gentile world who were previously 'far off'. Christ has abolished the law of commandments, created a single new humanity in place of the two, reconciled both to God, and preached peace to those near and far. *So then*, what is the result of Christ's achievement and announcement of peace? It is this: *you* (Gentiles) *are no longer* what you used to be, *strangers and sojourners*, 'aliens in a foreign land' (NEB), visitors without legal rights. On the contrary, your status has dramatically changed. Now you 'belong' in a way you never did before. You used to be refugees; at least now you have a home.

In order to indicate the richness of their changed position and their new privileges in Christ, Paul resorts to three familiar models of the church, which are developed in many other passages of Scripture. He pictures the new Jew-Gentile community as God's kingdom, God's family and God's temple.

a. God's kingdom (verse 19a)

According to verse 12 the Gentiles used to be stateless and disenfranchised outsiders, 'alienated from the commonwealth (*politeia*) of Israel'. But now, he says to them, *you are fellow citizens (sumpolitai) with the saints*, which seems here to mean the Jewish people, the 'saints' or 'holy nation'. Only a few years previously the word *politeia* had been used of Roman citizenship in Paul's conversation with the tribune in Jerusalem.[6] Now he writes of another citizenship. Although he does not develop the metaphor, he appears to be alluding to citizenship of God's kingdom. The kingdom of God is neither a territorial jurisdiction nor even a spiritual structure. God's kingdom is God himself ruling his people, and bestowing upon them all the privileges and responsibilities which his rule implies. To this new international God-ruled community, which had replaced the Old Testament national theocracy, Gentiles and Jews belonged on equal terms. Paul is writing while the Roman Empire is at the zenith of its splendour; no signs had yet appeared of its coming decline, let alone of its fall. Yet he sees this other kingdom, neither Jewish nor Roman but international and interracial, as something more splendid and more enduring than any earthly empire.[7] And he rejoices in its citizenship more even than in his Roman citizenship. Its citizens are free and secure. The words *no longer strangers and sojourners but ... citizens* emphasize the contrast between the rootlessness of a life outside Christ and the stability of being a part of God's new society. 'We no longer live on a passport, but ... we really have our birth certificates, ... we really do belong.'[8]

b. God's family (verse 19b)

The metaphor changes and becomes more intimate: *you are ... members of the household of God*. A kingdom is one thing; a household or family is another. And in Christ Jews and Gentiles find themselves more than fellow citizens under his rule; they are together children in his family. Paul has just written in the previous verse of the new and privileged access 'to the Father' which Jews and Gentiles

[6] Acts 22:25–29.

[7] Similarly, in 1 Cor. 10:32 Paul refers to 'the church of God' as a third community, distinct from both 'Jews' and 'Greeks'. It was doubtless on the basis of such texts as these that Clement of Alexandria could distinguish Christians from Greeks and Jews as those who worship God 'in the third form' and 'the one race of the saved people' (*Miscellanies*, VI.5), while the second-century *Letter to Diognetus* calls Christians 'a new race' (ch.1).

[8] Lloyd-Jones, *God's Way*, p. 302.

enjoy through Christ (verse 18), and earlier in the letter he has enlarged on the blessings of 'adoption' into his family (1:5). Soon he will have more to say about God's archetypal fatherhood (3:14–15) and about the 'one God and Father of us all' (4:6). But here his emphasis seems to be less on God's fatherhood than on the brotherhood into which, across racial barriers, the Father's children are brought. 'Brethren' (meaning 'brothers and sisters') is the commonest word for Christians in the New Testament. It expresses a close relationship of affection, care and support. *Philadelphia*, 'brotherly love', should always be a special characteristic of God's new society.

c. God's temple (verses 20–22)

Paul comes now to his third picture. Essentially the church is a community of people. Nevertheless, it may be likened in a number of respects to a building, and especially to the temple. The temple in Jerusalem—first Solomon's, then Zerubbabel's, then Herod's—had for nearly a thousand years been the focal point of Israel's identity as the people of God. Now there was a new people; would there be a new temple, as Jesus had hinted? The new people was not a new nation but a new humanity, international and worldwide. A geographically localized centre would therefore not be appropriate for it. What then could be its temple, its focus of unity? Here in verses 20–22 Paul elaborates his vision of the new temple in greater detail than elsewhere; it will repay careful study. As he develops his image, he refers to the foundation and cornerstone of the building, the structure as a whole and its individual stones, its cohesion and growth, its present function and (at least implicitly) its future destiny.

First, the foundation. Nothing is more important to any edifice than a solid, stable foundation. And Jesus' well-known parable of the two house builders, with which he concluded his sermon on the mount, taught the need for rock. On what rock, then, is the church built? Paul replies: it is *built upon the foundation of the apostles and prophets, Christ Jesus himself being the cornerstone* (verse 20).

Since apostles and prophets were both groups with a

teaching role, it seems clear that what constitutes the church's foundation is neither their person nor their office but their instruction. Moreover, we are to think of them as inspired teachers, organs of divine revelation, bearers of divine authority. The word 'apostles' here cannot therefore be a generic term for missionaries or church planters or bishops or other church leaders; instead it must denote that small and special group whom Jesus chose, called and authorized to teach in his name, and who were eyewitnesses of his resurrection, consisting of the Twelve plus Paul and James and perhaps one or two others. What they taught they expected the church to believe and preserve, what they commanded they expected the church to obey. The word 'prophets' also indicates inspired teachers to whom the word of God came and who conveyed that word to others faithfully. The couplet 'apostles and prophets' may bring together the Old Testament (prophets) and New Testament (apostles) as the basis of the church's teaching. But the inverted order of the words (not 'prophets and apostles' but 'apostles and prophets') suggests that probably New Testament prophets are meant. If so, their bracketing with the apostles as the church's foundation is significant. The reference must again be to a small group of inspired teachers, associated with the apostles, who together bore witness to Christ and whose teaching was derived from revelation (3:5) and was foundational.

In practical terms this means that the church is built on the New Testament Scriptures. They are the church's foundation documents. And just as a foundation cannot be tampered with once it has been laid and the superstructure is being built upon it, so the New Testament foundation of the church is inviolable and cannot be changed by any additions, subtractions or modifications offered by teachers who claim to be apostles or prophets today. The church stands or falls by its loyal dependence on the foundation truths which God revealed to his apostles and prophets, and which are now preserved in the New Testament Scriptures.

The cornerstone is also of crucial importance to a building. It is itself part of and essential to the foundation; it helps to hold the building steady, and it also sets it and keeps it in line. The temple in Jerusalem had massive cornerstones. Armitage Robinson mentions one ancient monolith excavated from the southern wall of the temple which measured 38 feet 9 inches (about 12 metres) in length.[9] *The chief cornerstone* of the new temple is *Christ Jesus himself.* Elsewhere he is also the foundation stone.[1] But here Paul has particularly in mind the function of Jesus Christ in holding the growing temple together as a unity. For he is *the chief cornerstone, in whom the whole structure is joined together and grows. . .* The unity and growth of the church are coupled, and Jesus Christ is the secret of both. Since the 'in Christ' concept is of an organic union, the most natural metaphors to illustrate it are organic metaphors such as the branches 'in' the vine and the members 'in' the body. Here the concept is transferred to construction work. As a building depends for both its cohesion and its development on being tied securely to its cornerstone, so Christ the cornerstone is indispensable to the church's unity and growth. Unless it is constantly and securely related to Christ, the church's unity will disintegrate and its growth either stop or run wild.

Paul moves on from the whole structure of the temple to its individual stones. In both cases union with Christ is indispensable: *Christ . . . the chief cornerstone in whom the whole structure is joined together . . . in whom you also are built into it. . .* The apostle Peter, who also develops the picture of the church as a building, describes individual church members as 'living stones' needing to 'come to him (Jesus) . . . and be . . . built into a spiritual house'.[2] Here in Paul's picture the extra stones being built into the structure are *you also*, by which he means his Gentile readers. The Jerusalem temple was an exclusively Jewish edifice, as we have seen, which all Gentiles were forbidden to enter. But now Gentiles are not only admitted; they are themselves constituent parts of the temple of God. And since one of the cornerstone's functions was to bind two walls together, it may be that Paul is using this imagery

[9] Armitage Robinson, p. 69.
[1] *Cf.* Is. 28:16; Ps. 118:22; 1 Cor. 3:11; 1 Pet. 2:4–8.
[2] 1 Pet. 2:4–5.

to set Christ forth as the key to Jewish-Gentile solidarity.

What is the purpose of the new temple? In principle, it is the same as the purpose of the old, namely to be a dwelling place of God (verse 22). Of course spiritually minded Israelites knew that God did not dwell in man-made temples and that the whole universe could not contain his infinite being.[3] Nevertheless, he promised to manifest his glory (the shekinah) in the temple's inner sanctuary, in order to symbolize the truth that he dwelt among his people. The new temple, however, is neither a material building, nor a 'national shrine, nor has it a localized site. It is a spiritual building (God's household) and an international community (embracing Gentiles as well as Jews), and it has a worldwide spread (wherever God's people are to be found). This is where God dwells. He is not tied to holy buildings but to holy people, to his own new society. To them he has pledged himself by a solemn covenant. He lives in them, individually and as a community.[4] What, then, has replaced the shekinah glory in the temple, as the symbol of God's presence and the means of its manifestation? Paul answers the question here. The church is both *a holy temple in the Lord* (meaning, as always in the New Testament when not otherwise stated, 'the Lord Jesus') and *a dwelling place of God in the Spirit*. Once more the Holy Trinity claims our attention. For God dwells in his people as his temple 'in the Lord' and 'in the Spirit', or through his Son and by his Spirit.

As Paul was dictating his letter, there stood in Ephesus the magnificent marble temple of Artemis ('great is Diana of the Ephesians'), one of the seven wonders of the ancient world, and in whose inner shrine there was a statue of the goddess. At the same time in Jerusalem there stood the Jewish temple built by Herod the Great, barricading itself against the Gentiles, and now also against God, whose shekinah glory it had housed in its inner sanctuary for centuries, but whose glory as revealed in its Messiah it had sought to extinguish. Two temples, one pagan and the other

[3] Cf. 1 Kgs. 8:27; Acts 7:48,49; 17:24.
[4] Contrast 1 Cor. 6:19; 3:16 and Eph. 2:21–22, where the temple of God is identified successively as the individual Christian's body, the local church and the universal church.

Jewish, each designed by its devotees as a divine residence, but both empty of the living God. For now there is a new temple, *a dwelling place of God in the Spirit*. It is his new society, his redeemed people scattered throughout the inhabited world. They are his home on earth. They will also be his home in heaven. For the building is not yet complete. *It grows into a holy temple in the Lord*. Only after the creation of the new heaven and the new earth will the voice from the throne declare with emphatic finality: 'Behold, the dwelling of God is with men.'[5]

Conclusion

It is marvellous to look back and trace the sequence of the apostle's teaching. He paints on a large canvas with bold brush strokes. Once, he reminds his Gentile readers, you were alienated from God and from his people. But Christ died to reconcile you to both. So now you are no longer the aliens you were, but the kingdom over which God rules, the family which he loves and the temple in which he dwells. More simply still: you were alienated, you have been reconciled, and Christ has brought you home.

It would be hard to exaggerate the grandeur of this vision. The new society God has brought into being is nothing short of a new creation, a new human race, whose characteristic is no longer alienation but reconciliation, no longer division and hostility but unity and peace. This new society God rules and loves and lives in.

That is the vision. But when we turn from the ideal portrayed in Scripture to the concrete realities experienced in the church today, it is a very different and a very tragic story. For even in the church there is often alienation, disunity and discord. And Christians erect new barriers in place of the old which Christ has demolished, now a colour bar, now racism, nationalism or tribalism, now personal animosities engendered by pride, prejudice, jealousy and the unforgiving spirit, now a divisive system of caste or class, now a clericalism which sunders clergy from laity as if they were separate breeds of human being, and now

[5] Rev. 21:1–5.

a denominationalism which turns churches into sects and contradicts the unity and universality of Christ's church.

These things are doubly offensive. First, they are an offence to Jesus Christ. How dare we build walls of partition in the one and only human community in which he has destroyed them? Of course there are barriers of language and culture in the world outside, and of course new converts feel more comfortable among their own kind, who speak and dress and eat and drink and behave in the same way that they do and have always done. But deliberately to perpetuate these barriers in the church, and even to tolerate them without taking any active steps to overcome them in order to demonstrate the trans-cultural unity of God's new society, is to set ourselves against the reconciling work of Christ and even to try to undo it.

What is offensive to Christ is offensive also, though in a different way, to the world. It hinders the world from believing in Jesus. God intends his people to be a visual model of the gospel, to demonstrate before people's eyes the good news of reconciliation. But what is the good of gospel campaigns if they do not produce gospel churches? It is simply impossible, with any shred of Christian integrity, to go on proclaiming that Jesus by his cross has abolished the old divisions and created a single new humanity of love, while at the same time we are contradicting our message by tolerating racial or social or other barriers within our church fellowship. I am not saying that a church must be perfect before it can preach the gospel, but I am saying that it cannot preach the gospel while acquiescing in its imperfections.

We need to get the failures of the church on our conscience, to feel the offence to Christ and the world which these failures are, to weep over the credibility gap between the church's talk and the church's walk, to repent of our readiness to excuse and even condone our failures, and to determine to do something about it. I wonder if anything is more urgent today, for the honour of Christ and for the spread of the gospel, than that the church should be, and should be seen to be, what by God's purpose and Christ's achievement it already is—a single new humanity, a model of human community, a family

111

of reconciled brothers and sisters who love their Father and love each other, the evident dwelling place of God by his Spirit. Only then will the world believe in Christ as Peacemaker. Only then will God receive the glory due to his name.

5. Paul's unique privilege

For this reason I, Paul, a prisoner for Christ Jesus on behalf of you Gentiles—²assuming that you have heard of the stewardship of God's grace that was given to me for you, ³how the mystery was made known to me by revelation, as I have written briefly. ⁴When you read this you can perceive my insight into the mystery of Christ, ⁵which was not· made known to the sons of men in other generations as it has now been revealed to his holy apostles and prophets by the Spirit; ⁶that is, how the Gentiles are fellow heirs, members of the same body, and partakers of the promise in Christ Jesus through the gospel.

⁷Of this gospel I was made a minister according to the gift of God's grace which was given me by the working of his power. ⁸To me, though I am the very least of all the saints, this grace was given, to preach to the Gentiles the unsearchable riches of Christ, ⁹and to make all men see what is the plan of the mystery hidden for ages in God who created all things; ¹⁰that through the church the manifold wisdom of God might now be made known to the principalities and powers in the heavenly places. ¹¹This was according to the eternal purpose which he has realized in Christ Jesus our Lord, ¹²in whom we have boldness and confidence of access through our faith in him. ¹³So I ask you not to lose heart over what I am suffering for you, which is your glory.

At this stage in his argument Paul introduces himself, and explains his unique personal role in God's purpose for the

113

Gentiles. It is not for nothing that he has come to be known as 'the apostle to the Gentiles'.

In the second half of Ephesians 2, as we saw in the last chapter, he painted a vivid contrast between the double alienation the Gentiles endured before Christ (from God and from Israel) and their double reconciliation through Christ. For by his death Christ demolished the Jew-Gentile and God-man barriers, and is now creating in relation to himself a single, new multi-cultural human society, which is both the family God loves and the temple he lives in. Paul's Gentile readers must have read with joyful amazement this exposition of the gospel of peace.

Now, abruptly, he turns their attention away from themselves to himself. In doing so, he styles himself *I Paul, a prisoner for Christ Jesus on behalf of you Gentiles* (verse 1). Humanly speaking, he was not Christ's prisoner but Nero's. He had appealed to the Emperor, and so to the Emperor he had been committed for trial.[1] But Paul never did think or speak in purely human terms. He believed in the sovereignty of God over the affairs of men. Therefore he called himself (literally) a 'prisoner of Christ Jesus' (verse 1)[2] or a 'prisoner in the Lord',[3] so convinced was he that the whole of his life, including his wearisome imprisonment, was under the lordship of Jesus. He may also have thought of himself as 'Christ's prisoner' much as he thought of himself as 'Christ's slave', in which case his self-description expressed a 'combination of external and internal captivity'.[4]

He then adds a second descriptive phrase, to indicate the nature and purpose of his imprisonment. He was Jesus Christ's prisoner *on behalf of you Gentiles*. This was a matter of fact. What had led to his arrest in Jerusalem, his imprisonment there and in Caesarea, his successive trials and his subsequent appeal to Caesar which had brought him to Rome, was fanatical Jewish opposition to his mission to the Gentiles. Luke, his friend, doctor and travelling companion, was with him at the time and faithfully recorded the details in his Acts record. He

---

[1] Acts 25:11–12.   [2] Also Phm. 1,9; and *cf.* 2 Tim. 1:8.
[3] 4:1.   [4] Barth *Ephesians, I* p. 361.

114

explains that what prompted the Jews to stir up the crowd against Paul was his reputation for 'teaching men everywhere against the people and the law and this place' (*viz.* the temple). How can he have acquired such a reputation? Doubtless by teaching exactly what he has just taught in Ephesians 2, namely that by abolishing the divisive elements of the law Jesus was creating a new people and building a new temple. So he was arrested. And when the tribune allowed him to make his public defence to the Jewish people, they listened to him quietly until he got to the point in his story where Jesus had said to him: 'Depart; for I will send you far away to the Gentiles.' At this they shouted 'Away with such a fellow from the earth.'[5]

So what led to Jewish opposition to Paul was his bold, uncompromising espousal of the Gentile cause. He not only preached his vision of the new and undivided humanity and wrote about it; he was at that moment suffering for the very truths he was expounding.

It seems likely that the apostle was intending to go on to pray for his Gentile readers. He began his sentence: *For this cause I Paul* ... But he interrupted himself, and did not begin his prayer until verse 14. Meanwhile, he elaborated his self-description in order to emphasize the unique privileges God had given him in the outworking of his purpose for the Gentiles.

Twice in these verses he uses the same expression, indeed an identical combination of Greek words, which are translated *God's grace that was given to me* (verses 2 and 7). He is referring to two privileges which God in unmerited favour had given to him.

The first was a certain revelation, as a result of which he had come to know something. Verses 2-3: *You have heard of ... God's grace that was given to me for you, how the mystery was made known to me by revelation.*

The second was a certain commission, as a result of which he had a responsibility to make something known to others. Verses 7-8: *Of this gospel I was made a minister according to the gift of God's grace which was given me by the working of his power.*

[5] Acts 21:17ff; 22:21ff.

It is clear that these two gifts of divine grace, the revelation and the commission, the 'mystery' revealed to him and the 'ministry' entrusted to him, were closely related to each other. For once he had received his special revelation from God, he knew that he was under obligation to make known to others what had been made known to him.

1. The divine revelation to Paul, or the mystery made known to him (verses 1–6)

Three times in this short paragraph Paul uses the word 'mystery': *how the mystery was made known to me by revelation* (verse 3) . . . *you can perceive my insight into the mystery of Christ* (verse 4) . . . *to make all men see what is the plan of the mystery* (verse 9). It is a key word for our understanding of the apostle Paul. We need to realize that the English and Greek words do not have the same meaning. In English a 'mystery' is something dark, obscure, secret, puzzling. What is 'mysterious' is inexplicable, even incomprehensible. The Greek word *mystērion* is different, however. Although still a 'secret', it is no longer closely guarded but open. Originally, the Greek word referred to a truth into which someone had been initiated. Indeed it came to be used of the secret teachings of the heathen mystery religions, teachings which were restricted to initiates. But in Christianity there are no esoteric 'mysteries' reserved for a spiritual élite. On the contrary, the Christian 'mysteries' are truths which, although beyond human discovery, have been revealed by God and so now belong openly to the whole church. More simply, *mystērion* is a truth hitherto hidden from human knowledge or understanding but now disclosed by the revelation of God.

If that is the general meaning of 'mystery' in the New Testament, what is the particular open secret or revealed truth, which was *not made known to the sons of men in other generations* but *has now been revealed to his holy apostles and prophets by the Spirit* (verse 5) and uniquely, Paul adds, *made known to me by revelation* (verse 3)? He calls it in verse 4, as in Colossians 4:3, *the mystery of*

Christ. So evidently it is a specially revealed truth 'of which Christ is both the source and the substance'.[6] Its exact nature Paul spells out with force and clarity in verse 6. It is *how the Gentiles are fellow heirs, members of the same body, and partakers of the promise in Christ Jesus through the gospel.* Thus the mystery concerns Christ and his one Jewish-Gentile people. In order to define it more precisely, Paul assembles (and in one case invents) three parallel, composite expressions. Each has the same prefix *syn*, 'together with', and indicates what Gentile believers now have and are in partnership with Jewish believers. What is this? Gentiles are 'co-heirs' (*synklēronoma*), 'concorporate' (*syssōma*) and 'co-sharers' (*symmetocha*) of the promise. But these three unusual Greek words need to be spelled out a little. What Paul is declaring is that Gentile and Jewish Christians together are now fellow-heirs of the same blessing, fellow-members of the same body and fellow-partakers of the same promise. And this shared privilege is both *in Jesus Christ* (because it is enjoyed equally by all believers, whether Jews or Gentiles, provided that they are in union with Christ) and *through the gospel* (because the gospel proclamation includes this unity and so makes it available to those who believe).

To sum up, we may say that 'the mystery of Christ' is the complete union of Jews and Gentiles with each other through the union of both with Christ. It is this double union, with Christ and with each other, which was the substance of the 'mystery'. God had revealed it specially to Paul, as he had written briefly (verse 3) in the previous chapter. But it had also been made known to God's *holy apostles and prophets by the Spirit* (verse 5), and through them 'to his saints' (Col. 1:26).[7] It was now therefore the common possession of the universal church.

It was a new revelation. For it was *not made known . . . in other generations* (verse 5) but was *hidden for ages* (verse 9). These statements have puzzled Bible readers because the Old Testament did reveal that God had a purpose for the Gentiles. It promised, for example, that

[6] Hendriksen, p. 153.
[7] An example was the special revelation to the apostle Peter of God's purpose to include the Gentiles, as recorded in Acts 10 and 11.

all the families of the earth would be blessed through Abraham's posterity; that the Messiah would receive the nations as his inheritance; that Israel would be given as a light to the nations; and that one day the nations would make a pilgrimage to Jerusalem and even 'flow to it' like a mighty river.[8] Jesus also spoke of the inclusion of the Gentiles and commissioned his followers to go and make them his disciples. But what neither the Old Testament nor Jesus revealed was the radical nature of God's plan, which was that the theocracy (the Jewish nation under God's rule) would be terminated, and replaced by a new international community, the church; that this church would be 'the body of Christ', organically united to him; and that Jews and Gentiles would be incorporated into Christ and his church on equal terms without any distinction. It was this complete union of Jews, Gentiles and Christ which was radically new, and which God revealed to Paul, overcoming his entrenched Jewish prejudice.[9]

2. The divine commission to Paul or the ministry entrusted to him (verses 7–13)

At the end of verse 6 Paul has virtually equated 'the mystery' with 'the gospel'. At least he writes that it is 'through the gospel' that Jewish and Gentile Christians become united to Christ. This can be so only because the gospel announces the mystery, so that people come to hear it, to believe it and to experience it.

Now this equation of 'mystery' and 'gospel' is significant, because the mystery was essentially truth revealed *to* Paul, while the gospel was essentially truth proclaimed *by* Paul. Paul himself made the connection, because he was convinced that the good news had been revealed to him only in order to be communicated. He says so plainly: *Of this gospel I was made a minister according to the gift of God's grace which was given me* (verse 7). Thus if the first gift of God's grace to him was 'the mystery' itself which had been revealed to him (verses 2–3), the second was the

---

[8] Gn. 12:1–3; Ps. 2:8; Is. 42:6; 49:6; 2:2–4.
[9] *Cf.* his claim to direct revelation in Gal. 1:12.

ministry which had been entrusted to him and by which he would share it with others. He had received it by God's grace, and would exercise it *by the working of his power.*

This commission or ministry Paul regards as an enormous privilege. For what he calls *this grace*, which we might call 'this privileged gift of God', had been given to him, in spite of the fact that he was *the very least of all the saints* (verse 8), or 'the meanest member of the holy people'.[1] It is a very striking expression. He takes the superlative (*elachistos*, 'least' or 'smallest') and does what is impossible linguistically but possible theologically; he turns it into a comparative (*elachistoteros*, 'leaster' or 'less than the least'). Perhaps he was deliberately playing on the meaning of his name. For his Roman surname 'Paulus' is Latin for 'little' or 'small', and tradition says he was a little man. 'I *am* little,' he may be saying, 'little by name, little in stature, and morally and spiritually littler than the littlest of all Christians.' In affirming this he is neither indulging in hypocrisy nor grovelling in self-depreciation. He means it. He is deeply conscious both of his own unworthiness because he 'formerly blasphemed and persecuted and insulted' Jesus Christ[2] and of Christ's overflowing mercy towards him. A good indication that his modesty was neither sham nor morbid is that it did not hinder him from taking responsibility as an apostle. On the contrary, in this very passage he twice uses the self-conscious apostolic *egō* 'I' (3:1; 4:1). Thus, he combined personal humility with apostolic authority. Indeed, while 'minimizing himself he magnified his office'.[3]

The privileged ministry of spreading the gospel, entrusted to him by the grace of God, he now elaborates in three stages:

a. Making known Christ's riches to the Gentiles (verse 8)

Since the mystery revealed to him concerned God's plan to incorporate the Gentiles in Christ, it was only logical that the ministry entrusted to him should be directed first and foremost to them. He was commissioned *to preach to the Gentiles*. 'Preach' here is *euangelizō*, to 'announce good

[1] Armitage Robinson, p. 169.　　[2] 1 Tim. 1:13.　　[3] Simpson, p. 70.

119

news', for he was well aware that his gospel was a message of great good news for the Gentiles. It consisted of *the unsearchable riches of Christ*, the riches which he possesses in himself and which he bestows on those who come to him. What these riches are we may judge from Paul's exposition in Ephesians 1 and 2. They are riches freely available because of the cross. They include resurrection from the death of sin, victorious enthronement with Christ in the heavenlies, reconciliation with God, incorporation with Jewish believers in his new society, the end of hostility and the beginning of peace, access to the Father through Christ and by the Spirit, membership of his kingdom and household, being an integral part of his dwelling place among men, and all this only a foretaste of yet more riches to come, namely the riches of the glory of the inheritance which God will give to all his people on the last day.

No wonder Paul terms Christ's riches *unsearchable*. The word *anexichniastos* means literally 'not to be tracked out'. In the Greek version of Job 5: 9 and 9: 10 it was applied to the wonders of God's creation and providence, which are beyond our understanding, and Paul himself has already used it in Romans 11: 33 of the deep mysteries of God's plan of salvation. The riches of Christ are similar. Like the earth they are too vast to explore, like the sea too deep to fathom. Translators and commentators compete with one another in their attempt to find a dynamic equivalent in English. The riches of Christ, they say, are 'unsearchable', 'inexplorable', 'untraceable', 'unfathomable', 'inexhaustible', 'illimitable', 'inscrutable' and 'incalculable'. Perhaps GNB's 'infinite' is the simplest, for what is certain about the wealth Christ has and gives is that we shall never come to an end of it.

Indirectly in these past verses the apostle has indicated two of the strongest incentives to evangelism. He began by emphasizing that the revelation and the commission which had been given to him belong indissolubly together, for what had been made known to him he must without fail make known to others. All revealed truth is held in stewardship. It is given to be shared, not monopolized. If men cannot keep their scientific discoveries to themselves, how much less should we keep to ourselves the divine disclosures? Paul then went on to emphasize the valuable content of the message itself. He was convinced, as we must be, that Christ never impoverishes those who put their trust in him, but always immeasurably enriches them. Here then was the double obligation Paul felt, first to share God's truth and secondly to share Christ's riches. So what is needed today for a recovery of evangelistic zeal in the church is the same apostolic conviction about the gospel. Once we are sure that the gospel is both truth from God and riches for mankind, nobody will be able to silence us.

b. Making known the mystery to all men (verse 9)

The second part or stage of Paul's privileged ministry he expresses in these terms: *to make all men see what is the plan of the mystery hidden for ages in God who created all things*. Verse 9 does not simply repeat verse 8. There are three significant differences.

First, the preaching of the gospel is now defined not as *euangelizō* (to 'announce good news') but as *phōtizō* (to 'enlighten'). Paul has already used the verb in his prayer in 1:18. So the thought shifts from the content of the message (good news) to the condition of those to whom it is proclaimed (in the darkness of ignorance). Jesus himself had characterized Paul's commission in these terms, since he told him he was sending him to the Gentiles 'to open their eyes, that they may turn from darkness to light and from the power of Satan to God'.[4] Paul never forgot this. His own conversion on the road to Damascus had resulted from the bright shining of a light from heaven, not just externally but internally. As he put it later: 'It is the God who said "Let light shine out of darkness" who has shone in our hearts.'[5] Indeed, *phōtismos* is the word he uses there to describe his 'enlightenment' involved in his conversion. We ourselves must always remember in our evangelism that 'the prince of darkness' holds men and women in darkness, and that only by a divine enlightenment will their eyes be opened to see. Our responsibility is to be

[4] Acts 26:17–18.   [5] 2 Cor. 4:6.

faithful in spreading the gospel, since this is the means which God has ordained by which to bring light to those in darkness.

A second difference between verse 8 and verse 9 lies in Paul's description of his message. In verse 8 he calls it *the unsearchable riches of Christ*, in verse 9 *the plan of the mystery*. These are not just divergent expressions for the same thing; again they indicate a shift of emphasis. One may say that Christ's 'unsearchable riches' is the broader of the two concepts. It embraces Christ's remedy for the two Gentile alienations (from God and from Israel) and therefore the totality of his salvation. The 'mystery' concentrates on only one of the two reconciliations. True, the mystery is 'the mystery of Christ'; it centres on Christ. But what it declares about Christ is that through him and in him Jews and Gentiles are incorporated on equal terms in the same single community. Let me point the difference more sharply in this way: according to verse 8 Paul's message was Christ, according to verse 9 it was the church.

The third difference between verses 8 and 9 is that Paul directs his ministry in the former verse to *the Gentiles*, and in the latter to *all men*. This was necessary because the mystery concerned both Jews and Gentiles. It was a message of mutual reconciliation and of joint membership in God's new society, which was also the new humanity he was creating. Perhaps this is the reason why in verse 9 Paul describes God as the One *who created all things*. He who created the universe has now begun a new creation and will one day finish it. Indeed, the 'mystery' includes the great promise that finally God will unite all things in and under Christ.[6] So in verse 9 Paul brings creation and redemption together in his mind. The God who created all things in the beginning will recreate all things in the end.

c. Making known God's wisdom to the cosmic powers (verse 10)

The apostle's perspective broadens further. He tells us that,

[6] 1:9–10.

although the gospel is addressed primarily and directly to humans, it brings a message indirectly to angels also, *to the principalities and powers in the heavenly places*. What does he mean?

The first result to be expected from the preaching of 'Christ's unsearchable riches' and 'the mystery' would be the birth and growth of the church. Gentiles and Jews would embrace the gospel, be converted, and find themselves joint members of the family of God and the body of Christ. Indeed, this had already happened, as Paul was writing. He was not theorizing. 'The mystery' was not an abstraction. It was taking concrete shape before people's eyes. And in this new phenomenon, this new multi-racial humanity, the wisdom of God was being displayed. Indeed, the coming into existence of the church, as a community of saved and reconciled people, is at one and the same time a public demonstration of God's power, grace and wisdom: first of God's mighty resurrection power,[7] next of his immeasurable grace and kindness,[8] and now thirdly of his *manifold wisdom*. The word for 'manifold' (*polupoikilos*) means 'many-coloured', and was used to describe flowers, crowns, embroidered cloth and woven carpets. The simpler word *poikilos* was used in the LXX of the 'coat of many colours' (AV) or 'richly ornamented robe' (NIV) which Jacob gave to his youngest son Joseph (Gn. 37:3,23,32). The church as a multi-racial, multi-cultural community is like a beautiful tapestry. Its members come from a wide range of colourful backgrounds. No other human community resembles it. Its diversity and harmony are unique. It is God's new society. And the many-coloured fellowship of the church is a reflection of the many-coloured (or 'many-splendoured', to use Francis Thompson's word) wisdom of God.

So then, as the gospel spreads throughout the world, this new and variegated Christian community develops. It is as if a great drama is being enacted. History is the theatre, the world is the stage, and church members in every land are the actors. God himself has written the play, and he directs and produces it. Act by act, scene by

[7] 1:19 – 2:6.   [8] 2:7.

scene, the story continues to unfold. But who are the audience? They are the cosmic intelligences, *the principalities and powers in the heavenly places*. We are to think of them as spectators of the drama of salvation. Thus 'the history of the Christian church becomes a graduate school for angels'.[9]

Our knowledge of these spiritual beings is limited, and we must be careful not to go beyond what Scripture teaches into idle speculation. It is clear, however, that they are not omniscient. The apostle Peter tells us that they did not fully understand the teaching of either the Old Testament prophets or the New Testament apostles regarding the good news of salvation in Christ, for these are 'things into which angels long to look'.[1] Similarly, we may infer from verse 10 here that God had not revealed to them directly his master plan for the church, but intended rather to make it known to them *through the church* itself, as it came into being and grew. It is through the old creation (the universe) that God reveals his glory to humans; it is through the new creation (the church) that he reveals his wisdom to angels. It seems legitimate to say that though we cannot see them, they can see us. They watch fascinated as they see Gentiles and Jews being incorporated into the new society as equals. Indeed, they learn from the composition of the church not only *the manifold wisdom of God* (verse 10) but also his *eternal purpose* (verse 11). This purpose *he has realized in Christ Jesus our Lord*, in the arena of history, through his death and resurrection, the gift of his Spirit, the preaching of the gospel and the emergence of the church. For *in* him (Christ) and *through our faith in him* all of us, whether Jews or Gentiles. *have boldness and confidence of access* (verse 12). This universal access of all Christian people to God through Christ is what the sixteenth-century reformers termed 'the priesthood of all believers'; it is a foundation privilege of all who are in Christ, in fact of 'the church', the universal Jew-Gentile community, of which Paul has just been writing.

I do not think I can leave these verses, especially verse 10, without at least mentioning a quite different interpret-

[9] Mackay, p. 84.   [1] 1 Pet. 1:10–12.

ation which is gaining popularity. It rests on an understanding of 'the principalities and powers' as being not cosmic intelligences (*i.e.* angels and demons) but rather the politico-economic structures of human society. I shall reserve a full exposition and critique of this view until we reach the warfare with the 'principalities and powers' in 6:12, but I cannot altogether ignore it here. Its importance may be gauged by G. B. Caird's statement about verse 10: 'It is hardly an exaggeration to say that any interpretation of Ephesians stands or falls by this verse.' He believes that God's purpose is to use the church not only to *inform* 'the powers' but actually to *redeem* them, since 'even such structures of power and authority as the secular state are capable of being brought into harmony with the love of God'.[2] Markus Barth elaborates this concept of the far flung, 'cosmic' influence of the church: 'Political and social, cultural and religious forces, also all other institutions, traditions, majorities and minorities are exposed to her testimony.' Dictatorships and democracies, organizations promoting racism and civil rights, *etc., etc.* 'all these and other powers are given a unique chance by God: they are entitled to see in their midst the beginning of a new heaven and a new earth'.[3] He is referring to the church's role as indicated in verse 10. Naturally, I feel very diffident about disagreeing with scholars of this calibre but, having weighed the matter carefully, I feel bound to declare myself on it: I do not believe either that Paul was referring to social structures on earth when he wrote of principalities and powers in the heavenlies, or that, whatever their identity, he intended the making known to them of God's manifold wisdom to be understood as a redemptive (as opposed to an informative) activity. But I will say no more on this topic here.

Looking back over Paul's exposition of the peculiar privilege which had been given him by God's grace to be the apostle to the Gentiles, it is instructive to note the different media and phases of God's communication. First, he made known the mystery of his plan to Paul himself (and the other apostles and prophets, verse 5) by revelation.

---

[2] Caird, pp. 66–67.   [3] Barth, *Ephesians, I*, p. 365.

Secondly, he commissioned Paul (and others) to preach the gospel to everybody throughout the world. Thirdly, his manifold wisdom and eternal purpose were made known to the principalities and powers through the fact of the church as they watched it grow. This is the circle of divine communication, for the good news was passed from God to Paul, from Paul and others to all mankind, and from the church on earth back to heaven again, to the cosmic powers. At each stage the medium changes. It is by direct revelation that God disclosed his plan to Paul, by the verbal proclamation of the gospel that the message spreads today, and by a visual model (the multi-cultural Christian community) that it finally reaches the unseen angelic spectators. Nothing is more honouring to the gospel, or more indicative of its surpassing importance, than this programme for its universal communication.

Conclusion

The major lesson taught by this first half of Ephesians 3 is the biblical centrality of the church. Some people construct a Christianity which consists entirely of a personal relationship to Jesus Christ and has virtually nothing to do with the church. Others make a grudging concession to the need for church membership, but add that they have given up the ecclesiastical institution as hopeless. Now it is understandable, even inevitable, that we are critical of many of the church's inherited structures and traditions. Every church in every place at every time is in need of reform and renewal. But we need to beware lest we despise the church of God, and are blind to his work in history. We may safely say that God has not abandoned his church, however displeased with it he may be. He is still building and refining it. And if God has not abandoned it, how can we? It has a central place in his plan. What then does this passage teach about the biblical centrality of the church?

a. The church is central to history

Verse 11, as we saw, alludes to *the eternal purpose* of God.

It is also called his 'plan' or 'the plan of the mystery' (verse 9). What we are told is that this plan or purpose of God, which was conceived in eternity, kept 'hidden for ages' (verse 9) and 'not made known to the sons of men in other generations' (verse 5), he has now *realized in Christ Jesus our Lord*, first through his historical work of salvation and then through its subsequent proclamation in the world. What is this eternal purpose which is now being worked out in history, this divine plan which thus belongs to both history and eternity? It concerns the church, the creating of a new and reconciled humanity in union with Jesus Christ. This is the 'mystery', hidden for ages but now revealed.

Is this our view of history? We have all studied history at school and may have found it (as I did) abominably dull. Perhaps we had to memorize lists of dates or of the kings and queens who ruled our country. But what is the point of history? Was Henry Ford right when in 1919, during his libel suit with the *Chicago Tribune*, he said, 'History is bunk'? Is history just the random succession of events, each effect having its cause and each cause its effect, yet the whole betraying no overall pattern but appearing rather as the meaningless development of the human story? Was Marx right in his dialectical understanding of the historical process? Or has history some other clue?

Christians affirm, in contrast to all other views, that history is 'his story', God's story. For God is at work, moving from a plan conceived in eternity, through a historical outworking and disclosure, to a climax within history, and then on beyond it to another eternity of the future. The Bible has this linear understanding of time. And it tells us that the centre of God's eternal-historical plan is Jesus Christ, together with his redeemed and reconciled people. In order to grasp this, it may be helpful to contrast the perspective of secular historians with that of the Bible.

Secular history concentrates its attention on kings, queens and presidents, on politicians and generals, in fact on 'VIPs'. The Bible concentrates rather on a group it calls 'the saints', often little people, insignificant people, unimportant people, who are however at the same time God's

127

people—and for that reason are both 'unknown (to the world) and yet well-known (to God)'.[4]

Secular history concentrates on wars, battles and peace-treaties, followed by yet more wars, battles and peace-treaties. The Bible concentrates rather on the war between good and evil, on the decisive victory won by Jesus Christ over the powers of darkness, on the peace-treaty ratified by his blood, and on the sovereign proclamation of an amnesty for all rebels who will repent and believe.

Again, secular history concentrates on the changing map of the world, as one nation defeats another and annexes its territory, and on the rise and fall of empires. The Bible concentrates rather on a multi-national community called 'the church', which has no territorial frontiers, which claims nothing less than the whole world for Christ, and whose empire will never come to an end.

No doubt I have painted the contrast between the secular and the biblical views of history too starkly. For the Bible does not ignore the great empires of Babylon, Egypt, Greece and Rome; and a true secular history cannot ignore the fact of the church. Yet it is a question of perspective, of priorities. The living God is the God of all the nations of the world, yet within the universal human community there exists a 'covenant community', his own new society, the beginning of his new creation. It is to this people only that he has pledged himself with the everlasting promise: 'I will be their God, and they shall be my people.'

b. The church is central to the gospel

The gospel which some of us proclaim is much too individualistic. 'Christ died for me,' we say, and then sing of heaven: 'Oh, that will be glory for me.' Both affirmations are true. As for the first, the apostle Paul himself could write, 'The Son of God . . . loved me and gave himself for me.'[5] As for the so-called 'glory song', the gospel does promise 'glory' for believers in heaven. But this is far from being the full gospel. For it is evident from Ephesians 3 that the full gospel concerns both Christ and the 'mystery' of Christ. The good news of the unsearchable riches of

[4] 2 Cor. 6:9.   [5] Gal. 2:20.

Christ which Paul preached is that he died and rose again not only to save sinners like me (though he did), but also to create a single new humanity; not only to redeem us from sin but also to adopt us into God's family; not only to reconcile us to God but also to reconcile us to one another. Thus the church is an integral part of the gospel. The gospel is good news of a new society as well as of a new life.

c. The church is central to Christian living

It is noteworthy that Paul concludes this section as he began it (verse 1), namely with a reference to his own sufferings in the Gentile cause. He addresses to them the following exhortation: *So I ask you not to lose heart over what I am suffering for you, which is your glory* (verse 13). Now 'suffering' and 'glory' are constantly coupled in the New Testament. Jesus said that he would enter his glory through suffering, and that his followers would have to tread the same path. Here, however, Paul writes something different, namely that *his* sufferings will bring *them* (his Gentile readers) glory. He is suffering in prison on their behalf, as their champion, standing firm for their inclusion in God's new society. So convinced is he of the divine origin of his vision that he is prepared to pay any price to see it become a reality. That is the measure of Paul's concern for the church.

Now of course it may be argued that Paul was exceptional. He was after all the apostle to the Gentiles. He had received a special revelation and a special commission. So one would expect him to have to suffer for the church. Nevertheless, the principle is applicable to all Christians. If the church is central to God's purpose, as seen in both history and the gospel, it must surely also be central to our lives. How can we take lightly what God takes so seriously? How dare we push to the circumference what God has placed at the centre? No, we shall seek to become responsible church members, active in some local manifestation of the universal church. We shall not be able to acquiesce in low standards which fall far short of the New Testament ideals for God's new society, whether mechanical, meaningless worship services, or fellowship which is icy cold and even spoiled by rivalries which make the Lord's Supper a farce, or such inward-looking isolationism as to turn the church into a ghetto which is indifferent to the outside world and its pain. If instead (like Paul) we keep before us the vision of God's new society as his family, his dwelling place and his instrument in the world, then we shall constantly be seeking to make our church's worship more authentic, its fellowship more caring and its outreach more compassionate. In other words (like Paul again), we shall be ready to pray, to work and if necessary to suffer in order to turn the vision into a reality.

6. Confidence in God's power

For this reason I bow my knees before the Father, ¹⁵from whom every family in heaven and on earth is named, ¹⁶that according to the riches of his glory he may grant you to be strengthened with might through his Spirit in the inner man, ¹⁷and that Christ may dwell in your hearts through faith; that you, being rooted and grounded in love, ¹⁸may have power to comprehend with all the saints what is the breadth and length and height and depth, ¹⁹and to know the love of Christ which surpasses knowledge, that you may be filled with all the fullness of God.

²⁰Now to him who by the power at work within us is able to do far more abundantly than all that we ask or think, ²¹to him be glory in the church and in Christ Jesus to all generations, for ever and ever. Amen.

One of the best ways to discover a Christian's chief anxieties and ambitions is to study the content of his prayers and the intensity with which he prays them. We all pray about what concerns us, and are evidently not concerned about matters we do not include in our prayers. Prayer expresses desire. For example, when Paul prayed for the salvation of his Israelite kinsfolk, he wrote of his 'heart's desire and prayer to God for them'.[1] As the hymn puts it, 'Prayer is the soul's sincere desire, uttered or unexpressed.'

This is certainly true of this second prayer of Paul's in Ephesians in which he pours out his soul to God. He has

[1] Rom. 10:1.

been explaining both Christ's peace-making work, which resulted in the creation of the new society, and his personal involvement in this because of the special revelation and commission he had received. Now he turns from exposition to intercession. He prays that God's wonderful plan which he has been elaborating may be even more completely fulfilled in his readers' experience. Prayer and preaching should always go together. As Jesus watered with prayer the good seeds of instruction he had sown in the Upper Room,[2] so Paul follows up his teaching with earnest prayer, and by recording it enables us to overhear him. As Bishop Handley Moule put it: 'Who has not read and re-read the closing verses of the third chapter of the Ephesians with the feeling of one permitted to look through parted curtains into the Holiest Place of the Christian life?'[3]

1. The introduction to his prayer (verses 14–16a)

The apostle begins *For this reason* . . ., resuming his train of thought where he had left it in verse 1. What 'reason' is in his mind? What is it that moves him to pray? Surely it is both the reconciling work of Christ and his own understanding of it by special revelation? These are the convictions which undergird his prayer. This being so, an important principle of prayer emerges. The basis of Paul's prayer was his knowledge of God's purpose. It was because of what God had done in Christ and revealed to Paul that he had the necessary warrant to pray. For the indispensable prelude to all petition is the revelation of God's will. We have no authority to pray for anything which God has not revealed to be his will. That is why Bible reading and prayer should always go together. For it is in Scripture that God has disclosed his will, and it is in prayer that we ask him to do it.[4]

Paul goes on: *I bow my knees*. The normal posture for prayer among the Jews was standing. In Jesus' parable of the Pharisee and the Publican both men stood to pray (Lk. 18:11,13). So kneeling was unusual. It indicated an exceptional degree of earnestness, as when Ezra confessed

[2] Jn. 13–17. [3] Moule, *Veni Creator*, p. 228.
[4] See *e.g.* Jn. 15:7 and 1 Jn. 5:14.

Israel's sins of penitence, Jesus fell on his face to the ground in the Garden of Gethsemane, and Stephen faced the ordeal of martyrdom.[5] Scripture lays down no rule about the posture we should adopt when we pray. It is possible to pray kneeling, standing, sitting, walking and even lying, although we may feel inclined to agree with William Hendriksen that 'the slouching position of the body while one is supposed to be praying is an abomination to the Lord'.[6]

I bow my knees before the Father. Already the apostle has called God 'the Father of our Lord Jesus Christ' and therefore because we are in Christ 'our Father', from whom all blessings flow.[7] He has also declared that Jews and Gentiles are fellow members of the Father's family, who enjoy equal access to their Father in prayer.[8] Here he goes on to affirm that from this Father, before whom he kneels in reverent humility, *every family in heaven and on earth is named.* At least, this is the RSV and NEB translation, and *pasa patria* may quite properly be rendered 'every family'. Yet there is something inherently inappropriate about this reference to a multiplicity of families, since the dominant theme of these chapters is that through Christ the 'one God and Father of us all' (4:6) has only one family or household to which Jewish and Gentile believers equally belong. It seems better, therefore, to translate *pasa patria* 'the whole family' (AV), 'his whole family' (NEB margin) or 'the whole family of believers' (NIV). Then the addition of the words *in heaven and on earth* will indicate that the church militant on earth and the church triumphant in heaven, though separated by death, are nevertheless only two parts of the one great family of God.

At the same time, there is a deliberate play on words in the Greek sentence, since 'father' is *patēr* and 'family' is *patria*. In consequence, some translators have tried to preserve the verbal assonance in English, and have rendered the phrase 'the Father from whom all fatherhood . . . derives its name' (JBP, NIV margin). Commentators point out that the word *patria* does not normally mean 'fatherhood', but rather 'family'. Nevertheless, it is a family

[5] Ezr. 9:5ff; Mt. 26:39; Lk. 22:41; Acts 7:59, 60.
[6] Hendriksen, p. 166.   [7] 1:2–3.   [8] 2:18–19.

descended from the same father, and so the concept of fatherhood is implied and 'the abstract idea of *paternity* seems uppermost here'.[9] It may be, then, that Paul is saying not only that the whole Christian family is named from the Father, but that the very notion of fatherhood is derived from the Fatherhood of God. In this case, the true relation between human fatherhood and the divine fatherhood is neither one of analogy ('God is a father like human fathers'), nor one of projection (Freud's theory that we have invented God because we needed a heavenly father figure), but rather one of derivation (God's fatherhood being the archetypal reality, 'the source of all conceivable fatherhood').[1]

To this Father Paul prays that he will give his readers certain gifts *according to the riches of his glory*. Both 'riches' and 'glory' are characteristic words of this letter, and here as in 1:18 are in combination. Paul has no doubt either that God has inexhaustible resources at his disposal or that out of them he will be able to answer his prayer.

2. The substance of his prayer (verses 16b–19)

I like to think of the apostle's petition as a staircase by which he climbs higher and higher in his aspiration for his readers. His prayer-staircase has four steps, whose key words are 'strength', 'love', 'knowledge' and 'fullness'. More precisely, he prays first that they may be *strengthened* by the indwelling of Christ through his Spirit; secondly that they may be rooted and grounded in *love*; thirdly that they may *know* Christ's love in all its dimensions, although it is beyond knowledge; and fourthly that they may be *filled* right up to the very fullness of God.

a. Strengthened with might

The prayer opens: *that ... he may grant you to be strengthened with might through his Spirit in the inner man, and that Christ may dwell in your hearts through faith* (verses 16–17a). These two petitions clearly belong together. Both refer to the Christian's innermost being, his

[9] F. F. Bruce in Simpson, p. 78.   [1] Armitage Robinson, p. 84.

'inner man' on the one hand and his 'heart' on the other. Then, although one specifies the strength of the *Spirit* and the other the indwelling of *Christ*, both surely refer to the same experience. For Paul never separates the second and third persons of the Trinity. To have Christ dwelling in us and to have the Spirit dwelling in us are the same thing. Indeed, it is precisely by the Spirit that Christ dwells in our hearts,[2] and it is strength which he gives us when he dwells there. Moreover, the experience of 'Christ in you' was a part of the 'mystery' and so of the privilege of Gentile believers.[3]

Some are puzzled by this first petition when they remember that Paul is praying for Christians. 'Surely', they say, 'Christ dwells by his Spirit within every believer? So how can Paul ask here that Christ may dwell in their hearts? Was Christ not already within them?'. To these questions we begin by replying that indeed every Christian is indwelt by Christ and is the temple of the Holy Spirit.[4] Nevertheless as Charles Hodge rightly comments, 'The indwelling of Christ is a thing of degrees'.[5] So also is the inward strengthening of the Holy Spirit. What Paul asks for his readers is that they may be 'fortified, braced, invigorated',[6] that they may 'know the strength of the Spirit's inner reinforcement' (JBP), and may lay hold ever more firmly 'by faith' of this divine strength, this divine indwelling.

That this is Paul's meaning is further confirmed by his choice of word for the 'dwelling' of Christ in the heart. There are two similar Greek verbs, *paroikeō* and *katoikeō*. The former is the weaker. It means to 'inhabit (a place) as a stranger' (AG), to live in fact as a *paroikos*, the very word Paul has used in 2:19 for an alien who is living away from his home. *Katoikeō*, on the other hand, means to settle down somewhere. It refers to a permanent as opposed to a temporary abode, and is used metaphorically both for the fullness of the Godhead abiding in Christ[7] and for Christ's abiding in the believer's heart (here in verse 17). Bishop Handley Moule draws out the implications: 'The

[2] See Jn. 14:16–18 and Rom. 8:9–11.   [3] Col. 1:27.
[4] Rom. 8:9, 10; 1 Cor. 6:19.   [5] Hodge, p. 186.
[6] F. F. Bruce in Simpson, p. 78.   [7] Col. 2:9.

word selected (*katoikein*) . . . is a word made expressly to denote residence as against lodging, the abode of a master within his own home as against the turning aside for a night of the wayfarer who will be gone tomorrow.' Again, it is 'the residence always in the heart of its Master and Lord, who where he dwells must rule; who enters not to cheer and soothe alone but before all things else to reign'.[8] Thus Paul prays to the Father that Christ by his Spirit will be allowed to settle down in their hearts, and from his throne there both control and strengthen them. For the fourth time in the letter one is struck by the natural trinitarian structure of the apostle's thought.[9]

b. Rooted and grounded in love

If we had the opportunity to ask Paul for what purpose he prayed that Christ would control and strengthen his readers, I think he would reply that he wanted them to be strengthened to love. For in the new and reconciled humanity which Christ is creating love is the pre-eminent virtue. The new humanity is God's family, whose members are brothers and sisters, who love their Father and love each other. Or should do. They need the power of the Spirit's might and of Christ's indwelling to enable them to love each other, especially across the deep racial and cultural divide which previously had separated them.

To express how fundamental Paul longs for their love to be, he joins two metaphors (one botanical, the other architectural), both of which emphasize depth as opposed to superficiality. These Christians are to be *rooted and grounded*, or to have 'deep roots and firm foundations' (NEB). Thus Paul likens them first to a well-rooted tree, and then to a well-built house. In both cases the unseen cause of their stability will be the same: love. Love is to be the soil in which their life is to be rooted; love is to be the foundation on which their life is built. One might say that their love is to be of both a 'radical' and a 'fundamental' nature in their experience, for these English words refer to our roots and our foundations.

[8] Moule, *Veni Creator*, pp. 235 and 240.
[9] Cf. 1:3, 17 and 2:18.

c. Knowing Christ's love

We observe that the apostle now passes from our love (in which we are to be rooted and grounded) to Christ's love (which he prays we may know). Indeed, he acknowledges that we need strength or power for both, strength to love and power to comprehend Christ's love. Certainly the two cannot be separated, and it is partly by loving that we learn the meaning of his love.

Paul prays that we *may have power to comprehend* the love of Christ in its full dimensions—its *breadth and length and height and depth*. Modern commentators warn us not to be too literal in our interpretation of these, since the apostle may only have been indulging in a little rhetoric or poetic hyperbole. Yet it seems to me legitimate to say that the love of Christ is 'broad' enough to encompass all mankind (especially Jews and Gentiles, the theme of these chapters), 'long' enough to last for eternity, 'deep' enough to reach the most degraded sinner, and 'high' enough to exalt him to heaven. Or, as Leslie Mitton expresses it, finding a parallel to Romans 8:37–39: 'Whether you go forward or backward, up to the heights or down to the depths, nothing will separate us from the love of Christ.'[1] Ancient commentators went further. They saw these dimensions illustrated on the cross. For its upright pole reached down into the earth and pointed up to heaven, while its crossbar carried the arms of Jesus, stretched out as if to invite and welcome the whole world. Armitage Robinson calls this a 'pretty fancy'.[2] Perhaps he is right and it is fanciful, yet what it affirms about the love of Christ is true.

We shall have power to comprehend these dimensions of Christ's love, Paul adds, only *with all the saints*. The isolated Christian can indeed know something of the love of Jesus. But his grasp of it is bound to be limited by his limited experience. It needs the whole people of God to understand the whole love of God, *all the saints* together, Jews and Gentiles, men and women, young and old, black and white, with all their varied backgrounds and experiences.

[1] Mitton, p. 134.   [2] Armitage Robinson, p. 176.

Yet even then, although we may 'comprehend' its dimensions to some extent with our minds, we cannot 'know' it in our experience. It is too broad, long, deep and high even for all the saints together to grasp. It *surpasses knowledge.* Paul has already used this 'surpassing' word of God's power[3] and grace;[4] now he uses it of his love. Christ's love is as unknowable as his riches are unsearchable (verse 8). Doubtless we shall spend eternity exploring his inexhaustible riches of grace and love.

d. *Filled up to God's fullness*

'Fullness' is a characteristic word of Ephesians, as it is of Colossians. In Colossians Paul tells us not only that God's fullness dwells in Christ, but also that in Christ we ourselves have come to fullness.[5] At the same time, he makes it plain in Ephesians that we still have room for growth. As individuals we are to go on being filled with the Spirit,[6] and the church, although already the fullness of Christ,[7] is still to 'grow up into him' till it reaches his fullness.[8] 'Growth into fullness' is therefore the theme of Paul's fourth and last petition for his Asian readers. He prays that they *may be filled with all the fullness of God.* It is uncertain how this genitive should be understood. If it is objective, then God's fullness is the abundance of grace which he bestows. If it is subjective, it is the fullness which fills God himself, in other words his perfection. Staggering as the thought may be, the latter seems the more probable because the Greek preposition is *eis*, which indicates that we are to be filled not 'with' so much as 'unto' the fullness of God. God's fullness or perfection becomes the standard or level up to which we pray to be filled. The aspiration is the same in principle as that implied by the commands to be holy as God is holy, and to be perfect as our heavenly Father is perfect.[9]

Such a prayer must surely look on to our final state of perfection in heaven when together we enter the completeness of God's purpose for us, and are filled to capacity,

---

[3] 1:19.   [4] 2:7.
[5] Col. 1:19; 2:9–10.   [6] 5:18.   [7] 1:23.
[8] 4:13–16.   [9] 1 Pet. 1:15–16; Mt. 5:48.

filled up to that fullness of God which human beings are capable of receiving without ceasing to be human. Another way of expressing the prospect is that we shall become like Christ, which is God's purpose and promise,[1] for Christ is himself the fullness of God. Yet another way of putting it is to say that we shall attain the fullness of love, of which Paul has just spoken in his prayer. Then Jesus' own prayer will be fulfilled: 'That the love with which thou hast loved me may be in them, and I in them.'[2]

In saying that Paul's last petition points to heavenly perfection, we have no liberty to try to evade its contemporary challenge. For God expects us to be growing daily towards that final fullness, as we are being transformed by the Holy Spirit into Christ's image from one degree of glory to another.[3]

As we now look back down the staircase which we have been climbing with Paul, we cannot fail to be struck by his audacity. He prays that his readers may be given the strength of the Spirit and the ruling presence of Christ, the rooting of their lives in love, the knowledge of Christ's love in all its dimensions, and the fullness of God himself. These are bold petitions. Climbers of this staircase become short of breath, even a little giddy. But Paul does not leave us in suspense.

3. The conclusion of his prayer (verses 20–21)

We notice now that the apostle's four petitions are sandwiched between two references to God. In verses 14–16 he is the Father of the whole family and possesses infinite riches in glory; in verses 20 and 21 he is the one who works powerfully within us. Such a God can answer prayer.

God's ability to answer prayer is forcefully stated by the apostle in a composite expression of seven stages. (1) He is able to *do* or to work (*poiēsai*), for he is neither idle, nor inactive, nor dead. (2) He is able to do what *we ask*, for he hears and answers prayer. (3) He is able to do what

[1] Rom. 8:29; 1 Jn. 3:2.   [2] Jn. 17:26.
[3] 2 Cor. 3:18.

139

we ask *or think*, for he reads our thoughts, and sometimes we imagine things for which we dare not and therefore do not ask. (4) He is able to do *all* that we ask or think, for he knows it all and can perform it all. (5) He is able to do *more . . . than* (*hyper*, 'beyond') all that we ask or think, for his expectations are higher than ours. (6) He is able to do much more, or *more abundantly* (*perissōs*), than all that we ask or think, for he does not give his grace by calculated measure. (7) He is able to do very much more, *far more abundantly*, than all that we ask or think, for he is a God of super-abundance. This adverb *hyperekperissou* is one of Paul's coined 'super-superlatives'.[4] English equivalents which have been proposed are 'immeasurably more' (NIV) or 'vastly more than more',[5] but perhaps the feel of it is best conveyed by 'infinitely more' (AG, JBP). It states simply that there are no limits to what God can do.

The infinite ability of God to work beyond our prayers, thoughts and dreams is *by the power at work within us*, within us individually (Christ dwelling in our hearts by faith) and within us as a people (who are the dwelling place of God by his Spirit). It is the power of the resurrection, the power which raised Christ from the dead, enthroned him in the heavenlies, and then raised and enthroned us there with him. That is the power which is at work within the Christian and the church.

Paul's prayer relates to the fulfilment of his vision for God's new society of love. He asks that its members may be strengthened to love and to know the love of Christ, though this surpasses knowledge. But then he turns from the love of God past knowing to the power of God past imagining, from limitless love to limitless power. For he is convinced, as we must be, that only divine power can generate divine love in the divine society.

To add anything more would be inappropriate, except the doxology. *To him be glory*, Paul exclaims, to this God of resurrection power who alone can make the dream come true. The power comes from him; the glory must go to him. To him be glory *in the church and in Christ Jesus*

---

[4] Bruce, p. 70.   [5] Simpson, p. 84.

140

together, in the body and in the Head, in the bride and in the Bridegroom, in the community of peace and in the Peacemaker, *to all generations* (in history), *for ever and ever* (in eternity), *Amen.*

III New standards

Ephesians 4:1 – 5:21

7. Unity and diversity in the church

*I therefore, a prisoner of the Lord, beg you to lead a life
worthy of the calling to which you have been called, ²with
all lowliness and meekness, with patience, forbearing one
another in love, ³eager to maintain the unity of the Spirit
in the bond of peace. ⁴There is one body and one Spirit,
just as you were called to the one hope that belongs to your
call, ⁵one Lord, one faith, one baptism, ⁶one God and
Father of us all, who is above all and through all and in
all. ⁷But grace was given to each of us according to the
measure of Christ's gift. ⁸Therefore it is said,*

> *'When he ascended on high he led a host of captives,*
> *and he gave gifts to men.'*

*⁹(In saying, 'He ascended,' what does it mean but that he
had also descended into the lower parts of the earth? ¹⁰He
who descended is he who also ascended far above all the
heavens, that he might fill all things.) ¹¹And his gifts were
that some should be apostles, some prophets, some evangelists,
some pastors and teachers, ¹²to equip the saints, for the
work of ministry, for building up the body of Christ, ¹³until
we all attain to the unity of the faith and of the knowledge
of the Son of God, to mature manhood, to the measure
of the stature of the fullness of Christ; ¹⁴so that we may
no longer be children tossed to and fro and carried about
with every wind of doctrine, by the cunning of men, by
their craftiness in deceitful wiles. ¹⁵Rather, speaking the
truth in love, we are to grow up in every way into him*

145

who is the head, into Christ, ¹⁶from whom the whole body, joined and knit together by every joint with which it is supplied, when each part is working properly, makes bodily growth and upbuilds itself in love.

For three chapters Paul has been unfolding for his readers the eternal purpose of God being worked out in history. Through Jesus Christ, who died for sinners and was raised from death, God is creating something entirely new, not just a new life for individuals but a new society. Paul sees an alienated humanity being reconciled, a fractured humanity being united, even a new humanity being created. It is a magnificent vision.

Now the apostle moves on from the new society to the new standards which are expected of it. So he turns from exposition to exhortation, from what God has done (in the indicative) to what we must be and do (in the imperative), from doctrine to duty, 'from the *credenda* ... *to the agenda*',[1] from mind-stretching theology to its down-to-earth, concrete implications in everyday living.

He begins: *I therefore, a prisoner for the Lord, beg you* ... He has taught them, and he has prayed for them (1:15–23 and 3:14–19); now he addresses to them a solemn appeal. Instruction, intercession and exhortation constitute a formidable trio of weapons in any Christian teacher's armoury. Besides, Paul was no ordinary teacher. He uses the emphatic personal pronoun, the *egō* of self-conscious apostolic authority, as in 3:1. And he again describes himself as *a prisoner for the Lord*, using a slightly different grammatical construction but the same *double entendre*, that he is both a prisoner of Christ and a prisoner for Christ, both bound to him by the chains of love and in custody out of loyalty to his gospel. Thus the authority of one of Christ's apostles and the passionate conviction of a man under house arrest because of his vision of a united church, together undergird his exhortation. *I beg you*, he writes, *to lead a life worthy of the calling to which you have been called.*

What this life is to be like can be determined only by the nature of the divine call of which it is to be worthy.

[1] Simpson, p. 87.

What is this? The new society which God is calling into being has two major characteristics. First, it is 'one' people, composed equally of Jews and Gentiles, the single family of God. Secondly, it is a 'holy' people, distinct from the secular world, set apart (like Israel in Old Testament days) to belong to God. Therefore, because God's people are called to be one people, they must manifest their unity, and because they are called to be a holy people, they must manifest their purity. Unity and purity are two fundamental features of a life worthy of the church's divine calling. The apostle treats the unity of the church in verses 1–16 and the purity of the church from 4:17 to 5:21.

During the last half-century and more a great deal has been said and written about the unity of the church. The modern preoccupation with it may be traced to the influential 'Appeal to all Christian People' which was issued by the 1920 Lambeth Conference of Anglican bishops under the chairmanship of Randall Davidson, Archbishop of Canterbury. Following this the movement towards reunion gathered speed, two notable milestones being the inauguration of the Church of South India in 1947 and of the World Council of Churches in 1948. Since then some more united churches have come into being, while other union schemes have foundered; and the movement may be said to be in the doldrums. It is all the more important, therefore, to look with fresh eyes at Ephesians 4:1–16, since this is one of the two classic New Testament passages on the subject of Christian unity (the other being John 17). It should prove both a strong stimulus to concern ourselves with Christian unity and a healthy corrective to a number of misleading notions about it.

Paul elaborates four truths about the kind of oneness which God intends his new society to enjoy. They may be stated in the following four propositions:

1. It depends on the *charity* of our character and conduct (verse 2)
2. It arises from the *unity* of our God (verses 3–6)
3. It is enriched by the *diversity* of our gifts (verses 7–12)
4. It demands the *maturity* of our growth (verses 13–16)

147

UNITY AND DIVERSITY IN THE CHURCH

It will be observed that charity, unity, diversity and maturity appear to be the key concepts of this section.

1. Christian unity depends on the charity of our conduct (verse 2)

Paul immediately portrays the life worthy of our calling as being characterized by five qualities—lowliness, meekness, patience, mutual forbearance and love. He has prayed to God that we may be 'rooted and grounded in love' (3:17); now he addresses his appeal to us to see to it that we live a life of love. This is where he begins, and this is also where we should begin. Too many start with structures (and structures of some kind are indispensable), but the apostle starts with moral qualities. Certainly, in the quest for Christian unity, if we have to choose, we must say that the moral is more important than the structural.

Lowliness was much despised in the ancient world. The Greeks never used their word for humility (*tapeinotēs*) in a context of approval, still less of admiration. Instead they meant by it an abject, servile, subservient attitude, 'the crouching submissiveness of a slave'.[2] Not till Jesus Christ came was a true humility recognized. For he humbled himself. And only he among the world's religious and ethical teachers has set before us as our model a little child.

Moreover, the word Paul uses here is *tapeinophrosynē*, which means 'lowliness of mind', the humble recognition of the worth and value of other people, the humble mind which was in Christ and led him to empty himself and become a servant.[3]

Now humility is essential to unity. Pride lurks behind all discord, while the greatest single secret of concord is humility. It is not difficult to prove this in experience. The people we immediately, instinctively like, and find it easy to get on with, are the people who give us the respect we consider we deserve, while the people we immediately, instinctively dislike are those who treat us like dirt. In other words, personal vanity is a key factor in all our

[2] F. F. Bruce in Simpson, p. 88 note.
[3] Phil. 2:3–8, the same noun being used in verse 3.

148

relationships. If, however, instead of manoeuvring for the respect of others (which is pride) we give them our respect by recognizing their intrinsic God-given worth (which is humility), we shall be promoting harmony in God's new society.

Meekness (*praōtēs*) was warmly applauded by Aristotle. Because he hated extremes and loved 'the golden mean', he saw in *praōtēs* the quality of moderation, 'the mean between being too angry and never being angry at all'.[4] The word was also used of domesticated animals. So 'meekness' is not a synonym for 'weakness'. On the contrary, it is the gentleness of the strong, whose strength is under control. It is the quality of a strong personality who is nevertheless master of himself and the servant of others. Meekness is 'the absence of the disposition to assert personal rights, either in the presence of God or of men'.[5] It is particularly appropriate in pastors who should also use their authority only in a spirit of gentleness.[6]

'Lowliness' and 'meekness' form a natural couple. For 'the meek man thinks as little of his personal claims, as the humble man of his personal merits'.[7] They were found together in perfect balance in the character of the Lord Jesus who described himself as 'gentle and lowly in heart'.[8]

The third and fourth qualities also form a natural pair, for *patience* (*makrothymia*) is longsuffering towards aggravating people, such as God in Christ has shown towards us,[9] while *forbearing one another* speaks of that mutual tolerance without which no group of human beings can live together in peace. *Love* is the final quality, which embraces the preceding four, and is the crown and sum of all virtues. Since to love is constructively to seek the welfare of others and the good of the community, its 'binding' properties are celebrated in Colossians 3:14.

Here, then, are five foundation stones of Christian unity. Where these are absent no external structure of unity can stand. But when this strong base has been laid, then there

---

[4] Barclay, p. 162.   [5] Findlay, p. 265.
[6] 1 Cor. 4:21; 2 Tim. 2:25.   [7] Dale, p. 215.
[8] Mt. 11:29 (*praōs . . . kai tapeinos*); cf. 2 Cor. 10:1.
[9] E.g. Rom. 2:4; 1 Tim. 1:16.

is good hope that a visible unity can be built. We may be quite sure that no unity is pleasing to God which is not the child of charity.

2. Christian unity arises from the unity of our God (verses 3–6)

Even the casual reader of verses 3–6 (thought by some to be part of a Christian hymn or a creed for catechumens) is struck by Paul's repetition of the word 'one'; in fact, it occurs seven times. A more careful reading discloses that three of these seven unities allude to the three Persons of the Trinity (*one Spirit,* verse 4; *one Lord,* verse 5, *i.e.* the Lord Jesus; and *one God and Father of us all,* verse 6), while the remaining four allude to our Christian experience in relation to the three Persons of the Trinity. This truth can be expressed in three simple affirmations.

First, there is *one body* because there is only *one Spirit* (verse 4). The one body is the church, the body of Christ (1:23), comprising Jewish and Gentile believers; and its unity or cohesion is due to the one Holy Spirit who indwells and animates it. As Paul writes elsewhere, 'By one Spirit we were all baptized into one body—Jews or Greeks, slaves or free—and all were made to drink of one Spirit.'[1] Thus, it is our common possession of the one Holy Spirit that integrates us into one body.

Secondly, there is *one hope* belonging to our Christian calling (verse 4), *one faith* and *one baptism* (verse 5) because there is only *one Lord.* For the Lord Jesus Christ is the one object of the faith, hope and baptism of all Christian people. It is Jesus Christ in whom we have believed, Jesus Christ into whom we have been baptized,[2] and Jesus Christ for whose coming we wait with expectant hope.

Thirdly, there is one Christian family, embracing *us all* (verse 6) because *there is one God and Father . . . who is above all and through all and in all.* A few manuscripts read 'in *you* all', clarifying that the 'all' of whom God is Father means 'all Christians', not 'all people' indiscriminately, or 'all things' (the universe). Armitage Robinson

---

[1] 1 Cor. 12:13.   [2] *E.g.* 1 Cor. 1:13; Gal. 3:27.

calls this addition of the word 'you' 'a timid gloss'.[3] Perhaps it is; and certainly the overwhelming manuscript evidence omits it. Nevertheless, it is a correct gloss. For the 'all' *above, through* and *in* whom God is Father, are his family or household, his redeemed children.[4]

We are now in a position to repeat the three affirmations, this time the other way round and in the order in which the Persons of the Trinity are normally mentioned. First, the one Father creates the one family. Secondly, the one Lord Jesus creates the one faith, hope and baptism. Thirdly, the one Spirit creates the one body.

Indeed, we can go further. We must assert that there *can* be only one Christian family, only one Christian faith, hope and baptism, and only one Christian body, because there is only one God, Father, Son and Holy Spirit. You can no more multiply churches than you can multiply Gods. Is there only one God? Then he has only one church. Is the unity of God inviolable? Then so is the unity of the church. The unity of the church is as indestructible as the unity of God himself. It is no more possible to split the church than it is possible to split the Godhead.

In stating the matter thus baldly and dogmatically (as the apostle Paul himself did), it is not difficult to imagine what the reader is thinking. You will be saying to me something like this: 'It is all very well declaring that we cannot split the church; the truth is we have been extremely successful in doing the very thing you say we cannot do!' How, then, can the evident phenomenon of the disunity of the church be reconciled with the biblical insistence on the indestructibility of its unity?

At this point a necessary distinction needs to be drawn. It is not just between the 'visible' and the 'invisible' church. That distinction is true, but the concept of the invisible church (whose members are known only to God) has been misused by some as an excuse for opting out of responsible membership in the visible church. So the distinction needs to be somewhat refined. It is between the church's unity as an invisible reality present to the mind of God (who

[3] Armitage Robinson, p. 93.   [4] *Cf.* 1:2, 17; 2:18–19; 3:14–15.

says to himself 'I have only one church') and the church's disunity as a visible appearance which contradicts the invisible reality (causing us to say to ourselves, 'There are hundreds of separated and competing churches'). We are one, for God says so, and in interdenominational conventions and congresses we sense our underlying unity in Christ. Yet outwardly and visibly we belong to different churches and different traditions, some of which are not even in communion with one another, while others have strayed far from biblical Christianity.

The apostle himself recognizes this paradoxical combination of unity and disunity. For in this very passage, in which the indestructible unity of the church is so emphatically asserted, the possibility of disunity is also acknowledged. Consider verse 3, which we have so far omitted and in which we are told to be *eager to maintain the unity of the Spirit in the bond of peace*. This is a very strange exhortation. Paul first describes the church's unity as 'the unity of the Spirit' (meaning a unity which the Holy Spirit creates) and then argues that this unity is as indestructible as God himself. Yet in the same context he also tells us that we have to maintain it! What can he mean? What is the sense of urging the maintenance of something indestructible, and of urging *us* to maintain it, when it is 'a unity of the Spirit', which he created and is therefore presumably himself responsible for preserving?

There seems to be but one possible answer to these questions, namely that to *maintain* the church's unity must mean to maintain it visibly. Here is an apostolic exhortation to us to preserve in actual concrete relationships of love (*in the bond of peace*, that is, by the peace which binds us together) that unity which God has created and which neither man nor demon can destroy. We are to demonstrate to the world that the unity we say exists indestructibly is not the rather sick joke it sounds but a true and glorious reality.

Perhaps the analogy of a human family will help us to grasp our responsibility more clearly. We will imagine a couple called Mr and Mrs John Smith, and their three sons, Tom, Dick and Harry. They are one family; there is no doubt about that. Marriage and parenthood have united them. But in the course of time the Smith family disintegrates. Father and mother quarrel, keep up an uneasy truce for several years, become increasingly estranged and finally get a divorce. The three boys also quarrel, first with their parents and then with each other, and separate. Tom goes to live in Canada, Dick in South Africa and Harry in Australia. They never meet, write or telephone. They lose contact with each other altogether. More than that. So determined are they to repudiate each other that they actually change their names by deed poll. It would be hard to imagine a family which has experienced a more disastrous disintegration than this. All mutual relationships have been severed.

Now supposing we were cousins of the Smith family, how would we react? Would we shrug our shoulders, smile complacently and mutter 'Oh, well, never mind, they are still one family, you know'? We would be quite correct. In God's sight I reckon they are still one family, indestructibly. Mr and Mrs Smith are still husband and wife and still parents of their three sons, who are still brothers. For simply nothing can alter the unity of the family which the circumstances of marriage and birth have imposed upon it. But would we acquiesce in this situation? Would we try to excuse or minimize the tragedy of their disunity by appealing to the indestructibility of their family ties? No, this would not satisfy either our mind or our heart or our conscience. What, then, would we do? Surely we would seek to be peacemakers. We would urge them to 'maintain the unity of the family by means of the bond of peace', that is, to demonstrate their family unity by repenting and getting reconciled to one another.

Just so, the fact of the church's indestructible unity is no excuse for acquiescing in the tragedy of its actual disunity. On the contrary, the apostle tells us to be *eager to maintain the unity of the Spirit*. The Greek verb for 'eager' (*spoudazontes*) is emphatic. It means that we are to 'spare no effort' (NEB), and, being a present participle, it is a call for continuous, diligent activity. Markus Barth expresses the sense vividly: 'It is hardly possible to render exactly the urgency contained in the underlying Greek verb. Not only haste and passion, but a full effort of the

153

whole man is meant, involving his will, sentiment, reason, physical strength, and total attitude. The imperative mood of the participle found in the Greek text excludes passivity, quietism, a wait-and-see attitude, or a diligence tempered by all deliberate speed. Yours is the initiative! Do it now! Mean it! *You* are to do it! I mean it!—Such are the overtones in verse 3.'[5]

Where, I ask myself, is this eagerness for unity to be found among evangelical Christians today? Is this an apostolic command we are guilty of largely ignoring?

Take the local church first, for presumably it is to this that Paul is primarily referring. Some Christian fellowships are marred by rivalries between individuals or groups which have been allowed to fester for years. How can we possibly condone such things? We need to be 'eager' for love, unity and peace, and more active in seeking it.

But Ephesians, as we have seen, may have been a circular letter addressed to several churches. Perhaps even in the city of Ephesus itself there were now so many Christians that they met in several distinct house churches. We know, for example, that Aquila and Priscilla had a church in their home when they lived in Rome (Rom.16:3–5), and probably also when they moved to Ephesus (Acts 18:26). So Paul may have in mind the need for unity *between* as well as *within* the churches. If so, his concern would apply to inter-church relationships today. This is not the place to go into the technical terms which are used for various kinds of relations between churches, such as 'open communion', 'intercommunion', 'full communion' and 'organic union'. There is room for differences of conviction among us as to the precise form or forms in which God wants Christian unity to be expressed. But we should all be eager for some visible expression of Christian unity, provided always that we do not sacrifice fundamental Christian truth in order to achieve it. Christian unity arises from our having one Father, one Saviour, and one indwelling Spirit. So we cannot possibly foster a unity which pleases God either if we deny the doctrine of the Trinity or if we have not come personally to know God

[5] Barth, p. 428.

the Father through the reconciling work of his Son Jesus Christ and by the power of the Holy Spirit. Authentic Christian 'unity' in truth, life and love is far more important than 'union' schemes of a structural kind, although ideally the latter should be a visible expression of the former.

3. Christian unity is enriched by the diversity of our gifts (verses 7–12)

The contrast between verses 6 and 7 is striking. Verse 6 speaks of God as the Father of us *all*, who is above *all*, through *all* and in *all*. Verse 7, however, begins: *But grace was given to each of us* . . . Thus Paul turns from 'all of us' to 'each of us', and so from the unity to the diversity of the church.

He is, in fact, deliberately qualifying what he has just written about the church's unity. Although there is only one body, one faith and one family, this unity is not to be misconstrued as a lifeless or colourless uniformity. We are not to imagine that every Christian is an exact replica of every other, as if we had all been mass-produced in some celestial factory. On the contrary, the unity of the church, far from being boringly monotonous, is exciting in its diversity. This is not just because of our different cultures, temperaments and personalities (which, though true, is not Paul's point here), but because of the different gifts which Christ distributes for the enrichment of our common life.

Verse 7 refers to Christ's *grace* in bestowing different gifts. Although Paul does not here employ the term *charismata* for 'gifts' (as he does in Rom. 12:6 and 1 Cor. 12:4), yet clearly it is to these that he is referring. For 'grace' is *charis*, and 'gifts' are *charismata*. Moreover, it is very important to understand the difference between them. 'Saving grace', the grace which saves sinners, is given to all who believe;[6] but what might be termed 'service grace', the grace which equips God's people to serve, is given in differing degrees *according to the measure of Christ's gift* (verse 7). The unity of the church is due to

[6] See 2:5, 8: 'By grace you have been saved.'

charis, God's grace having reconciled us to himself; but the diversity of the church is due to *charismata*, God's gifts distributed to church members.

It is, of course, from this word *charismata* that the adjective 'charismatic' is derived. The so-called 'charismatic movement', although controversial in a number of its distinctive emphases, has without doubt been used by God to bring spiritual renewal to many churches and individual Christians. Nevertheless, we should register a biblical protest against the designation 'charismatic movement', whether its adherents themselves chose it or were given it. 'Charismatic' is not a term which can be accurately applied to any group or movement within the church, since according to the New Testament the whole church is a charismatic community. It is the body of Christ, every single member of which has a gift (*charisma*) to exercise or function to perform.

What, then, does this paragraph teach us about *charismata* or spiritual gifts? It tells us about their giver, their character and their purpose.

a. The giver of spiritual gifts is the ascended Christ
(verse 7–10)

According to verse 7 each gift is Christ's gift, and this truth is now enforced in the following verse by a quotation from Psalm 68:18: *When he ascended on high he led a host of captives, and he gave gifts to men.*

Psalm 68 is a call to God to come to the rescue of his people and vindicate them again, as in olden days. For he went in triumph before his people after the exodus (verse 7), so that Mount Sinai trembled (verse 8) and kings were scattered (verses 11–14). Then, desiring Mount Zion as his abode (verse 16), he came from Sinai to his holy place (verse 17) and ascended the high mount, leading captives in his train. It is all very vivid imagery. It seems that the transfer of the ark to Zion is likened to the triumphant march of Yahweh into his capital.

Paul applies this picture to Christ's ascension, not arbitrarily because he detected a vague analogy between the two, but justifiably because he saw in the exaltation of

Jesus a further fulfilment of this description of the triumph of God. Christ ascended as conqueror to the Father's right hand, his train of captives being the principalities and powers he had defeated, dethroned and disarmed.[7]

In the application of Psalm 68:18 to Christ, however, there is .a textual problem. For the Psalm reads that God ascended the mount, 'receiving gifts among men', whereas Paul's quotation is that Christ 'gave gifts to men'. Some commentators do not hesitate to say that Paul changed the wording to suit his purpose. For example, J. H. Houlden writes: 'There is no need to suppose that the alteration was other than deliberate.'[8] Others think it was 'an unintentional misquotation'.[9] Because of the apostle's known regard for Scripture both these explanations seem *a priori* unlikely.

The place to begin an explanation is surely to see that the two renderings are only formally but not substantially contradictory. Words cannot be interpreted by themselves, but only in context. So we need to remember that after every conquest in the ancient world there was invariably both a receiving of tribute and a distributing of largesse. What conquerors took from their captives, they gave away to their own people. The spoils were divided, the booty was shared.[1] It seems possible that the Hebrew text itself may imply this, since the verb could be translated 'brought' rather than 'received', and it is not without significance that two ancient versions or translations, one Aramaic and the other Syriac, render it 'gave'. So evidently this was already a traditional interpretation.

One other interesting point needs to be made. Liturgical custom in the synagogues associated Psalm 68 with Pentecost, the Jewish feast commemorating the giving of the law. Paul's use of it in reference to the Christian Pentecost then makes a remarkable analogy. As Moses received the law and gave it to Israel, so Christ received the Spirit and gave him to his people in order to write God's law in their hearts and through the pastors he appointed (verse 11) to teach them the truth. This whole argument that 'receiving' and 'giving' belong indissolubly

[7] 1:20–22; *cf.* Col. 2:15.   [8] Houlden, p. 310.   [9] *E.g.* Mitton, p. 146.
[1] For Old Testament examples see Gn. 14; Jdgs. 5:30; 1 Sa. 30:26–31; Ps. 68:12 and Is. 53:12.

to each other is aptly illustrated in Acts 2:33 where Peter on the day of Pentecost said: 'Being therefore exalted at the right hand of God, and having received from the Father the promise of the Holy Spirit; he (*sc.* Jesus) has poured out this which you see and hear'. Christ could only give the gift he had received.

After the quotation from Psalm 68:18 Paul adds in parenthesis that Christ's having *ascended* into heaven implies that *he had also descended into the lower parts of the earth* (verse 9). Because of the immediate context, which concerns the gifts of Christ to his church following his ascension, G. B. Caird makes the novel suggestion that his 'descent' was his 'return at Pentecost to give his Spirit to the church'.[2] But, ingenious as this is, the natural interpretation of the words suggests that his descent preceded his ascent rather than followed it. The early fathers understood this as a reference to his descent into hades.[3] They associated it with 1 Peter 3:19 ('he went and preached to the spirits in prison') which they interpreted as his spoiling or 'harrowing' hell. But, whatever the 1 Peter text means, there is no obvious reference to hades or hell in Ephesians 4:9. Calvin (followed by Reformed commentators like Charles Hodge) argued from the 'ascended into heaven' of John 3:13 that 'the lower parts of the earth' is a genitive of apposition or definition, that what it means is simply 'the earth', and that Christ's descent refers to his incarnation. NEB takes it this way too, namely that he descended 'to the lowest level, down to the very earth'. Perhaps, however, the reference is more general still, namely that Christ descended to the depths of humiliation when he came to earth. Or possibly the allusion is to the cross, and 'to the experience of the nethermost depths, the very agonies of hell'[4] which Christ endured there.

Such an interpretation would fit well with Philippians 2:5–11, where 'even death on a cross' describes his deepest humiliation, which was followed by his supreme exaltation. This was 'far above all rule and authority and power and dominion, and above every name that is named' according

---

[2] Caird, pp. 73–74.   [3] Acts 2:25 ff. and Rom. 10:7.
[4] Hendriksen, p. 193.

to 1:21, and here 'far above all the heavens, that he might fill all things' (verse 10), or 'so that he might fill the universe' (NEB). What is in Paul's mind, therefore, is not so much descent and ascent in spatial terms, but rather humiliation and exaltation, the latter bringing Christ universal authority and power, as a result of which he bestowed on the church he rules both the Spirit himself to indwell it and the gifts of the Spirit to edify it or bring it to maturity.

In the light of this emphasis on Christ, ascended, exalted, filling the universe, ruling the church, bestowing gifts, it would clearly be a mistake to think of *charismata* as being exclusively 'gifts of the Spirit' and to associate them too closely with the Holy Spirit or with experiences of the Holy Spirit. For here they are the gifts of Christ, while in Romans 12 they are the gifts of God the Father. It is always misleading to separate the three Persons of the Trinity, the Father, the Son and the Holy Spirit. Together they are involved in every aspect of the church's wellbeing.

b. *The character of spiritual gifts is extremely varied*

Paul specifically says so in 1 Cor.12:4: 'Now there are varieties of gifts'. It is important to recall this because many today have a very restricted view of *charismata*. For example, some people speak and write of 'the nine gifts of the Spirit', presumably to make a neat but artificial parallel with the Spirit's ninefold fruit.[5] Others seem to be pre-occupied, even obsessed, with only three of the more spectacular gifts ('tongues', 'prophecy' and 'healing'). In fact, however, the five lists given in the New Testament mention between them at least twenty distinct gifts, some of which are very prosaic and unsensational (like 'doing acts of mercy', Rom. 12:8). Moreover, each list diverges widely from the others, and gives its selection of gifts in an apparently haphazard fashion. This suggests not only that no one list is complete, but that even all five together do not represent an exhaustive catalogue. Doubtless there are many more which are unlisted.

In our text Paul selects only five for mention. Christ

[5] Gal. 5:22–23.

(*autos*, 'he', is emphatic, verse 11) gave *some* to be *apostles, some prophets, some evangelists, some pastors and teachers.* The word 'apostle' has three main meanings in the New Testament. Once only it seems to be applied to every individual Christian, when Jesus said: 'A servant is not greater than his master; nor is he who is sent (*apostolos*) greater than he who sent him.'[6] So every Christian is both a servant and an apostle. The verb *apostello* means to 'send', and all Christian people are sent out into the world as Christ's ambassadors and witnesses, to share in the apostolic mission of the whole church.[7] This cannot be the meaning here, however, for in this sense all Christians are 'apostles', whereas Paul writes that Christ gave only 'some' to be apostles.

Secondly, there were 'apostles of the churches',[8] messengers sent out by a church either as missionaries or on some other errand. And thirdly there were the 'apostles of Christ', a very small and distinctive group, consisting of the Twelve (including Matthias who replaced Judas), Paul, James the Lord's brother, and possibly one or two others. They were personally chosen and authorized by Jesus, and had to be eyewitnesses of the risen Lord.[9] It must be in this sense that Paul is using the word 'apostles' here, for he puts them at the top of his list, as he does also in 1 Corinthians 12:28 ('first apostles'), and this is how he has so far used the word in his letter, referring to himself (1:1) and to his fellow apostles as the foundation of the church and the organs of revelation (2:20; 3:5).

We should not hesitate, therefore, to say that *in this sense* there are no apostles today. In 1975 John Noble wrote and published a booklet entitled *First Apostles, Last Apostles.* In it his concern is 'to arouse my fellow Christians to look for apostles to shape church life in our day', who will 'unite and release an army under God which will accomplish his purpose in these end-times'. His reading of history is that when the original apostles died, 'they left a vacuum of authority into which the wrong men stepped', *i.e.* the bishops. He criticizes both Catholicism and

[6] Jn. 13:16.   [7] Jn. 17:18; 20:21.   [8] 2 Cor. 8:23; *cf.* Phil. 2:25.
[9] Acts 1:21, 22; 10:40–41; 1 Cor. 9:1; 15:8–9.

Protestantism, the former for 'investing absolute authority in one man' and the latter for 'giving every individual the right to rule in the church'. We can certainly agree with him that throughout the long and chequered history of the church there have been many misuses of authority, but he misses in his exposition the vitally important truths (1) that the original apostles as eyewitnesses of the historic risen Jesus can in the nature of the case have no successors, and (2) that their authority is preserved today in the New Testament, which is the essential 'apostolic succession'. Once we have insisted, however, that there are today no apostles of Christ with an authority comparable to that of the apostles Paul, Peter and John, it is certainly possible to argue that there are people with apostolic ministries of a different kind, including episcopal jurisdiction, pioneer missionary work, church planting, itinerant leadership, *etc.*

What about *prophets*? Here again it is necessary to make a distinction. In the primary sense in which the Bible uses the word, a prophet was a person who 'stood in the council of God', who heard and even 'saw' his word, and who in consequence 'spoke from the mouth of the Lord' and spoke his word 'faithfully'.[1] In other words, a prophet was a mouthpiece or spokesman of God, a vehicle of his direct revelation. *In this sense* we must again insist that there are no prophets today. Nobody can presume to claim an inspiration comparable to that of the canonical prophets, or use their introductory formula 'Thus says the Lord'. If this were possible, we would have to add their words to Scripture, and the whole church would need to listen and obey. Yet this is the sense in which Paul appears to be using the word here. He puts the prophets next after the apostles (as in 1 Cor. 12:28; 'second prophets'), and he brackets 'apostles and prophets' as the church's foundation and the recipients of fresh revelation from God (2:20; 3:6). As the foundation on which the church is being built the prophets have no successors, any more than the apostles have, for the foundation was laid and finished centuries ago and we cannot tamper with it in any way today.

[1] *Cf.* Je. 23:16–32.

But, as with apostles so with prophets, having first established the uniqueness of the original teachers of the church, we then have to ask if there is a subsidiary gift of some kind. It seems right to answer 'yes', but then to confess that we do not know for certain what it is! Some see it as a special gift of biblical exposition, an unusual degree of insight into the Word of God, so that by the ministry of the Holy Spirit modern 'prophets' hear and receive the Word of God, not however as a new revelation but as a fresh understanding of the old. Others see it as a sensitive understanding of the contemporary world, a reading of the signs of the times, together with an indignant denunciation of the social sins of the day and a perceptive application of Scripture to them. Those who hold this view draw attention to the socio-political oracles of the Old Testament prophets. A third view concentrates on the effect which the ministry of New Testament prophets had on their listeners, bringing to unbelievers a conviction of sin and to believers 'upbuilding and encouragement and consolation'.[2] In these three views the 'prophetic' gift is detected in the handling of the Word of God, for one cannot think of God's prophets in isolation from God's Word. It is understood as a gift of insight into either the biblical text or the contemporary situation, or both, namely a powerful combination of accurate exposition and pertinent application.

There is another view, however, popularized by 'pentecostal' and 'charismatic' Christians, namely that God is again raising up prophets and prophetesses today, who speak his word in his name and by his direct inspiration. I have to confess my own grave hesitation about this claim. Those who make it seldom seem to recognize either the uniqueness of the original apostles and prophets or that successors were superfluous since the New Testament Scriptures became available to the church. Besides, there have been many similar claims in the history of the church, which do not encourage one's confidence in the modern phenomenon. In those churches in which the possibility of such a gift is accepted, however, it is important to insist

[2] 1 Cor. 14:3; *cf.* Acts 15:32.

that so-called 'prophetic utterances' could never be of more than local and limited value (to individuals or a particular congregation, not the whole church), that they must always be carefully tested by Scripture and by the known character of the speaker, and that the regular, systematic, thoughtful exposition of the Bible is much more important for the building up of the people of God.

After apostles and prophets Paul mentions *evangelists*. This noun occurs only three times in the New Testament (here, in Acts 21:8 of Philip and in 2 Tim. 4:5 of Timothy himself), although of course the verb 'to evangelize' is frequently used to describe the spreading of the gospel. Since all Christians are under obligation, when they have an appropriate opportunity, to bear witness to Christ and his good news, the gift of an 'evangelist' (bestowed only upon some) must be something different. It may refer to the gift of evangelistic preaching, or of making the gospel particularly plain and relevant to unbelievers, or of helping timorous people to take the plunge of commitment to Christ, or of effective personal witnessing. Probably the gift of an evangelist may take all these different forms and more. It must relate in some way to an evangelistic ministry, whether in mass evangelism, personal evangelism, literature evangelism, film evangelism, radio and television evangelism, musical evangelism or in the use of some other medium. There is a great need for gifted evangelists today who will pioneer new ways of exercising and developing their gift, so as to penetrate the vast unreached segments of society for Christ.

Since the definite article is not repeated in the expression *some pastors and teachers*, it may be that these are two names for the same ministry. Calvin did not think so, for he suggested that the administration of discipline, the sacraments, warning and exhortation belonged particularly to pastors. Yet it is clear that 'pastors' (that is, 'shepherds'), who are called to 'tend' God's flock, do so in particular by 'feeding it', *i.e.* by teaching.[3] Perhaps one should say that, although every pastor must be a teacher, gifted in the ministry of God's Word to people (whether a congregation

---

[3] *cf.* Jn. 21:15–17; Acts 20:28; 1 Pet. 5:2.

or groups or individuals), yet not every Christian teacher is also a pastor (since he may be teaching only in a school or college rather than in a local church).

Looking back, we observe that all five gifts relate in some way to the ministry of teaching. Although there are neither apostles nor prophets in the original sense today, there are evangelists to preach the gospel, pastors to tend the flock, and teachers to expound the word. Indeed, they are urgently needed. Nothing is more necessary for the building up of God's church in every age than an ample supply of God-gifted teachers. Yet I wonder if this need has ever been greater than it is in our own day. In some areas of the third world great 'people movements' are taking place. Large numbers, in some cases whole villages and tribes, are accepting Christ, and the church growth rate exceeds the population growth rate. This exciting fact brings with it both problems and dangers, however. The newly baptized converts are spiritual babies. As such they are prone to sin and error, and almost defenceless against false teaching. Above all else they need teaching from the Word of God. In some situations, believe it or not, missionaries are calling for a moratorium on converts. 'For heaven's sake', they pray to God, 'don't give us any more, for we don't know what to do with the thousands we already have.' I sometimes urge my charismatic friends, therefore, some of whom seem to me to be preoccupied with the less important gifts, to remember Paul's dictum 'earnestly to desire the higher gifts',[4] and to consider whether these are not the teaching gifts. It is teaching which builds up the church. It is teachers who are needed most.

Another important question is raised by this verse (11). There is no mention in it of presbyter-bishops or deacons (to whom reference is made, for example, in Phil. 1:1 and 1 Tim. 3:1, 12), still less of the threefold order 'bishops, presbyters and deacons' which came to be developed in the second century and is widely acknowledged in Christendom today. How should we account for their omission here? Is this just an earlier stage before the more developed

[4] 1 Cor. 12:31.

164

situation reflected in the Pastoral Epistles? Alternatively, should we distinguish between an 'institutional' ministry appointed by the church ('bishops, presbyters and deacons') and a 'charismatic' ministry appointed by Christ ('apostles, prophets, evangelists, pastors and teachers')? No, neither of these explanations should commend itself to us. To separate the 'institutional' from the 'charismatic', or ministerial 'order' from ministerial 'gifts', is a false distinction and a disastrous one. That there is such a thing by God's intention as an institutional ministry or a ministerial order (whether threefold or twofold does not matter for our purposes here) is clear from the Pastoral Epistles. Timothy was to select and ordain presbyters and deacons for every church. But how would he select them? What were to be their qualifications? Partly he was to assure himself of the integrity of their moral character, partly of their doctrinal orthodoxy, and partly of their gifts (*e.g.* 'an apt teacher', *didaktikos*).[5] It is inconceivable that the church should select, train and ordain people who lack the appropriate God-given gifts. Ordination to the pastoral ministry of any church should signify at least (1) the public recognition that God has called and gifted the person concerned, and (2) the public authorization of this person to obey the call and exercise the gift, with prayer for the enabling grace of the Holy Spirit. So we must not separate what God has united. On the one hand, the church should acknowledge the gifts which God has given people, and should publicly authorize them and encourage their exercise in ministry. On the other, the New Testament never contemplates the grotesque situation in which the church commissions and authorizes people to exercise a ministry for which they lack both the divine call and the divine equipment. No, gift and office, divine enabling and ecclesiastical commissioning, belong together. It seems to me that Paul indicates this by numbering 'pastors and teachers' among Christ's gifts to his church, since the work of ordained presbyters is precisely to shepherd and teach Christ's flock. 'They therefore are insane', writes Calvin without mincing his words, 'who, neglecting this means

[5] 1 Tim. 3:2.

165

(*sc.* of building up the church), hope to be perfect in Christ, as is the case with fanatics who pretend to secret revelations of the Spirit, and the proud, who content themselves with the private reading of the Scripture, and imagine they do not need the ministry of the Church.'[6]

c. The purpose of spiritual gifts is service

In verse 12 Paul states clearly why Christ gave these gifts to his church. The RSV first edition (1946) read: *for the equipment of the saints, for the work of ministry, for building up the body of Christ.* It will be noted that according to this translation, Christ had three distinct purposes in mind. I think Armitage Robinson was the first commentator to insist that this was a mistake. 'The second of these clauses', he wrote, 'must be taken as dependent on the first, and not . . . as coordinate with it.'[7] In other words, the first comma ('the fatal comma'[8])—which is 'without linguistic authority but with undoubted ecclesiological bias'[9]—must be erased. If it is allowed to stand, we are faced with 'a saddening result', for 'the verse then means that only the special ministers, not all the saints, are called to do "the work of ministry" and to cooperate in the "building of the body".' This interpretation 'has an aristocratic, that is, a clerical and ecclesiastical flavour, it distinguishes the (mass of the) "saints" from the (superior class of the) officers of the church'.[1]

If the comma is erased, however, we are left with two purposes—one immediate and the other ultimate—for which Christ gave gifts to his church. His immediate purpose was 'to equip the saints for the work of ministry' (RSV second edition 1971) or better 'to equip God's people for work in his service' (NEB), and his ultimate purpose 'for building up the body of Christ'.

The former expression about equipping God's people is of far-reaching significance for any true understanding of Christian ministry. For the word *ministry* (*diakonia*) is

[6] Quoted by Hodge, p. 230. *Cf.* Calvin's *Institutes*, IV. 3, 4.
[7] Armitage Robinson, p. 99. [8] Mackay, p. 185. [9] *Ibid.*
[1] Markus Barth. The first quotation comes from *Broken Wall*, p. 165, and the second from the longer discussion in *Ephesians*, II, *viz.* Comment VI entitled 'The Church without Laymen and Priests' pp. 477–484.

here used not to describe the work of pastors but rather the work of so-called laity, that is, of all God's people without exception. Here is incontrovertible evidence that the New Testament envisages ministry not as the prerogative of a clerical élite but as the privileged calling of all the people of God. Thank God that in our generation this biblical vision of an 'every-member ministry' is taking a firm hold in the church.

It does not mean that there is no distinctive pastoral ministry left for clergy; rather it establishes its character. The New Testament concept of the pastor is not of a person who jealously guards all ministry in his own hands, and successfully squashes all lay initiatives, but of one who helps and encourages all God's people to discover, develop and exercise their gifts. His teaching and training are directed to this end, to enable the people of God to be a servant people, ministering actively but humbly according to their gifts in a world of alienation and pain. Thus, instead of monopolizing all ministry himself, he actually multiplies ministries.

What model of the church, then, should we keep in our minds? The traditional model is that of the pyramid, with the pastor perched precariously on its pinnacle, like a little pope in his own church, while the laity are arrayed beneath him in serried ranks of inferiority. It is a totally unbiblical image, because the New Testament envisages not a single pastor with a docile flock but both a plural oversight and an every-member ministry. Not much better is the model of the bus, in which the pastor does all the driving while the congregation are the passengers slumbering in peaceful security behind him. Quite different from either the pyramid or the bus is the biblical model of the body. The church is the body of Christ, every member of which has a distinctive function. Although the body metaphor can certainly accommodate the concept of a distinct pastorate (in terms of one ministry—and a very important one—among many), there is simply no room in it either for a hierarchy or for that kind of bossy clericalism which concentrates all ministry in the hands of one man and denies the people of God their own rightful ministries.

I saw the principle of the every-member ministry well

illustrated when I visited St Paul's Church, Darien, Connecticut, a few years ago. It is an American Episcopal church, which has been influenced by the charismatic movement. On the front cover of their Sunday bulletin I read the name of the Rector, the Reverend Everett Fullam, then the names of the Associate Rector and of the Assistant to the Rector. Next came the following line: 'Ministers: the entire congregation'. It was startling, but undeniably biblical.

So Christ's immediate purpose in the giving of pastors and teachers to his church is through their ministry of the word to equip all his people for their varied ministries. And the ultimate purpose of this is to build up his body, the church. For clearly the way the whole body grows is for all its members to use their God-given gifts. These gifts are so beneficial both to those who exercise their ministry faithfully and to those who receive it that the church becomes steadily more healthy and mature. If the sixteenth century recovered 'the priesthood of all believers' (every Christian enjoying through Christ a direct access to God), perhaps the twentieth century will recover 'the ministry of all believers' (every Christian receiving from Christ a privileged ministry to men).

All spiritual gifts, then, are service-gifts. This is their purpose. They are not given for selfish but for unselfish use, namely for the service of other people. Each of the lists of *charismata* in the New Testament emphasizes this. 'To each is given the manifestation of the Spirit for the common good'.[2] It follows that their comparative importance (Paul is quite clear that some are 'higher' or 'greater' than others)[3] is to be assessed by the degree to which they 'edify' or build up the church. This is why the teaching gifts are of paramount importance, for nothing builds up the church like the truth of God's Word.

To recapitulate, we have seen that it is the exalted Christ who bestows gifts on his church, that his gifts are very diverse in character, that the teaching gifts are primary, and that their purpose is to equip God's people for their ministries and so build up Christ's body.

[2] 1 Cor. 12:7.   [3] 1 Cor. 12:31.

4. Christian unity demands the maturity of our growth (verses 13–16)

The apostle goes on to elaborate what he means by *building up the body of Christ*. It will evidently be a lengthy process, leading (in three pregnant phrases) to *the unity of the faith and of the knowledge of the Son of God*, *mature manhood*, and *the measure of the stature of the fullness of Christ*. This is the goal to which the church will one day *attain*.

Because this verb *attain* means literally 'to come to meet' (*katantaō*), and because the first and third phrases refer explicitly to the Lord Jesus ('Son of God' and 'Christ'), Markus Barth interprets the second ('mature manhood') as referring to him too. He translates it 'the Perfect Man' and pictures the church as the bride of Christ going out in a joyful festival procession to meet her Bridegroom at his triumphant appearing.[4] It is an attractive reconstruction, and certainly accords with the development of the bride and bridegroom imagery of 5:25–27. On the other hand, it seems somewhat forced, since what we are said to 'attain' or 'meet' is not simply 'the Son of God' but 'the unity of the faith and of the knowledge of the Son of God', not simply 'Christ' but 'the measure of the stature of the fullness of Christ'. In other words, the church's goal is not Christ but its own maturity in unity which comes from knowing, trusting and growing up into Christ.

We pause to note that the church's unity, although already in one sense given and inviolable, as we have seen, yet needs in another sense to be both 'maintained' (verse 3) and 'attained' (verse 13). Both verbs are surprising. If unity already exists as a gift, how can it be attained as a goal? Probably we need to reply that just as unity needs to be maintained *visibly*, so it needs to be attained *fully*. For there are degrees of unity, just as there are degrees of sanctity. And the unity to which we are to come one day is that full unity which a full faith in and knowledge of the Son of God will make possible. This expression effectively disposes of the argument that unity can grow

---

[4] Barth, *Ephesians*, II, Comment VII, 'Meeting the Perfect Man', pp. 484–496.

without Christian faith or knowledge. On the contrary, it is precisely the more we know and trust the Son of God that we grow in the kind of unity with one another which he desires.

This full unity is also called *mature manhood*. Some interpret this individually of each Christian growing into maturity in Christ, which is certainly a New Testament concept. But the context seems to demand that we understand it corporately. The church is represented as a single organism, the body of Christ, and is to grow up into adult stature. Indeed, Paul has referred to it as the new humanity which God is creating, or as 'one new man' (2:15). To the oneness and the newness of this 'man' he now adds matureness. The *one new man* is to attain *mature manhood*, which will be nothing less than *the measure of the stature of the fullness of Christ*, the fullness which Christ himself possesses and bestows.

Although it seems that this growth into maturity is a corporate concept, describing the church as a whole, yet it clearly depends on the maturing of its individual members, as Paul proceeds to say: *so that we may no longer be children* (verse 14). Of course we are to resemble children in their humility and innocence,[5] but not in their ignorance or instability. Unstable children are like little boats in a stormy sea, entirely at the mercy of wind and waves. Paul paints a graphic picture, tossed to and fro (*klydōnizomenoi*, from *klydōn*, rough water or surf) meaning 'tossed here and there by waves' (AG) and *carried about* (*peripheromenoi*) meaning 'swung round by shifting winds'.[6] Apparently Plato used this latter word of tops, which led E. K. Simpson to dub such people 'whirligigs'.[7] NEB brings the two storm pictures together by translating 'tossed by the waves and whirled about by every fresh gust of teaching'. Such are immature Christians. They never seem to know their own mind or come to settled convictions. Instead, their opinions tend to be those of the last preacher they heard or the last book they read, and they fall an easy prey to each new theological fad. They cannot resist

[5] Mt. 18:3; 1 Cor. 14:20.   [6] Armitage Robinson, p. 183.
[7] Simpson, p. 97 note, and p. 98.

the cunning of men (*kybia* means 'dice-playing' and so 'trickery') or *their craftiness in deceitful wiles.*

In contrast to doctrinal instability, which is a mark of immaturity, we should be *speaking the truth in love* in order that we may *grow up in every way into him who is the head, into Christ, from whom the whole body, joined and knit together by every joint with which it is supplied, when each part is working properly, makes bodily growth and upbuilds itself in love* (verses 15–16)

We must not look in these verses for inspired instruction on human anatomy and physiology. The apostle's intention is not to teach us how the human body works, but rather how the body of Christ grows. True, he uses some terms employed by ancient Greek medical writers like Hippocrates and Galen. 'We can almost see him turn to "the beloved physician", of whose presence he tells us in the companion epistle (Col. 4:14), before venturing to speak—technical language of "every ligament of the whole apparatus" of the human frame.'[8] But his emphasis is on the head 'into' whom we are to grow up (verse 15) and 'from' whom the body grows when 'each part is working properly'. Markus Barth brings out clearly in his translation this focusing of attention on the initiative and work of the Head, Christ: 'He is at work fitting and joining the whole body together. He provides sustenance to it through every contact according to the needs of each single part. He enables the body to make its own growth so that it builds itself up in love.'[9]

If now we drop the body metaphor and enquire exactly how the church grows into maturity, Paul is ready with his answer. It grows by truth and love. To allow ourselves to be hurled hither and thither by the fierce blasts of false teaching is to condemn ourselves and the church to perpetual immaturity (verse 14). Instead, what we need is 'the truth', provided we speak it 'in love' (verse 15). For it is 'in love' that the church grows and builds itself up (verse 16). What Paul calls for is a balanced combination of the two. 'Speaking the truth in love' is not the best rendering of his expression, for the Greek verb makes no

---

[8] Armitage Robinson, p. 104.   [9] Barth, *Ephesians*, II, p. 426.

reference to our speech. Literally, it means, 'truthing (*alētheuontes*) in love', and includes the notions of 'maintaining', 'living' and 'doing' the truth. Thank God there are those in the contemporary church who are determined at all costs to defend and uphold God's revealed truth. But sometimes they are conspicuously lacking in love. When they think they smell heresy, their nose begins to twitch, their muscles ripple, and the light of battle enters their eye. They seem to enjoy nothing more than a fight. Others make the opposite mistake. They are determined at all costs to maintain and exhibit brotherly love, but in order to do so are prepared even to sacrifice the central truths of revelation. Both these tendencies are unbalanced and unbiblical. Truth becomes hard if it is not softened by love; love becomes soft if it is not strengthened by truth. The apostle calls us to hold the two together, which should not be difficult for Spirit-filled believers, since the Holy Spirit is himself 'the Spirit of truth', and his firstfruit is 'love'.[1] There is no other route than this to a fully mature Christian unity.

Conclusion

Here, then, is Paul's vision for the church. God's new society is to display charity, unity, diversity and growing maturity. These are the characteristics of 'a life worthy of the calling' to which God has called us, and which the apostle begs us to lead (verse 1).

The more we share Paul's perspective, the deeper will be our discontent with the ecclesiastical *status quo*. Some of us are too conservative, too complacent, too ready to acquiesce in the present situation and to resist change. Others are too radical, wanting to dispense with the institution altogether. Instead we need to grasp more clearly the kind of new society God wants his church to be. Then we shall not be content either with things as they are, or with partial solutions, but rather will pray and work for the church's total renewal.

Some look mainly for structures of unity, but seem to have no comparable concern that the church should become

[1] *E.g.* Jn. 14:17; 15:26; 16:13; Gal. 5:22.

172

a truly caring community marked by humility, meekness, longsuffering, forbearance and love. Paul's primary concern is not for structures; he begins and ends with love (verses 2,16).

Others lay great stress on the fact of the church's unity as a theological concept clearly articulated in their minds, but appear to see nothing anomalous in the visible disunity which contradicts their theology.

Others are content with a uniformity of church life and liturgy which is dull, boring, colourless, monotonous and dead; they have never glimpsed the variety God intends or the diversity of ministries which should enrich and enliven their membership of the body of Christ.

Others have a static view of the church, and are well satisfied if the congregation manages to maintain its size and programme, without cutback; they have no vision of church growth either by evangelistic outreach or by the Christian maturing of their members.

All such complacency is unworthy of the church's calling. In contrast to it the apostle sets before us the picture of a deepening fellowship, an eagerness to maintain visible Christian unity and to recover it if it is lost, an active every-member ministry and a steady growth into maturity by holding the truth in love. We need to keep this biblical ideal clearly before us. Only then shall we live a life that is worthy of it.

8. A new set of clothes

The apostle continues to describe the new standards which are expected of God's new society, or the life which is worthy of God's call. Called to be 'one' people, he has argued, we must cultivate unity. Called to be a 'holy' people, he goes on to argue now, we must also cultivate purity. Purity is as indispensable a characteristic of the people of God as unity.

Paul opens this section on the church's purity, just as he opened the former section on the church's unity, with an assertion of his authority as an apostle of Christ.

> Verse 1   *I therefore, a prisoner for the Lord, beg you ...*
> Verse 17 *Now this I affirm and testify in the Lord ...*

The phrase *in the Lord* means 'in the Lord's name' (GNB). He is making the solemn claim that he writes to them with the authority of the Lord Jesus. NIV brings out this emphasis: 'I tell you this, and insist on it in the Lord.'

The gist of his message is plain: *you must no longer live as the Gentiles do.* He is generalizing of course. Not all pagans were (or are) as dissolute as those he is about to portray. Yet just as there is a typical Christian life, so there is a typical pagan life. When each life is true to its own principles, it is fundamentally opposed to the other. His readers knew from experience what he was saying; for they had been pagans themselves, and they were still living in a pagan environment. But they must live that way *no longer*, even if all around them others continued to do so (*as the Gentiles do*). Once they were pagans and so lived like pagans; now they were Christians and must live like Christians. They had become different people; they must behave differently. Their new status as God's new society involved new standards, and their new life in Christ a new lifestyle.

The way Paul handles his theme is to begin with the doctrinal basis of the new life (4:17–24), and then move on to its practical outworking in everyday behaviour (4:25 – 5:4).

1. The doctrinal basis (4:17–24)

It was essential at the outset for his readers to grasp the contrast between what they had been as pagans and what they now were as Christians, between their old and their new life, and further to grasp the underlying theological basis of this change.

Now this I affirm and testify in the Lord, that you must no longer live as the Gentiles do, in the futility of their minds; [18]*they are darkened in their understanding, alienated from the life of God because of the ignorance that is in them, due to their hardness of heart;* [19]*they have become callous and have given themselves up to licentiousness, greedy to practise every kind of uncleanness.* [20]*You did not so learn Christ!—*[21]*assuming that you have heard about him and were taught in him, as the truth is in Jesus.* [22]*Put off your old nature which belongs to your former manner of life and is corrupt through deceitful lusts,* [23]*and be renewed in the spirit of your minds,* [24]*and put on the new nature, created after the likeness of God in true righteousness and holiness.*

What is immediately noteworthy is the apostle's emphasis on the intellectual factor in everybody's way of life. While describing pagans, he draws attention to *the futility of their minds*, adds that they are *darkened in their understanding* and attributes their alienation from God to *the ignorance that is in them*. He thus refers to their empty minds, darkened understanding and inward ignorance, as a result

175

of which they had become callous, licentious and insatiably unclean. But in contrast to them the believers had 'learned' Christ, 'heard' him, been 'taught' in him, all according to the 'truth' which is in Jesus. Over against the darkness and ignorance of the heathen Paul thus sets the truth of Christ which the Christians had learned. Scripture bears an unwavering testimony to the power of ignorance and error to corrupt, and the power of truth to liberate, ennoble and refine.

a. The pagan life (verses 17–19)

But what is the origin of the darkness of heathen minds, when God himself is light, and he is continuously speaking to mankind through his creation, and both heaven and earth declare his glory? It is *due to their hardness of heart*, says Paul. The word he uses is *pōrōsis*, and on its derivation and history Armitage Robinson supplies a long additional note.[1] Pōros was 'a kind of marble' or in medical writers a 'callus' or a 'bony formation on the joints'. Hence the verb *pōroun* meant to petrify, to become hard and therefore insensible, and even (when 'transferred from the organs of feeling to the organ of sight') blind. But in his view it does not mean 'stubbornness'. It is rather 'intellectual obtuseness, not the steeling of the will'. He examines the eight New Testament occurrences of the word and then concludes: 'Obtuseness, or a dulling of the faculty of perception equivalent to moral blindness, always gives an appropriate sense. On the other hand, the context never decisively favours the meaning "hardness", and this meaning seems sometimes quite out of place.'[2] So he opts for 'blindness', as does the AV in this verse, as 'the least misleading' rendering.

Despite the careful arguing of his case, however, Armitage Robinson has not carried the translators and commentators with him. Certainly Mark 3:5 (where Jesus 'looked around at them with anger, grieved at their hardness of heart') seems to imply a wilful obtuseness. Coming back to our Ephesians text, NEB translates it 'their minds have grown hard as stone', GNB uses the word 'stubborn', and J. H.

---

[1] Armitage Robinson, pp. 264–274.   [2] *Ibid*, p. 267.

Houlden comments: 'Pagan immorality is seen as wilful and culpable . . . , the result of their deliberate refusal of the moral light available to them in their own thought and conscience.'[3] It is true that in biblical usage 'heart' and 'mind' cannot be separated, since the heart includes our capacity to think and understand. Nevertheless, there is a real distinction between 'ignorance' and 'hardness' or 'obstinacy'.

If we put Paul's expressions together, noting carefully their logical connections (especially *because of* and *due to*, both translating *dia*), he seems to be depicting the terrible downward path of evil, which begins with an obstinate rejection of God's known truth. First comes *their hardness of heart*, then *their ignorance*, being *darkened in their understanding*, next and consequently they are *alienated from the life of God*, since he turns away from them, until finally *they have become callous and have given themselves up to licentiousness, greedy to practise every kind of uncleanness*. NEB has 'They stop at nothing to satisfy their foul desire'. Thus hardness of heart leads first to darkness of mind, then to deadness of soul under the judgment of God, and finally to recklessness of life. Having lost all sensitivity, people lose all self-control. It is exactly the sequence which Paul elaborates in the latter part of Romans 1. Comparative tables may help to demonstrate this:

Romans 1:18–32	Ephesians 4:17–19

Stage 1: Obstinacy

Romans 1:18–32	Ephesians 4:17–19
18 'Men . . . by their wickedness suppress the truth'	18 'Due to their hardness (pōrōsis) of heart'
21 'Although they knew God they did not honour him as God'	
28 'They did not see fit to acknowledge God'	

[3] Houlden, p. 317.

Stage 2: Darkness

21 *'They became futile in their thinking and their senseless minds were darkened'*

22 *'They became fools'*

28 *'A base mind'*

17 *'The futility of their minds'*

18a *'They are darkened in their understanding'*

18b *'The ignorance that is in them'*

Stage 3: Death or judgment

24 *'Therefore God gave them up'*

26 *'For this reason God gave them up'*

28 *'God gave them up'*

18 *'They are . . . alienated from the life of God'*

Stage 4: Recklessness

God gave them up to—

24 *'Impurity'*

26 *'Dishonourable passions'*

27 *'Shameless acts'*

28 *'Improper conduct'*

29–31 *'All manner of wickedness . . .'*

19 *'They have become callous and have given themselves up to licentiousness* (aselgeia, *meaning public indecency of a shameless kind), greedy to practise every kind of uncleanness'*

b. The Christian life (verses 20–24)

The RSV does not adequately bring out the sharpness of the contrast, the 'but as for you' (*humeis de*) or 'you, however' (NIV) of the beginning of verse 20: *you did not so learn Christ!* Over against heathen hardness, darkness and recklessness Paul sets a whole process of Christian moral education. He uses three parallel expressions which centre on three verbs, all in the aorist tense, meaning to 'learn', to 'hear' and to 'be taught', with a final reference to 'the truth as it is in Jesus'.

First, 'you learned Christ' (verse 20, *emathete*)
Secondly, 'you heard him' (verse 21a, *ēkousate*)
Thirdly, 'you were taught in him' (verse 21b, *edidachthēte*)

These are remarkable expressions. They 'evoke the image of a school'[4] and refer to the catechetical instruction which Paul assumes, indeed knows, they have had. According to the first, Christ is himself the substance of Christian teaching. Just as evangelists 'preach Christ',[5] so their hearers 'learn' Christ, and 'receive' him, that is, a tradition about him.[6] But what sort of Christ do they learn? Not just the Word made flesh, the unique God-man, who died, rose and reigns. More than that. The implication of the context is that we must also preach his lordship, the kingdom or rule of righteousness he ushered in, and all the moral demands of the new life. The Christ whom the Ephesians had learned was calling them to standards and values totally at variance with their former pagan life.

Secondly, Christ who is the substance of the teaching ('you learned Christ') is himself also the teacher ('you heard him'). It is a pity that RSV translates the phrase *you heard about him*, for there is no preposition. Paul assumes that through the voice of their Christian teachers, they had actually heard Christ's voice. Thus, when sound biblical moral instruction is being given, it may be said that Christ is teaching about Christ.

Thirdly, they had been *taught in him*. That is to say, Jesus Christ, in addition to being the teacher and the teaching, was also the context, even the atmosphere within which the teaching was given. When Jesus Christ is at once the subject, the object and the environment of the moral instruction being given, we may have confidence that it is truly Christian. For *truth is in Jesus*. The change from his title 'Christ' to his human name 'Jesus' seems to be deliberate. The historical Jesus is himself the embodiment of truth, as he claimed.[7]

But what exactly is this truth that is in Jesus? If heathen

---

[4] Barth, *Ephesians*, II, p. 504.   [5] 2 Cor. 4:5.
[6] Col. 2:6.   [7] Jn. 14:6.

179

darkness leads to reckless uncleanness, what is the truth which sets Christians free and leads them to righteousness? The next verses (22–24) give the answer. To 'learn Christ' is to grasp the new creation which he has made possible, and the entirely new life which results from it. It is nothing less than putting off our old humanity like a rotten garment and putting on like clean clothing the new humanity recreated in God's image.

When does this take place? RSV is seriously misleading in that it renders the infinitive verbs as if they were imperatives, and thus represents Paul's written instruction as fresh commands to his readers: *Put off your old nature ... and put on the new nature* (verses 22,24). But this cannot be right, for two main reasons. First, in the parallel passage in Colossians[8] the verbs are aorist participles, indicating what the Colossian Christians did at the time of their conversion: 'Seeing that you have put off the old nature ... and have put on the new nature.' Secondly, if they are commands in Ephesians 4:22,24, then the command of verse 25 becomes a nonsense: *Therefore, putting away falsehood ...* Surely this 'therefore', which builds on what has just been written, can hardly base one command upon another, as if to say: 'Put off your old nature ... and put on the new ... Therefore put away falsehood'. The Colossians parallel, on the other hand, makes perfect sense, because it builds a present command on a past fact. It reads: 'Put all these things away—anger, malice, slander (*etc.*)—seeing that you have put off the old nature ... and have put on the new' (3:8–10). It is because we have already put off our old nature, in that decisive act of repentance called conversion, that we can logically be commanded to put away all the practices which belong to that old and rejected life. In Ephesians 4 as in Colossians 3, therefore, the same logic is to be found. The verbs 'put off' and 'put on' are not fresh commands which the apostle is now addressing to his readers, but old ones which he gave when he was with them and of which he now reminds them. Indeed, these commands are the very 'truth as it is in Jesus' which they had been taught and learned. So we

[8] Col. 3:9–10.

should repunctuate these sentences, and replace the full stop at the end of verse 21 with a colon or with the word 'namely', thus: 'You did not so learn Christ!—assuming that you . . . were taught in him, as the truth is in Jesus, namely that you were to put off your old nature . . . and put on the new . . .' JBP captures the sequence of thought well: 'What you learned was to fling off . . . and to put on. . .' So does NEB: 'Were you not . . . taught the truth as it is in Jesus?—that, leaving your former way of life, you must lay aside that old human nature.'

What had they been taught, then? They had been taught that becoming a Christian involves a radical change, namely 'conversion' (as the human side of the experience is usually called) and 're-creation' (the divine side). It involves the repudiation of our former self, our fallen humanity, and the assumption of a new self or re-created humanity. Each of these two Paul calls (literally) a 'man', the 'old man' which is put off, and the 'new man' which is put on. Charles Hodge explains their language: 'What is here called "the old man" Paul elsewhere calls himself, as in Rom. 7:14 "I am carnal" . . . or "the flesh" . . . as in Gal. 5:16,17 . . . It is called "man" because it is ourselves.'[9] Further, our former self and our new self are vividly contrasted with each other: 'As we are called to put off our corrupt nature as a ragged and filthy garment, so we are required to put on our new nature as a garment of light. And as the former was personified as an old man, decrepit, deformed, and tending to corruption, so the latter is personified as a new man, fresh, beautiful and vigorous, like God. . .' *i.e.* created in his image.[1]

The portraits Paul paints of both 'men' balance one another. The old was *corrupt*, in the process of degenerating, on its way to ruin or destruction; the new has been freshly *created after the likeness of God*. The old was dominated by *lusts*, uncontrolled passions; the new has been created in *righteousness and holiness*. The lusts of the old were *deceitful*; the righteousness of the new is *true*. Thus, corruption and creation, passion and holiness, deceit and truth are set in opposition to one another, indicating the

[9] Hodge, pp. 259–260.   [1] *Ibid*, pp. 264–265.

total incompatibility of the old and the new, what we were in Adam and what we are in Christ.

In between these contrasting portraits of the kind of person we 'put off' and 'put on' comes verse 23: *and be renewed in the spirit of your minds.* This verb is a present infinitive, in distinction to those of verses 22 and 24 which are aorists. It indicates that, in addition to the decisive rejection of the old and assumption of the new, implicit in conversion, a daily—indeed a continuous—inward renewal of our outlook is involved in being a Christian. If heathen degradation is due to the futility of their minds, then Christian righteousness depends on the constant renewing of our minds.

In all this teaching the divine and the human are beautifully blended. In the command to exchange our old humanity for a new one, Paul is not implying that we can bring about our own new birth. Nobody has ever given birth to himself. The very concept is ludicrous. No, the new humanity we assume is God's creation, not ours. Nevertheless, when God recreates us in Christ according to his own likeness, we entirely concur with what he has done. We 'put off' our old life, turning away from it in distate, and we 'put on' the new life he has created, embracing it and welcoming it with joy. In a word, recreation (what God does) and repentance (what we do by his grace) belong together and cannot be separated.

All this the Ephesian and other Asian Christians had been taught. They had been thoroughly grounded in the nature and consequences of the new creation and the new life. It was part of the 'truth in Jesus' which they had learned. They had not only been taught to 'put off' the old and 'put on' the new; they had done it. The reality took place at their conversion. Then the symbolism may have followed at their baptism, for some early baptisms included a ceremonial investiture with a white robe.[2] Now Paul reminds them what they had learned and done.

Looking back over these verses, we can perhaps grasp more clearly the two solid doctrinal foundations for Christian holiness which Paul has laid. They are like two

[2] *Cf.* Gal. 3:27.

roots from which holiness sprouts and grows. First, we have experienced a new creation, and secondly, in consequence, we have received a new mind which is constantly being renewed. Moreover, the two are organically related to one another. It is our new creation which has given us a new mind; and it is our new mind which understands our new creation and its implications. Since it is a new creation in God's holy image, it has involved for us the total putting away of our old fallenness and the thankful putting on of our new humanness.

Therefore, Paul continues, 'each of you must put off . . .' (verse 25, NIV). That is, because you did throw off your former self once and for all, you must now throw off all conduct which belonged to your old life. Your new behaviour must be completely consistent with the kind of person you have become. As we have already noted, the metaphor ('putting off' and 'putting on') is drawn from the way we dress. It can now be elaborated.

The kind of clothing we wear depends on the kind of role we are fulfilling. For example, when we go to a wedding we wear one kind of clothing; when we go to a funeral we wear another. I realize of course that some young people in the West wear blue jeans at all times. Nevertheless the custom of adapting our dress to suit the occasion still stands as a general principle. Many people's dress is also determined by their job. Soldiers and sailors wear different uniforms. Lawyers have special clothing, at least when they appear in court. So do some clergy. So do prisoners and convicts. But when we change our role, we change our dress. When prisoners are released from custody and become free people again (putting off one role and assuming another), they change what they are wearing (putting off prison garb and putting on ordinary clothes). Similarly, when a soldier leaves the army and becomes a civilian, he gets out of uniform into 'civvies'. Just so, since by a new creation we have put off the old humanity and put on the new, we must also put away the old standards and adopt new ones. Our new role will mean new clothing, our new life a new ethical lifestyle.

2. Six concrete examples (4:25 – 5:4)

It is marvellous to see how easily Paul can descend from lofty theological talk about our two humanities, about the Christ we have learned and the new creation we have experienced, to the nitty-gritty of Christian behaviour—telling the truth and controlling our anger, honesty at work and kindness of speech, forgiveness, love and sexual self-control. All very practical. And before we come to his six examples, we need to notice three features common to them all.

First, they all concern our relationships. Holiness is not a mystical condition experienced in relation to God but in isolation from human beings. You cannot be good in a vacuum, but only in the real world of people. Besides, 'all the qualities enjoined here are aspects of that unity in the church which it is our writer's prime concern to elucidate and to foster. To this matter he deliberately gives pride of place . . . Similarly, the evils to be avoided are all destroyers of human harmony.'[3]

Secondly, in each example a negative prohibition is balanced by a corresponding positive command. It is not enough to put off the old rags; we have to put on new garments. It is not enough to give up lying and stealing and losing our temper, unless we also start speaking the truth, working hard and being kind to people.

Thirdly, in each case a reason for the command is either given or implied, indeed a theological reason. For in the teaching of Jesus and his apostles doctrine and ethics, belief and behaviour are always dovetailed into one another.

a. Don't tell lies, but rather tell the truth (verse 25)

Therefore, putting away falsehood, let every one speak the truth with his neighbour, for we are members one of another.

Strictly speaking, the Greek word is not *falsehood* in the abstract but 'the lie' (*to pseudos*). It is possible, therefore, that Paul is referring here as in Romans 1:25 to 'the great

[3] Houlden, p. 320.

lie of idolatry', and that because his readers had renounced that supreme falsehood of paganism, the chief symptom of a futile and darkened mind (verses 17–18), he urges them now to forsake all lesser lies and speak the truth.[4] Certainly the avoidance of lies is of little use without the active pursuit of truth. The followers of Jesus (in whom is truth, verse 21) should be known in their community as honest, reliable people whose word can be trusted. The reason given is not only that the other person is our *neighbour*, whom we are commanded in Scripture to love, but that in the church our relationship is closer still, *for we are members one of another*. Paul brings us back to his doctrine of the church as the body of Christ (*cf.* verses 12–16), and implies that 'a lie is a stab into the very vitals of the Body of Christ'.[5] For fellowship is built on trust, and trust is built on truth. So falsehood undermines fellowship, while truth strengthens it.

b. Don't lose your temper, but rather ensure that your anger is righteous (verses 26–27)

Be angry but do not sin; do not let the sun go down on your anger, [27]and give no opportunity to the devil.

'Be angry, but sin not' is an echo of Psalm 4:4. It seems clear that this form of words is a Hebrew idiom which permits and then restricts anger, rather than actually commanding it. The equivalent English idiom would be 'in your anger do not sin' (NIV). Nevertheless, the verse recognizes that there is such a thing as Christian anger, and too few Christians either feel or express it. Indeed, when we fail to do so, we deny God, damage ourselves and encourage the spread of evil.

Scripture plainly teaches that there are two kinds of anger, righteous and unrighteous. In verse 31 'anger' is one of a number of unpleasant things which we are to 'put away' from us. Evidently unrighteous anger is meant. But in 5:6 we are told of the anger of God which will fall on the disobedient, and we know that God's anger is righteous. So was the anger of Jesus.[6] There must therefore be a good

[4] Findlay, p. 292.   [5] Mackay, p. 213.   [6] Mk. 3:5.

and true anger which God's people can learn from him and from their Lord Jesus.

I go further and say that there is a great need in the contemporary world for more Christian anger. We human beings compromise with sin in a way in which God never does. In the face of blatant evil we should be indignant not tolerant, angry not apathetic. If God hates sin, his people should hate it too. If evil arouses his anger, it should arouse ours also. 'Hot indignation seizes me because of the wicked, who forsake thy law.'[7] What other reaction can wickedness be expected to provoke in those who love God?

It is particularly noteworthy that the apostle introduces this reference to anger in a letter devoted to God's new society of love, and in a paragraph concerned with harmonious relationships. He does so because true peace is not identical with appeasement. 'In such a world as this,' comments E. K. Simpson, 'the truest peace-maker may have to assume the role of a peace-breaker as a sacred obligation.'[8]

At the same time, we need to remember our fallenness, and our constant proneness to intemperance and vanity. Consequently, we always have to be on our guard and act as censors of our own anger. If we are wise, we shall be 'slow to anger', remembering that 'the anger of man does not work the righteousness of God'.[9] So Paul immediately qualifies his permissive *be angry* by three negatives. First, *do not sin*. We have to make sure that our anger is free from injured pride, spite, malice, animosity and the spirit of revenge. Secondly, *do not let the sun go down on your anger*. This instruction illustrates well the folly of excessive literalism in interpreting the Bible. We are not to understand Paul 'so literally that we may take leave to be angry till sunset', for 'then might our wrath lengthen with the days, and men in Greenland, where days last above a quarter of the year, have plentiful scope of revenge'.[1] No, the apostle's intention is to warn us against nursing anger. It is seldom safe to allow the embers to smoulder. Certainly

[7] Ps. 119:53.   [8] Simpson, p. 108.   [9] Jas. 1:19–20.
[1] Quoted from an earlier commentator by Armitage Robinson, p. 112 note.

if we become aware of some sinful or selfish element in it (and if our *orgē*, anger, degenerates into *parorgismos*, resentment, the word used at the end of verse 26), then it is time for us to cease from it, and either apologize or be reconciled to the person concerned. In the Old Testament a moneylender who took a poor person's cloak as a pledge was required to restore it 'when the sun goes down', so that he might sleep in it, and an employer who had any servants who were poor and needy was required to pay them their wages daily 'before the sun goes down'.[2] There are many similar situations in which it is wise to live a day at a time. 'Never go to bed angry' is a good rule, and is seldom more applicable than to a married couple.

Paul's third qualification is *give no opportunity to the devil* (verse 27), for he knows how fine is the line between righteous and unrighteous anger, and how hard human beings find it to handle their anger responsibly. So he loves to lurk round angry people, hoping to be able to exploit the situation to his own advantage by provoking them into hatred or violence or a breach of fellowship.

c. *Don't steal, but rather work and give* (verse 28)

Let the thief no longer steal, but rather let him labour, doing honest work with his hands, so that he may be able to give to those in need.

'Do not steal' was the eighth commandment of Moses' law. It had and still has a wide application, not only to the stealing of other people's money or possessions, but also to tax evasions and customs dodges which rob the government of their dues, to employers who oppress their workers, and to employees who give poor service or work short time.

In echoing the commandment (*let the thief no longer steal*), however, the apostle goes beyond the prohibition and draws out its positive implications. It is not enough that the thief stops stealing. Let him start working, *doing honest work with his hands*, earning his own living. Then he will *be able* not only to support himself and his family,

[2] Dt. 24:13–15.

but also *to give to those in need*. Instead of sponging on the community, as thieves do, he will start contributing to it. And none but Christ can transform a burglar into a benefactor!

d. Don't use your mouth for evil, but rather for good (verses 29–30)

Let no evil talk come out of your mouths, but only such as is good for edifying, as fits the occasion, that it may impart grace to those who hear. [30]*And do not grieve the Holy Spirit of God, in whom you were sealed for the day of redemption.*

The apostle turns from the use of our hands to the use of our mouths. Speech is a wonderful gift of God. It is one of our human capacities which reflect our likeness to God. For our God speaks, and like him we also speak. Speech distinguishes us from the animal creation. Cows can moo, dogs bark, donkeys bray, pigs grunt, lambs bleat, lions roar, monkeys squeal and birds sing, but only human beings can speak.

So *let no evil talk come out of your mouths*, Paul says. 'Evil' here is *sapros*, a word used of rotten trees and rotten fruit.[3] When applied to rotten talk, whether this is dishonest, unkind or vulgar, we may be sure that in some way it hurts the hearers. Instead, we are to use our unique gift of speech constructively, *for edifying*, that is to build people up and not damage or destroy them, *as fits the occasion*. Then our words will *impart grace to those who hear*.

Jesus taught the great significance of speech. Our words reveal what is in our hearts, he said, and we shall have to give an account on judgment day of every careless word we have uttered.[4] So James was only echoing the teaching of his Master when he emphasized the immense power of the human tongue for good or evil.[5] If we are truly a new creation of God, we shall undoubtedly develop new standards of conversation. Instead of hurting people with our words, we shall want to use them to help, encourage, cheer, comfort and stimulate them. I have myself often

---

[3] Mt. 7:17–18 and 12:33.   [4] Mt. 12:33–37.   [5] Jas. 3:1–12.

been challenged by the contrasting speech of the wise man and the fool in Proverbs 12:18: 'There is one whose rash words are like sword thrusts, but the tongue of the wise brings healing'.

It is not immediately clear why Paul now introduces the Holy Spirit: *Do not grieve the Holy Spirit of God, in whom you were sealed for the day of redemption* (verse 30). But the apostle was constantly aware that behind the actions of human beings invisible personalities are present and active. He has just warned us to give no opportunity to the devil (verse 27); now he urges us not to grieve the Holy Spirit. It is evident from this that the Holy Spirit is fully personal, for *lypeō* is to cause sorrow, pain or distress, and only persons can feel these things. But what grieves him? Since he is the 'holy Spirit', he is always grieved by unholiness, and since he is the 'one Spirit' (2:18; 4:4), disunity will also cause him grief. In fact, anything incompatible with the purity or unity of the church is incompatible with his own nature and therefore hurts him. One might add that because he is also the 'Spirit of truth', through whom God has spoken, he is upset by all our misuse of speech, which has been Paul's topic in the preceding verse.

We notice also in verse 30 the references to being *sealed* with the Spirit and to *the day of redemption*. The sealing (as Paul has already explained in 1:13) took place at the beginning of our Christian life; the Holy Spirit himself, indwelling us, is the seal with which God has stamped us as his own. The day of redemption, however, although we already have redemption in the sense of forgiveness (verse 1:7), looks on to the end when our bodies will be redeemed, for only then will our redemption or liberation be complete. So the 'sealing' and the 'redemption' refer respectively to the beginning and the end of the salvation process. And in between these two termini we are to grow in Christlikeness and to take care not to grieve the Holy Spirit. For the Holy Spirit is a sensitive Spirit. He hates sin, discord and falsehood, and shrinks away from them. Therefore, if we wish to avoid hurting him, we shall shrink from them too. Every Spirit-filled believer desires to bring him pleasure, not pain.

e. Don't be unkind or bitter, bur rather kind and loving
(4:31 – 5:2)

Let all bitterness and wrath and anger and clamour and slander be put away from you, with all malice, [32]and be kind to one another, tenderhearted, forgiving one another, as God in Christ forgave you.

[5:1]*Therefore be imitators of God, as beloved children. [2]And walk in love, as Christ loved us and gave himself up for us, a fragrant offering and sacrifice to God.*

Here is a whole series of six unpleasant attitudes and actions which are to be *put away* from us entirely. *Bitterness (pikria)* is a sour spirit and sour speech. We sometimes talk about a 'sour puss', and I guess there are sour tomcats too. Little is sadder in elderly people than a negative and cynical outlook on life. Quoting Aristotle, Armitage Robinson defines it as 'an embittered and resentful spirit which refuses to be reconciled'.[6] *Wrath (thymos)* and *anger (orgē)* are obviously similar, the former denoting a passionate rage and the latter a more settled and sullen hostility. *Clamour (kraugē)* describes people who get excited, raise their voices in a quarrel, and start shouting, even screaming, at each other, while *slander (blasphēmia)* is speaking evil of others, especially behind their backs, and so defaming and even destroying their reputation. The sixth word is *malice (kakia)*, or ill will, wishing and probably plotting evil against people. Alternatively, it may be inclusive of the five preceding vices, namely 'silently harboured grudge, indignant outburst, seething rage, public quarrel and slanderous taunt.'[7] There is no place for any of these horrid things in the Christian community; they have to be totally rejected.

In their place we should welcome the kind of qualities which characterize the behaviour of God and his Christ. We are to *be kind to one another*. The word is *chrēstos*, and because of the obvious assonance with the name of Christ *(Christos)*, Christians from the beginning saw its peculiar appropriateness. It occurs in the Sermon on the

---

[6] Armitage Robinson, p. 194.   [7] Caird, p. 83.

Mount for God's kindness towards even 'the ungrateful and the selfish'.[8] *Tenderhearted* is 'compassionate', while *forgiving one another* (*charizomenoi*) is literally 'acting in grace' towards one another, as God in Christ has acted in grace towards us. *Therefore*, because of God's gracious attitude and generous actions towards us, we are to *be imitators* (*mimētai*) *of God, as beloved children*. Just as children copy their parents, so we are to copy our Father God, as Jesus himself told us to.[9] We are also to follow Christ, to *walk in love as Christ loved us and gave himself up for us*. The same verb for self-giving (*paradidōmi*) is used of the heathen in 4:19. They give themselves up to licentiousness; we like Christ are to give ourselves up to love. Such self-giving for others is pleasing to God. As with Christ so with us, self-sacrificial love is a *fragrant offering and sacrifice to God*. It is thus a striking truth that sacrificial love for others becomes a sacrifice acceptable to God.

It is noteworthy how God-centred Paul's ethic is. It is natural for him, in issuing his moral instructions, to mention the three Persons of the Trinity. He tells us to 'copy God', to 'learn Christ' and not to 'grieve the Holy Spirit'.

f. Don't joke about sex, but rather give thanks for it
(verses 3–4)

But fornication and all impurity or covetousness must not even be named among you, as is fitting among saints. ⁴Let there be no filthiness, nor silly talk, nor levity, which are not fitting; but instead let there be thanksgiving.

Paul turns from 'self-sacrifice . . . to its very opposite, self-indulgence',[1] from genuine 'love' to that perversion of it called 'lust'. The Greek words for *fornication* (*porneia*) and *impurity* (*akatharsia*) together cover every kind of sexual sin, in other words all sexual intercourse outside its God-ordained context of a loving marriage. To them Paul adds *covetousness*, surely because they are an especially

---

[8] Lk. 6:35.   [9] Mt. 5:45, 48.   [1] Hendriksen, p. 227.

degrading form of it, namely the coveting of somebody else's body for selfish gratification. The tenth commandment had specifically prohibited coveting a neighbour's wife, and earlier in this letter Paul has written of the 'greed' involved in unclean practices (4:19).[2] So all forms of sexual immorality, he writes, *must not even be named among you*. We are not only to avoid their indulgence, but also to avoid thinking and talking about them, so completely are they to be banished from the Christian community. This was a high and holy standard to demand, for immorality was rife in Asia. And since the Greek goddess Artemis, 'Diana of the Ephesians', was regarded as a fertility goddess, sexual orgies were regularly associated with her worship.

Verse 4 goes beyond immorality to vulgarity. For *filthiness* means obscenity, and both *silly talk* and *levity* are probably an allusion to coarse jesting, which is the cheapest form of wit. All three refer to a dirty mind expressing itself in dirty conversation. But these things *are not fitting. Instead*, Paul says, *let there be thanksgiving*. The contrast is striking and beautiful. In itself thanksgiving is not an obvious substitute for vulgarity, since the latter is essentially self-centred, and the former God-centred. But perhaps this is the point that Paul is making: 'Whereas sexual impurity and covetousness both express self-centred acquisitiveness, thanksgiving is the exact opposite, and so the antidote required; it is the recognition of God's generosity'.[3] It seems to me probable, however, that Paul is setting vulgarity and thanksgiving even more plainly in opposition to each other, namely as alternative pagan and Christian attitudes to sex. Of course Christians have a bad reputation for being negative towards sex. Dr Michel Fourcault, since 1970 Professor of the History of Thought Systems at the Collège de France, is apparently writing a *History of Sexuality* in six volumes. Explaining his work in *Le Monde* in January 1977 he spoke of 'Christianity's most intolerably burdensome legacy, sex as sin'. And it is true that some of our Victorian forefathers came close

[2] See also 1 Cor. 5:10–11; 6:9–10 and Col. 3:5 for other passages in which the apostle associates covetousness with immorality.
[3] Houlden, p. 324.

to this identification. But the reason why Christians should dislike and avoid vulgarity is not because we have a warped view of sex, and are either ashamed or afraid of it, but because we have a high and holy view of it as being in its right place God's good gift, which we do not want to see cheapened. All God's gifts, including sex, are subjects for thanksgiving, rather than for joking. To joke about them is bound to degrade them; to thank God for them is the way to preserve their worth as the blessings of a loving Creator.

Conclusion

What is the theme which has run right through chapter 4 and spilled over into chapter 5? These chapters are a stirring summons to the unity and purity of the church; but they are more than that. Their theme is the integration of Christian experience (what we are), Christian theology (what we believe) and Christian ethics (how we behave). They emphasize that being, thought and action belong together and must never be separated. For what we are governs how we think, and how we think determines how we act. We are God's new society, a people who have put off the old life and put on the new; that is what he has made us. So we need to recall this by the daily renewal of our minds, remembering how we 'learned Christ . . . as the truth is in Jesus', and thinking Christianly about ourselves and our new status. Then we must actively cultivate a Christian life. For holiness is not a condition into which we drift. We are not passive spectators of a sanctification God works in us. On the contrary, we have purposefully to 'put away' from us all conduct that is incompatible with our new life in Christ, and to 'put on' a lifestyle compatible with it.

Two words stand out as summarizing this theme. In 4:1 Paul begs us to lead a life that is *worthy* of God's call, and in 5:3 he tells us to avoid immorality, 'as is *fitting* among saints'. It is most unfortunate that the word 'saints' has come to be used, if not for the heroes of the church who have been canonized, then at least for exceptional and often eccentric people who are distinguished from others

193

by their pallid countenance, heavenward look and invisible halo. But 'the saints' are all God's people who have been reconciled to him and to each other. Therefore, certain kinds of behaviour are 'worthy', or 'fitting', being appropriate to who we are, while certain others are 'unworthy' or 'unfitting', being inappropriate.

Let no-one say that doctrine does not matter! Good conduct arises out of good doctrine. It is only when we have grasped clearly who we are in Christ, that the desire will grow within us to live a life that is worthy of our calling and fitting to our character as God's new society.

5:5–21

9. More incentives to righteousness

It is somewhat arbitrary to suggest a break after verse 4 and the beginning of a new paragraph with verse 5, especially when the same topic of sexual morality is being handled in both. Yet verses 3 and 4 seem to belong to the previous section's practical examples of ethical conduct, each consisting of a balancing prohibition and commandment. After them, although verse 5 continues the topic of sex, we become aware that the emphasis has changed. Paul moves on in his treatment of Christian behaviour from models to motivation, and adds four powerful incentives to righteous living.

All employers in business and industry know the vital importance of incentives. How can workers be persuaded to work harder and better, and so increase productivity or sales? All kinds of inducement are offered in the form of higher wages, more attractive conditions, bonuses, holidays, recreational and educational facilities, and then retirement and pension prospects. The best incentives are neither material nor selfish, however. Wise employers of labour seek to give their work force a heightened interest in their job, a greater loyalty to the firm, and a feeling of pride in what they are making or selling. All this bears witness to the nature of men and women, made in God's likeness, who in addition to a job need reasons for doing it, ideals to inspire them and a sense of creative fulfilment. Not surprisingly, therefore, the Bible which gives us this doctrine of mankind is itself concerned not only with obligation but with motivation. People know what they

195

ought to do; how can they be motivated to do it? Here is an aspect of the doctrine of sanctification (that is, of the process of becoming like Christ) which is much emphasized in the Bible and much neglected in the contemporary church.

The apostle has been arguing that because we are God's new society we must adopt new standards, and because we have decisively 'put off' the old life and 'put on' the new, we must wear appropriate clothing. Now he adds more arguments for holiness. The first concerns the solemn certainty of judgment (verses 5–7), the second what he calls 'the fruit of light' (verses 8–14), *i.e.* the implications of being people who belong to the light, the third the nature of wisdom (verses 15–17) and the fourth the fullness of the Holy Spirit (verses 18–21).

1. The certainty of judgment (verses 5–7)

Be sure of this, that no fornicator or impure man, or one who is covetous (that is, an idolater), has any inheritance in the kingdom of Christ and of God. ⁶Let no one deceive you with empty words, for it is because of these things that the wrath of God comes upon the sons of disobedience. ⁷Therefore do not associate with them.

Many reasons are given in the New Testament why Christian people should abstain from immorality. There is, for example, the trinitarian theology of the human body as created by God, belonging to Christ and indwelt by the Spirit, which Paul develops in 1 Corinthians 6:12–20. Then there is the intrinsic inappropriateness of unholy practices in the holy people of God; in other words, sexual licence is simply 'not fitting among saints' (verses 3–4). And now there is the fear of judgment. Most immoral people get away with their immorality on earth, but they will not escape detection, conviction and sentence for ever. For *be sure of this*, Paul warns, since there is no uncertainty about it, *that no fornicator or impure man* ('person' would be better, for the words though masculine are not intended to limit the reference to men) . . . *has any inheritance in the kingdom of Christ and of God*. We note in passing

196

the remarkable bracketing of Christ and God in this expression. Since the definite article is not repeated, the kingdom is said to belong to him who is both 'Christ' and 'God'. And this divine kingdom is a righteous kingdom, from which all unrighteousness will be excluded.[1]

We must be cautious, however, in our application of this severe statement. It should not be understood as teaching that even a single immoral thought, word or deed is enough to disqualify us from heaven; otherwise, which of us would ever qualify for admission? No; for those who fall into such sins through weakness, but afterwards repent in shame and humility, there is forgiveness. The immoral or impure person envisaged here is one who has given himself up without shame or penitence to this way of life, *one who is covetous* in the sense already defined, namely sexually greedy (4:19; 5:3), *that is*, Paul adds in parenthesis, *an idolater*. Such people, whose lust has become an idolatrous obsession, will have no share in the perfect kingdom of God.

Let no one deceive you, the apostle continues. He has himself urged them to acknowledge the truth of divine judgment (*be sure of this*); now he warns them of the *empty words* of false teachers who would persuade them otherwise. In his day Gnostics were arguing that bodily sins could be committed without damage to the soul, and with impunity. In our day there are many deceivers in the world, and even in the church. They teach that God is too kind to condemn everybody, and that everybody will get to heaven in the end, irrespective of their behaviour on earth. But their words are empty and their teaching deceitful. Universalism (*i.e.* universal final salvation) is a lie. The truth is that *because of these things* (these evil, immoral, greedy, idolatrous practices) *the wrath of God comes upon the sons of disobedience*. The last phrase is a Hebraism already encountered in 2:2; it means simply 'the disobedient', those who know God's law and wilfully disobey it. God's wrath falls on such, beginning now, and culminating in the day of judgment.[2]

Therefore, Paul concludes, because God's kingdom is

[1] Cf. 1 Cor. 6:9, 10; Gal. 5:21.
[2] Cf. Rom. 1:18 ff; Eph. 4:17–19.

righteous and God's wrath will overtake the unrighteous, *do not associate with them*. The RSV rendering is unfortunate. Paul is not prohibiting all contact or association with such people. Otherwise we could not bring them the good news or seek to restrain them from their evil ways. And we would need to go out of the world altogether, which Christ has forbidden.[3] The Greek word *summetochoi* refers to participation, not just association, and the prohibition means 'do not be partners with them' (NIV). For if we share in their practices, as Lot was warned in Sodom, we run the risk of sharing in their doom.

It would be easy for Christians to speed-read a paragraph like this, without pausing for reflection, on the assumption that it applies to unbelievers, not to us. Has not Paul assured us in the earlier part of his letter of our heavenly inheritance, taught us that the Holy Spirit within us is God's guarantee, even foretaste and first instalment, of it 'until we acquire possession of it',[4] and prayed that our eyes might be opened to see 'the riches of the glory of the inheritance' which will one day be ours?[5] Yes, indeed he has. At the same time he also addresses to us this warning about the danger of forfeiting our inheritance in God's kingdom. How can we reconcile these things? Only by recalling that assurance of salvation is neither a synonym nor an excuse for presumption. And if we should fall into a life of greedy immorality, we would be supplying clear evidence that we are after all idolaters, not worshippers of God, disobedient people instead of obedient, and so the heirs not of heaven but of hell. The apostle gives us a solemn warning; we shall be wise to heed it.

2. The fruit of light (verses 8–14)

For once you were darkness, but now you are light in the Lord; walk as children of light[9]*(for the fruit of light is found in all that is good and right and true),* [10]*and try to learn what is pleasing to the Lord.* [11]*Take no part in the unfruitful works of darkness, but instead expose them.* [12]*For it is a shame even to speak of the things that they do in*

---

[3] Jn. 17:15; 1 Cor. 5:9–10.   [4] 1:13–14.   [5] 1:18.

secret; ¹³*but when anything is exposed by the light it becomes visible, for anything that becomes visible is light.* ¹⁴*Therefore it is said,*

> 'Awake, O sleeper, and arise from the dead,
> and Christ shall give you light.'

Paul goes on to give an additional reason for not getting involved in the evil conduct of immoral people. He bases it not now on the future (the coming judgment of God) but on the past and the present (the difference between what his readers once were and now are).

The whole paragraph plays on the rich symbolism of darkness and light, 'darkness' representing ignorance, error and evil, 'light' representing truth and righteousness. In 4: 17–18 he has portrayed the darkened understanding of pagans. Formerly his readers were the same: *Once you were darkness, but now you are light in the Lord.* Notice that he does not say they used to be *in* darkness, but now were *in* the light. This would have been true, as the New Testament writers say.⁶ But what Paul writes here is more striking still: they themselves were actually now 'light'. 'Their lives and not just their environment'⁷ had been changed from darkness to light. And this radical transformation had taken place *in the Lord*, by virtue of their union with him who claimed to be the light of the world.⁸ So then, because they had become 'light in the Lord', they must *walk as children of light* or 'like people who belong to the light' (GNB). Their behaviour must conform to their new identity. They must radiate the light they are, and 'live like men who are at home in daylight' (NEB).

What will this mean in practice? It will mean a life shining with *all that is good and right and true*, for these things are *the fruit of light* (some MSS read 'the fruit of the Spirit' but this is probably an assimilation to Gal. 5: 22, and 'the fruit of light' is the better reading). It is possible that Paul is following the metaphor through and likening the goodness and truth which grow by the light

---

⁶ *E.g.* Jn. 8:12; 1 Pet. 2:9; 1 Jn. 1:5–7; 2:9.
⁷ Bruce, p. 145.   ⁸ Jn. 8:12; *cf.* Mt. 5:14.

199

of Christ to a harvest ripening under the sun. Certainly if they are to live consistently as 'children of light', they will *try to learn* (*dokimazō* is to test, discern and approve) *what is pleasing to the Lord*. The light metaphor speaks vividly of Christian openness and transparency, of living joyfully in the presence of Christ, with nothing to hide or fear.

Unfortunately, however, it is not possible to live in the light and enjoy it, without also adopting some attitude towards those who still live in the darkness, and to their lifestyle. What attitude will this be? Negatively, *take no part in the unfruitful works of darkness*. While the light produces the fruit of goodness and truth, the works of darkness are unfruitful, unproductive, barren; they have no beneficial results. So we are to take no part in them, but *instead*, positively, *expose them*, 'show them up for what they are' (NEB). We may not wish to do this, but we cannot help it, for this is what light invariably does. Besides, evil deeds deserve to be exposed, that is, to be unmasked and rebuked, *for it is a shame even to speak of the things that they do in secret.*

Verse 13 elaborates the double value of a Christian exposure of evil. First, *when anything is exposed by the light it becomes visible*. This is always good. Darkness hides the ugly realities of evil; the light makes them visible. Then evil is seen for what it is without any possibility of concealment or subterfuge. Secondly, *anything that becomes visible is light*. Paul's economy of words makes it difficult to be certain what he means by this statement. But he seems to be describing a second stage in what light does: it actually transforms what it illumines into light. This may mean that Christians who lead a righteous life thereby restrain and reform evildoers, yes, and even convert them. For as their light shines, what it makes visible suddenly *is light*, just as the Ephesians themselves *are light* (verse 8). JBP paraphrases: 'It is possible (after all it happened to you) for light to turn the thing it shines upon into light.' If this is correct, then Paul has brought his argument about light and darkness to a fine climax. 'Exposure' sounds negative, showing people up for what they are, judgmental, condemning. And it is that. But the light which exposes has positive evangelistic power also, 'the light of one soul making another light'.[9] For it may bring people, as they see the ugliness of evil, to conviction of their sin and so to penitent faith in Jesus. This, then, is the twofold effect which a Christian's light has on the prevailing darkness: it makes visible and it makes light.

Verse 14 is a natural conclusion. Paul clinches his argument with an apt quotation, which either summarizes the teaching of an Old Testament verse like Isaiah 61:1 (since *legei*, *it is said*, normally introduces a quotation from Scripture) or, as many modern commentators suggest, is an extract from an Easter or baptismal hymn: *Awake, O sleeper, and arise from the dead, and Christ shall give you light.* Here our former condition in Adam is graphically described in terms of sleep, death and darkness, from all of which Christ rescues us. Conversion is nothing less than awaking out of sleep, rising from death and being brought out of darkness into the light of Christ. No wonder we are summoned to live a new life in consequence!

3. The nature of wisdom (verses 15–17)

Look carefully then how you walk, not as unwise men but as wise, ¹⁶making the most of the time, because the days are evil. ¹⁷Therefore do not be foolish, but understand what the will of the Lord is.

Paul's next little paragraph is based upon two assumptions, first that Christians are *sophoi*,—wise people, not fools—and secondly that Christian wisdom is practical wisdom, for it teaches us how to behave. His word for to 'behave' throughout the letter has been a Hebrew concept, to 'walk'. Our Christian walk or behaviour, he has written, must no longer be according to the world, the flesh and the devil (2:1–3), or like the pagans (4:17). Instead, it must be 'worthy' of God's call, 'in love', and 'as children of light' (4:1; 5:1; 5:8). Now he adds a more general exhortation to us to behave like the wise people he credits us with being: *look carefully how you walk*, he writes. Everything

[9] Foulkes, p. 148.

worth doing requires care. We all take trouble over the things which seem to us to matter—our job, our education, our home and family, our hobbies, our dress and appearance. So as Christians we must take trouble over our Christian life. We must treat it as the serious thing it is. 'Be most careful then how you conduct yourselves: like sensible men, not like simpletons' (NEB). What, therefore, are the marks of wise people who take trouble over their Christian discipleship?

First, *wise people make the most of their time*. The verb *exagorazō* can mean to 'redeem' or 'buy back', and if used in this way here, the appeal is to 'ransom the time from its evil bondage'.[1] But probably it means rather to 'buy up', in which case RSV is right to translate *making the most of the time*, 'time' (*kairos*) referring to every passing opportunity.

Certainly wise people know that time is a precious commodity. All of us have the same amount of time at our disposal, with sixty minutes in every hour and twenty-four hours in every day. None of us can stretch time. But wise people use it to the fullest possible advantage. They know that time is passing, and also that *the days are evil*. So they seize each fleeting opportunity while it is there. For once it has passed, even the wisest people cannot recover it. Somebody once advertised as follows: 'LOST, yesterday, somewhere between sunrise and sunset, two golden hours, each set with sixty diamond minutes. No reward offered, for they are gone for ever'.[2] By contrast, Jonathan Edwards, the philosopher-theologian who became God's instrument in the 'Great Awakening' in America in 1734–5, wrote in the seventieth of his famous *Resolutions* just before his twentieth birthday: 'Resolved: Never to lose one moment of time, but to improve it in the most profitable way I possibly can.' He was a wise man, for the first sign of wisdom which Paul gives here is a disciplined use of time.

Secondly, *wise people discern the will of God*. They are sure that, whereas wilfulness is folly, wisdom is to be

[1] Armitage Robinson, p. 201.
[2] Horace Mann, quoted by Ted W. Engstrom and Alex Mackenzie in *Managing Your Time* (Zondervan, 1967), p. 63.

found in God's will and nowhere else. *Therefore do not be foolish, but understand what the will of the Lord is* (verse 17). Jesus himself prayed, 'Not my will but yours be done,' and taught us to pray, 'May your will be done on earth as in heaven.' Nothing is more important in life than to discover and do the will of God. Moreover, in seeking to discover it, it is essential to distinguish between his 'general' and his 'particular' will. The former is so called because it relates to the generality of his people and is the same for all of us, *e.g.* to make us like Christ. His particular will, however, extending to the particularities of our life, is different for each of us, *e.g.* what career we shall follow, whether we should marry, and if so whom. Only after this distinction has been made can we consider how we may find out *what the will of the Lord is*. His 'general' will is found in Scripture; the will of God for the people of God has been revealed in the Word of God. But we shall not find his 'particular' will in Scripture. To be sure, we shall find general principles in Scripture to guide us, but detailed decisions have to be made after careful thought and prayer and the seeking of advice from mature and experienced believers.

4. The fullness of the Holy Spirit (verses 18–21)

And do not get drunk with wine, for that is debauchery; but be filled with the Spirit, [19]addressing one another in psalms and hymns and spiritual songs, singing and making melody to the Lord with all your heart, [20]always and for everything giving thanks in the name of our Lord Jesus Christ to God the Father.

[21]Be subject to one another out of reverence for Christ.

Paul has already told his readers that they have been 'sealed' with the Holy Spirit, and that they must not 'grieve' the Holy Spirit (1:13; 4:30). Now he bids them *be filled with the Spirit*. There is no greater secret of holiness than the infilling of him whose very nature and name are 'holy'.

Grammatically speaking, this paragraph consists of two imperatives (the commands not to get drunk but to be Spirit-filled), followed by four present participles (speaking, singing, thanking and submitting). Theologically speaking, it first presents us with our Christian duty (to avoid drunkenness but seek the Spirit's fullness) and then describes four consequences of this spiritual condition, in terms of our relationships. 'Being filled with the Spirit' is a topic much discussed and debated today; it is important for us to study Paul's teaching carefully.

The apostle begins by drawing a certain comparison between drunkenness and the Holy Spirit's fullness: *Do not get drunk with wine,* he says, . . . *but be filled with the Spirit.* And indeed there is a superficial similarity between the two conditions. A person who is drunk, we say, is 'under the influence' of alcohol; and certainly a Spirit-filled Christian is under the influence and power of the Holy Spirit. But there the comparison ends and the contrast begins. Of course in the heathen cult of Dionysus intoxication was regarded as a means to inspiration. But it is a serious mistake to suppose that to be filled with the Spirit of Jesus Christ is a kind of spiritual inebriation in which we lose control of ourselves. On the contrary, 'self-control' (*enkrateia*) is the final quality named as 'the fruit of the Spirit' in Galatians 5:22–23. Under the influence of the Holy Spirit we do not lose control; we gain it. It is true that on the day of Pentecost some said the Spirit-filled disciples were drunk; 'They are filled with new wine.' These were a minority, however, described by Luke as 'others'; the majority had no such thought in their minds, but were amazed to hear God's mighty works being announced in their own languages. It seems that the minority were not even sincere in attributing drunkenness to the Spirit-filled Christians. Luke says they were making fun of them, so that the work of the Holy Spirit was 'mockingly misinterpreted'.[3]

The first chapter of Dr Martyn Lloyd-Jones' exposition of Ephesians 5:18–6:9, *Life in the Spirit in Marriage, Home and Work,* is entitled 'The Stimulus of the Spirit'. Writing as both a physician and a pastor, he helpfully compares and contrasts the two states of drunkenness and the Spirit's fullness. He says: 'Wine—alcohol— . . . pharmacologically speaking is not a stimulant—it is a depressant. Take up

[3] Bruce, p. 110.

any book on pharmacology and look up 'alcohol', and you will find, always, that it is classified among the depressants. It is not a stimulant'.[4] Further, 'it depresses first and foremost the highest centres of all in the brain . . . They control everything that gives a man self-control, wisdom, understanding, discrimination, judgment, balance, the power to assess everything; in other words everything that makes a man behave at his very best and highest'.[5] What the Holy Spirit does, however, is the exact opposite. 'If it were possible to put the Holy Spirit into a textbook of Pharmacology, I would put him under the stimulants, for that is where he belongs. He really does stimulate. . . He stimulates our every faculty . . . the mind and the intellect . . . the heart . . . and the will. . .'[6]

Consider now how Paul paints the contrast. The result of drunkenness, he writes, is debauchery (*asōtia*). People who are drunk give way to wild, dissolute and uncontrolled actions. They behave like animals, indeed worse than animals. The results of being filled with the Spirit are totally different. If excessive alcohol dehumanizes, turning a human being into a beast, the fullness of the Spirit makes us more human, for he makes us like Christ.

The apostle now lists the four beneficial results of being filled with the Spirit.

a. Fellowship: addressing one another in psalms and hymns and spiritual songs (verse 19a)

The familiar AV version of this sentence begins, 'Speaking to yourselves in psalms . . .' This does not mean that Spirit-filled believers talk to themselves, however, for the Greek use of the reflexive here can equally be translated 'each other' (as in 4:32). Nor does it mean that, if we are filled with the Spirit, we stop speaking to one another and start singing to one another instead. No, the reference is to Christian fellowship, and the mention of 'psalms, hymns and spiritual songs' (which are not easily distinguishable, although the first word implies a musical accompaniment) indicates that the context is public worship. Whenever

[4] Lloyd-Jones, *Life in the Spirit*, p. 19.
[5] *Ibid.*, p. 15.   [6] *Ibid.*, pp. 20–21.

Christians assemble, they love to sing both to God and to each other. Sometimes we sing responsively, as the Jews did in temple and synagogue, and as the early Christians did also, meeting before daybreak 'to recite a hymn antiphonally to Christ as to a god'.[7] Also some of the psalms we sing are in reality not worship of God but mutual exhortation. A good example is Psalm 95, the *Venite*, in the singing of which we should turn to one another: 'O come, let us sing to the Lord; let us make a joyful noise to the rock of our salvation!' Here is fellowship in worship, a reciprocal invitation to praise.

b. Worship: singing and making melody (perhaps the verbs combine vocal and instrumental music) *to the Lord with all your heart* (verse 19)

Here the singing is not 'to one another' but 'to the Lord'. Although RSV may be right in translating the following words 'with all your heart', the Greek phrase probably means 'in your heart' (AV), as in Colossians 3:16, referring to either the sincerity or the inwardness of authentic Christian praise, or both. Perhaps JBP has caught the point with 'making music in your hearts for the ears of the Lord', an instruction from which unmusical people unable to sing in tune have always derived much comfort. In this case it may be silent worship, although at the same time inwardly joyful and melodious. Without doubt Spirit-filled Christians have a song of joy in their hearts, and Spirit-filled public worship is a joyful celebration of God's mighty acts, though J. Armitage Robinson suggests that Paul 'contrasts the merriment of wine with the sober gladness of sacred psalmody'.[8]

c. Gratitude: always and for everything giving thanks in the name of our Lord Jesus Christ to God the Father (verse 20)

The call to thanksgiving is not uncommon in Paul's letters.[9]

---

[7] Extract from the famous letter addressed to the Emperor Trajan, *c.* 112 AD, by Pliny the Younger, procurator of Bithynia.

[8] Armitage Robinson, p. 116.

[9] *Cf.* the three references to it in Col. 3:15–17; also 1 Thes. 5:18.

The grumbling spirit is not compatible with the Holy Spirit. Grumbling was one of the besetting sins of the people of Israel; they were always 'murmuring' against the Lord and against Moses. But the Spirit-filled believer is full not of complaining, but of thanksgiving.

Although the text reads that we are to give thanks *always and for everything*, we must not press these words literally. For we cannot thank God for absolutely 'everything', including blatant evil. The strange notion is gaining popularity in some Christian circles that the major secret of Christian freedom and victory is unconditional praise; that a husband should praise God for his wife's adultery and a wife for her husband's drunkenness; and that even the most appalling calamities of life should become subjects for thanksgiving and praise. Such a suggestion is at best a dangerous half-truth, and at worst ludicrous, even blasphemous. Of course God's children learn not to argue with him in their suffering, but to trust him, and indeed to thank him for his loving providence by which he can turn even evil to good purposes (*e.g.* Rom. 8:28). But that is praising God for being God; it is not praising him for evil. To do this would be to react insensitively to people's pain (when Scripture tells us to weep with those who weep) and to condone and even encourage evil (when Scripture tells us to hate it and to resist the devil). God abominates evil, and we cannot praise or thank him for what he abominates.

So then the 'everything' for which we are to give thanks to God must be qualified by its context, namely *in the name of our Lord Jesus Christ to God the Father*. Our thanksgiving is to be for everything which is consistent with the loving Fatherhood of God and the self-revelation he has given us in Jesus Christ. Once again the doctrine of the Trinity informs and directs our devotion. When we are filled with the Holy Spirit we give thanks to God our Father in the name of the Lord Jesus Christ.

d. Submission: be subject to one another out of reverence for Christ (verse 21)

Although RSV begins a new paragraph with this verse, and

translates it as an imperative, it is in fact another present participle (*hypotassomenoi*), dependent on the command 'be filled with the Spirit', like the preceding three. Sometimes a person who claims to be filled with the Spirit becomes aggressive, self-assertive and brash. But the Holy Spirit is a humble Spirit, and those who are truly filled with him always display the meekness and gentleness of Christ. It is one of their most evident characteristics that they submit to one another.

They also submit to Christ, for their mutual submissiveness is *out of reverence for Christ*, or in more familiar terminology 'in the fear of Christ'. Those who are truly subject to Jesus Christ do not find it difficult to submit to each other as well. Incidentally, this expression 'in the fear of Christ' is a notable if indirect testimony to Paul's belief in the deity of Jesus, since the regular Old Testament requirement was to live 'in the fear of God'. There are several other 'Christianizations' of Old Testament thought in this chapter. For example, God's kingdom is Christ's (verse 5). We are to please Christ and seek his will, just as before Christ people sought God's will and pleasure (verses 10, 17), and worshipping God becomes worshipping Christ (verse 19). For in the last three verses mentioned 'the Lord' is a title for Jesus.

Such are the wholesome results of the fullness of the Holy Spirit. They all concern our relationships. If we are filled with the Spirit, we shall be harmoniously related both to God (worshipping him with joy and thanksgiving) and to each other (speaking and submitting to one another). In brief, Spirit-filled believers love God and love each other, which is hardly surprising since the first fruit of the Spirit is love.

We need now to return to the imperative on which these four participles depend, that is, to the Christian duty and privilege from which these four Christian attitudes result. It is the command *Be filled with the Spirit*. The exact form of the verb *plērousthe* is suggestive.

First, it is in the *imperative mood*. 'Be filled' is not a tentative proposal, but an authoritative command. We have no more liberty to avoid this responsibility than the many others which surround it in Ephesians. To be filled with the Spirit is obligatory, not optional.

Secondly, it is in the *plural form*. In other words, it is addressed to the whole Christian community. None of us is to get drunk; all of us are to be Spirit-filled. The fullness of the Spirit is not an élitist privilege, but available for all the people of God.

Thirdly, it is in the *passive voice*. NEB renders it: 'Let the Holy Spirit fill you'. There is no technique to learn and no formula to recite. What is essential is such a penitent turning from what grieves the Holy Spirit and such a believing openness to him that nothing hinders him from filling us. It is significant that the parallel passage in Colossians reads not 'Let the Spirit fill you' but 'Let the word of Christ dwell in you richly' (3:16). We must never separate the Spirit and the Word. To obey the Word and to surrender to the Spirit are virtually identical.

Fourthly, it is in the *present tense*. In Greek there are two kinds of imperative, an aorist describing a single action, and a present when the action is continuous. Thus, when Jesus said during the wedding reception at Cana, 'Fill the jars with water' (Jn.2:7), the imperative is aorist, since the jars were to be filled only once. But when Paul says to us, 'Be filled with the Spirit', he uses a present imperative, implying that we are to go on being filled. For the fullness of the Spirit is not a once-for-all experience which we can never lose, but a privilege to be renewed continuously by continuous believing and ·obedient appropriation. We have been 'sealed' with the Spirit once and for all; we need to be filled with the Spirit and go on being filled every day and every moment of the day.

Here, then, is a message for both the defeated and the complacent, that is, for Christians at opposite ends of the spiritual spectrum. To the defeated Paul would say, 'Be filled with the Spirit, and he will give you a new love, joy, peace, patience, kindness, goodness, faithfulness, meekness and self-control.' To the complacent Paul would say 'go on being filled with the Spirit. Thank God for what he has given you thus far. But do not say you have arrived. For there is more, much more, yet to come.'

IV New relationships

Ephesians 5:21 – 6:24

10. Husbands and wives

Paul has been outlining the new standards which God expects of his new society, the church, especially in terms of its unity and purity. These two qualities are indispensable to a life which is both worthy of the calling and fitting to the status of the people of God. He moves on now to the new relationships in which God's new people inevitably find themselves, and in so doing he concentrates in the rest of his letter on two further dimensions of Christian living.

The first concerns the practical, down-to-earth relationships of the home. For the divine family ceases to be a credible concept if it is not itself subdivided into human families which display God's love. What is the point of peace in the church if there is no peace in the home? The second dimension concerns the enemy we face and therefore the equipment we need in our unremitting spiritual warfare.

These two responsibilities (home and work on the one hand, and spiritual combat on the other) are quite different from each other. Husband and wife, parents and children, masters and servants are visible, tangible human beings, while the 'principalities and powers' arrayed against us are invisible, intangible demonic beings. Nevertheless, if our Christian faith is to be of any practical value, it must be able to cope with both situations. It must teach us how to behave Christianly at home and at work, and it must enable us to fight against evil in such a way that we stand and do not fall. Thus harmony in the home and stability in the fight are the two final topics which the apostle handles.

Husbands and wives, parents and children, masters and

213

servants were to be found in the earliest Christian congregations. Moreover, these three pairs of relationship are basic to all human existence. Markus Barth expresses this well by suggesting that in the first we see the human person as 'a *sexual* being (before Dr Freud or Dr Kinsey had put their fingers on this fact)', in the second as 'a *temporal* being (tied to the generation to which he belongs)' and in the third as 'a *material* being and part of an economic structure', Paul thus anticipating Marx. 'So this is man: a sexual, temporal and material being who, without exception, is enmeshed and, as it seems, hopelessly trapped in the structures of these three dimensions.'[1]

Detailed, practical instruction on Christian family life and on Christian responsibility in what nowadays we call 'employment' seems to have been given by the apostles from the beginning. Examples occur in the letters of both Paul and Peter.[2] There is an urgent need in our day for similar plain moral education. Too much so-called 'holiness teaching' emphasizes a personal relationship to Jesus Christ without any attempt to indicate its consequences in terms of relationships with the people we live and work with. In contrast to such holiness-in-a-vacuum, which magnifies experiences and minimizes ethics, the apostles spelled out Christian duty in the concrete situations of everyday life and work.

Luther in his *Catechism* seems to have been the first person to refer to these lists as *Haustafeln*, meaning literally 'house tables' but often translated 'tables of household duties'. In recent years scholars have compared them with similar precepts both in the Jewish *halakah* (their corpus of law and tradition) and in Gentile literature, especially of the Stoics. That Jews, Stoics and Christians should all have been concerned about moral behaviour in the home should not surprise us. But the similarity between their *Haustafeln* has sometimes been exaggerated.[3] If the apostles

[1] Barth, *Broken Wall*, pp. 205–207. *Cf.* also his *Ephesians*, II, p. 755.

[2] *E.g.* Eph. 5:22 – 6:9; Col. 3:18 – 4:1; Tit. 2:1–10 and 1 Pet. 2:18 – 3:7.

[3] John Howard Yoder gives a list of eight 'very significant differences' between the Stoic and Christian *Haustafeln* in *The Politics of Jesus*, pp. 170–183.

of Jesus were conscious of taking over any material from Jewish or Gentile sources, they thoroughly Christianized what they borrowed. There is no better example of this than Paul's address to husbands and wives in Ephesians, which is based upon a developed doctrine of Christ and his church.

1. Authority and submission

The RSV may be right to begin the new paragraph with verse 21: *Be subject to one another out of reverence for Christ*. We have seen that the Greek verb is a present participle ('submitting') like 'addressing one another', 'singing and making melody' (verse 19) and 'giving thanks' (verse 20), and that all four participles depend on the command 'be filled with the Spirit' (verse 18) and describe the consequences of the Holy Spirit's fullness. Nevertheless, a Greek participle was sometimes used as an imperative, and undoubtedly the demand for mutual submissiveness leads on to the submission asked from wives, children and slaves. Moreover, there is no verb at all in verse 22, because the call for submission in verse 21 is intended to be carried over into it. So verse 21 is in fact a transition verse, forming a bridge between two sections, which is why the NEB puts it in a paragraph by itself.

What is beyond question is that the three paragraphs which follow are given as examples of Christian submission, and that the emphasis throughout is on submission. Thus, wives are addressed before their husbands and are told to *be subject* to them (verse 22); children are mentioned before their parents and are told to *obey* them (6:1); and slaves are addressed before their masters and are told to *be obedient* to them (6:5).

Now the very notion of submission to authority is out of fashion today. It is totally at variance with contemporary attitudes of permissiveness and freedom. Almost nothing is calculated to arouse more angry protest than talk of 'subjection'. Ours is an age of liberation (not least for women, children and workers), and anything savouring of oppression is deeply resented and strongly resisted. How are Christians to react to this modern mood?

215

Our initial reaction to these liberation movements, I do not hesitate to say (although I shall qualify it later), should be one of positive welcome. For we have to agree that women in many cultures have been exploited, being treated like servants in their own home; that children have often been suppressed and squashed, not least in Victorian England in which they were supposed to be 'seen and not heard'; and that workers have been unjustly treated, being given inadequate wages and working conditions, and an insufficient share in responsible decision-making, not to mention the appalling injustices and barbarities of slavery and the slave trade.

We who name Christ's name need to acknowledge with shame that we ourselves have often acquiesced in the *status quo* and so helped to perpetuate some forms of human oppression, instead of being in the vanguard of those seeking social change. Nothing in the paragraphs we are about to study is inconsistent with the true liberation of human beings from all humiliation, exploitation and oppression. On the contrary, to whom do women, children and workers chiefly owe their liberation? Is it not to Jesus Christ? It is Jesus Christ who treated women with courtesy and honour in an age in which they were despised. It is Jesus Christ who said 'Let the children come to me' in a period of history in which unwanted babies were consigned to the local rubbish dump (as they are today to the hospital incinerator), or abandoned in the forum for anybody to pick up and rear for slavery or prostitution. And it is Jesus Christ who taught the dignity of manual labour by working himself as a carpenter, washing his disciples' feet and saying, 'I am among you as one who serves.'

So then, we must not interpret what Paul writes to wives, children and servants in his *Haustafeln* about submission in a way which contradicts these fundamental attitudes of Jesus. Nor should we make Paul contradict himself, as some writers do, for to do this in biblical exegesis is a counsel of despair. No, we must set the *Haustafeln* squarely within the framework of the Ephesian letter, in which Paul has been describing the single new humanity which God is creating through Christ. He has

216

been emphasizing the complete oneness in Christ of people of all cultures, especially Jew and Gentile, while in his parallel letter to the Colossians he has added slave and free man (3:11) and in an earlier letter male and female (Gal. 3:28). We may be quite sure that in his *Haustafeln* he does not now destroy his own thesis by erecting new barriers of sex, age and rank in God's new society in which they have been abolished. We must give the apostle credit for a little consistency of thought and allow him to explain himself.

In the light of the teaching of Jesus and his apostles, we may confidently and repeatedly affirm at least three relevant truths: first, the *dignity* of womanhood, childhood and servanthood; secondly, the *equality* before God of all human beings, irrespective of their race, rank, class, culture, sex or age, because all are made in his image; and the even deeper *unity* of all Christian believers, as fellow-members of God's family and of Christ's body. It is only when these truths are firmly kept in the forefront of our minds that we are ready to consider the teaching of the *Haustafeln*.

Negatively, the submission which Paul enjoins on wives, children and servants is not another word for inferiority. Positively it is important to grasp the difference which Luther and his followers rightly make between persons on the one hand and their roles on the other. Here is one of Luther's expositions of this theme: 'I have often said that we must sharply distinguish between these two, the office and the person. The man who is called Hans or Martin is a man quite different from the one who is called elector or doctor or preacher. Here we have two different persons in one man. The one is that in which we are created and born, according to which we are all alike—man or woman or child, young or old. But once we are born, God adorns and dresses you up as another person. He makes you a child and me a father, one a master and another a servant, one a prince and another a citizen.'[4]

Once we see this distinction, then those who hold an office—whether rulers, magistrates, husbands, parents or

---

[4] From his exposition of 'Blessed are the meek' (Mt. 5:5) in *The Sermon on the Mount, Luther's Works*, Vol. 21 (Concordia, 1956), p. 23.

employers—have a certain God-given authority which they expect others to acknowledge. Husbands and wives, parents and children, masters and servants have equal dignity as God-like beings, but different God-appointed roles. As J. H. Yoder succinctly puts it, 'Equality of *worth* is not identity of *role*'.[5] The husband, the parent and the master have been invested with an authority to which others should submit.

Two questions immediately arise about this authority: Where does it come from? And how is it to be used?

In answer to the first question we reply that it comes from God. The God of the Bible is a God of order, and in his ordering of human life (*e.g.* in the state and the family) he has established certain authority or leadership roles. And since such authority, though exercised by human beings, is delegated to them by God, others are required conscientiously to submit to it. The Greek words imply this, for at the heart of *hypotassomai* ('submit') is *taxis* ('order'). Submission is a humble recognition of the divine ordering of society. This is plainly taught in Paul's *Haustafeln*. He tells wives to be submissive to their husbands *as to the Lord* (verse 22), children to obey their parents *in the Lord* (6:1), and slaves to be obedient to their earthly masters *as to Christ* (6:5). That is, behind the husband, the parent and the master they must discern the Lord himself who has given them their authority. Then, if they wish to submit to him, they will submit to them, since it is his authority which they exercise. The same is true of the mutual submission expected of all Christian people. It is *out of reverence for Christ* that we are to submit to one another, the Christ who both wields authority as Lord and humbled himself as servant.

We have to be very careful not to overstate this biblical teaching on authority. It does not mean that the authority of husbands, parents and masters is unlimited, or that wives, children and workers are required to give unconditional obedience. No, the submission required is to God's authority delegated to human beings. If, therefore, they misuse their God-given authority (*e.g.* by commanding

[5] Yoder, p. 177 note 23.

what God forbids or forbidding what God commands),
then our duty is no longer conscientiously to submit, but
conscientiously to refuse to do so. For to submit in such
circumstances would be to disobey God. The principle is
clear: we must submit right up to the point where obedience
to human authority would involve disobedience to God.
At that point 'civil disobedience' becomes our Christian
duty. In order to submit to God, we have to refuse to
submit to human beings. As Peter put it to the Sanhedrin:
'We must obey God rather than men.'[6] This is the exception,
however. The general rule on which the New Testament
insists is humble submission to God-given authority.

To the second question about the use of divinely
delegated authority, we reply that it must never be used
selfishly, but always for those others for whose benefit it
has been given. Perhaps the most striking feature of the
Haustafeln is that in each pair of relationships reciprocal
duties are laid down. It is true that wives are to submit
to their husbands, children to their parents and slaves to
their masters, and that this requirement of submission
(*hypotagē*) presupposes an authority (*exousia*) in the
husbands, parents and masters. Indeed, these two Greek
words complement each other. Yet the word *exousia* is not
used once in the passage. When Paul is describing the
duties of husbands, parents and masters, in no case is it
authority which he tells them to exercise. On the contrary,
explicit or implicitly, he warns them against the improper
use of their authority, forbids them to exploit their position,
and urges them instead to remember their responsibilities
and the other party's rights. Thus, husbands are to love
their wives and care for them, parents are not to provoke
their children but bring them up sensitively, and masters
are not to threaten their slaves, but treat them with justice.

It has seemed necessary, before coming to the actual text
of the *Haustafeln*, to open up in a general way this topic
of submission to authority. To sum up, 'authority' in
biblical usage is not a synonym for 'tyranny'. All those
who occupy positions of authority in society are responsible
both to the God who has entrusted it to them and to the

6 Acts 5:29.

person or persons for whose benefit they have been given it. In a word, the biblical concept of authority spells not tyranny but responsibility.

The first responsibilities which Paul elaborates are those of husbands and wives. The essence of his teaching is clear. Wives are to 'submit', and husbands are to 'love'.

Wives, be subject to your husbands, as to the Lord. ²³*For the husband is the head of the wife as Christ is the head of the church, his body, and is himself its Saviour.* ²⁴*As the church is subject to Christ, so let wives also be subject in everything to their husbands.* ²⁵*Husbands, love your wives, as Christ loved the church and gave himself up for her,* ²⁶*that he might sanctify her, having cleansed her by the washing of water with the word,* ²⁷*that he might present the church to himself in splendour, without spot or wrinkle or any such thing, that she might be holy and without blemish.* ²⁸*Even so husbands should love their wives as their own bodies. He who loves his wife loves himself.* ²⁹*For no man ever hates his own flesh, but nourishes and cherishes it, as Christ does the church,* ³⁰*because we are members of his body.* ³¹*'For this reason a man shall leave his father and mother and be joined to his wife, and the two shall become one flesh.'* ³²*This mystery is a profound one, and I am saying that it refers to Christ and the church;* ³³*however, let each one of you love his wife as himself, and let the wife see that she respects her husband.*

2. The duty of wives (verses 22–24)

Two reasons are given, or at least implied, for the wife's submission to her husband. The first is drawn from creation and concerns the husband's 'headship' of his wife, while the second is drawn from redemption and concerns Christ's 'headship' of the church.

Wives, be subject to your husbands, as to the Lord. For the husband is the head of the wife ... (verses 22–23a). The husband's headship is both stated as a fact and made the ground of his wife's submission. But its origin is not elaborated here. For a fuller understanding of Paul's argument we need to turn elsewhere, especially to 1

Corinthians 11:3–12 and 1 Timothy 2:11–13. In both these passages he goes back to the narrative of Genesis 2 and points out that woman was made after man, out of man and for man. He adds that man is also born from woman, so that man and woman are dependent on one another. Nevertheless, his emphasis is on the order, mode and purpose of the creation of Eve. And since it is mainly on these facts of creation that Paul bases his case for the husband's headship, his argument has permanent and universal validity, and is not to be dismissed as culturally limited. The cultural elements of his teaching are to be found in the applications of the principle, in the requirement of 'veiling' certainly, and I think also in the requirement of 'silence'. But the man's (and especially the husband's) 'headship' is not a cultural application of a principle; it is the foundation principle itself. This is not chauvinism, but creationism. The new creation in Christ frees us from the distortion of relations between the sexes caused by the fall (*e.g.* Gn. 3:16), but it establishes the original intention of the creation. It was to this 'beginning' that Jesus himself went back (*e.g.* Mt. 19:4–6). He confirmed the teaching of Genesis 1 and 2. So must we. What creation has established, no culture is able to destroy.

This is also why we should reject the facile argument that since slavery has been abolished, the wife's submission should by analogy be abolished too. If this were the case, then why not complete the trio and abolish a child's obedience as well? No, the parallels are inexact. Slavery is a dehumanizing institution, with no justification in any biblical doctrine. A husband's headship, however, is rooted in creation.

Turning from biblical revelation to contemporary experience, Christians will agree that our human sexuality is part and parcel of our humanness. Masculinity and feminity represent a profound distinction which is psychological as well as physiological. Of course the sexes are equal before God, but this does not mean that they are identical. God himself created man male and female in his likeness. So both equally bear his image,[7] but each also complements

[7] Gn. 1:26–27.

the other.[8] The biblical perspective is to hold simultaneously the equality and the complementarity of the sexes. 'Partnership' is a good word too, so long as it is remembered that the contribution which each brings to it is not identical but distinctive. Hence a man finds himself by being a man, and a woman finds herself by being a woman. Genuine self-discovery and self-fulfilment do not come from striving to be somebody else or from imitating the opposite sex.

What then are the complementary distinctives of the two sexes? The biblical teaching is that God has given to man (and specially to the husband in the marriage relationship) a certain headship, and that his wife will find herself and her true God-given role not in rebellion against him or his headship, but in a voluntary and joyful submission.

The modern understanding of sexual differentiation tends to confirm this biblical teaching. This at least is the thesis of the American sociologist Professor Steven Goldberg in his book *The Inevitability of Patriarchy*.[9] Although it is a conscious response to the feminist movement, he claims that his approach is scientific and not ideological, in that he rests his case on empirical evidence. Nor is his viewpoint to be dismissed as masculine, for the distinguished American anthropologist Dr Margaret Mead is quoted on the book's dust cover as supporting its thesis: 'All the claims so glibly made about societies ruled by women are nonsense. We have no reason to believe that they ever existed.'

The first part of his book is an anthropological study whose conclusion he expresses as follows: 'In every society that has ever existed one finds patriarchy (males fill the overwhelming percentage of upper hierarchical positions in political and all other hierarchies), male attainment (males attain the high-status roles, whatever these may be in any given society) and male dominance (both males and females feel that dominance in male-female encounters and relationships resides in the male, and social expectations and authority systems reflect this).'[1] He is at pains to point out that he is neither making any value judgments, nor

[8] Gn. 2:18–24.
[9] Published in the United States in 1973 and in Britain by Maurice Temple Smith in 1977.   [1] *Op. cit.*, p. 63.

measuring performance, nor pronouncing either sex
'superior' or 'inferior' to the other; his purpose is simply
to show that 'patriarchy', 'male dominance' and 'male
attainment'—in the technical sense in which he employs
these terms—are 'three universal realities',[2] since 'in no
society, anywhere or at any time, have these realities been
absent'.[3]

For the development of his second thesis Dr Goldberg
moves from anthropology to physiology. He argues that
the anthropological evidence for male dominance which he
has marshalled has a physiological cause. The 'three
universal realities' are the manifestation in society of a
basic male drive (often called 'aggression', though Dr
Goldberg prefers 'dominance tendency'), which is itself
'neuro-endocrinological' in origin. 'At its most basic, the
hypothesis at the core of the theory presented here simply
states that there are neuro-endocrinological differences
between men and women that engender different male and
female responses to the environment and, therefore, different
male and female behaviour'.[4] He is not denying that our
genetic code interacts with our environment and upbringing,
nor that there are individual exceptions to his generalization,
nor that many women are frustrated because they lack
opportunities to use their gifts. Instead, he is asserting that
there are basic differences between masculinity and feminity,
that masculinity means drive for dominance, and that
'dominance tendency is primarily a result of hormonal
development and not primarily of anatomy, gender identity
or the socialization that reflects anatomy and gender
identity'.[5]

A Christian who reads Professor Goldberg's thesis wants
to state it theologically in terms of creation. God has made
and makes men and women different, and one of their
basic differences lies in the 'headship' which he has given
to man. This may well have a genetic basis. If so, man's
natural 'drive' needs to be controlled if his 'headship' is
to be constructive. For 'patriarchy' sounds paternalistic and
'male dominance' oppressive. Even the biblical word

[2] *Op. cit.*, p. 60.   [3] *Op. cit.*, p. 62.
[4] *Op. cit.*, p. 121.   [5] *Op. cit.*, p. 81.

'submission' is often expounded as if it were a synonym for 'subjection', 'subordination' and even 'subjugation'. All these words have emotive associations. 'Submission' is no exception. We have to try to disinfect it of these and to penetrate into its essential biblical meaning. This we shall discover neither from its modern associations nor even from its etymology but primarily from the way it is used in its context in Ephesians 5.

There is little doubt what 'submission' meant in the ancient world in which disdain for women was almost universal. William Barclay sums it up: 'The Jews had a low view of women. In the Jewish form of morning prayer there was a sentence in which a Jewish man every morning gave thanks that God had not made him "a Gentile, a slave or a woman" . . . In Jewish law a woman was not a person, but a thing. She had no legal rights whatsoever; she was absolutely in her husband's possession to do with as he willed. . . The position was worse in the Greek world . . . The whole Greek way of life made companionship between man and wife next to impossible. The Greek expected his wife to run his home, to care for his legitimate children, but he found his pleasure and his companionship elsewhere . . . In Greece, home and family life were near to being extinct, and fidelity was completely non-existent . . . In Rome in Paul's day the matter was still worse . . . The degeneracy of Rome was tragic . . . It is not too much to say that the whole atmosphere of the ancient world was adulterous . . . The marriage bond was on the way to complete breakdown.'[6] Charles Seltman confirms this. In the Roman Empire, he writes, 'A girl was completely under her father's, a wife completely under her husband's, power. She was his chattel . . . Her life was one of legal incapacity which amounted to enslavement, while her status was described as 'imbecilitas', whence our word.'[7] True, this was not the whole picture. Markus Barth tries to redeem the balance: 'There was also a counter-movement which promoted equal rights for females', while 'different periods and different geographical areas

[6] Barclay, pp. 199–203.
[7] *Women in Antiquity* (Pan, 1956), pp. 136, 138.

224

produced differing views'. As for Ephesus and its environment, 'The cult of the Great Mother and the Artemis Temple stamped this city more than others as a bastion and bulwark of women's rights.'[8] Nevertheless, the oppression of women prevailed in the ancient world, and their emancipation had scarcely begun. It is against this dark background that Paul's teaching shines with such a bright light. Yet we still have to ask precisely what is meant by 'headship' and 'submission'.

To begin with, these words do not by themselves establish stereotypes of masculine and feminine behaviour. Different cultures assign different tasks to men and women, husbands and wives. In the West, for example, it has long been conventional for the wife to do the shopping, cooking and cleaning, together with the feeding, bathing, nappy-changing and minding of babies. In many parts of Africa and Asia the women also work in the fields and carry heavy loads on their heads. Nowadays, however, and rightly, these conventions are recognized as cultural and are therefore being challenged and in some cases changed. Many couples are learning to share the household chores.

In order to understand the nature of the husband's headship in the new society which God has inaugurated, we need to look at Jesus Christ. For Jesus Christ is the context in which Paul uses and develops the words 'headship' and 'submission'. Although he grounds the fact of the husband's headship in creation, he defines it in relation to the headship of Christ the redeemer: *for the husband is the head of the wife as Christ is the head of the church, his body, and is himself its saviour* (verse 23). Now Christ's headship of his church has already been described in 4:15–16. It is from Christ as head that the body derives its health and grows into maturity. His headship expresses care rather than control, responsibility rather than rule. This truth is endorsed by the surprising addition of the words *and is himself its saviour*. The head of the body is the saviour of the body; the characteristic of his headship is not so much lordship as saviourhood.

If the husband's headship of the wife resembles Christ's

[8] Barth, *Ephesians*, II, pp. 655–662.

225

of his church, then the wife's submission will resemble the church's: *As the church is subject to Christ, so let wives also be subject in everything to their husbands* (verse 24). There is nothing demeaning about this, for her submission is not to be an unthinking obedience to his rule but rather a grateful acceptance of his care. To quote Markus Barth again: 'The submission to, and respect for the husband, to which the wife is specifically admonished . . . is by no means the submissiveness of a pussycat or a crouching dog . . . Paul . . . is thinking of a voluntary, free, joyful and thankful partnership, as the analogy of the relationship of the church to Christ shows.'[9] Whenever the husband's headship mirrors the headship of Christ, then the wife's submission to the protection and provision of his love, far from detracting from her womanhood, will positively enrich it.

3. The duty of husbands (verses 25–33)

If the word which characterizes the wife's duty is 'submit', the word characterizing the husband's is 'love'. We might think that nature itself would teach husbands this priority obligation, but many cultures both ancient and modern prove the contrary. Of course a certain tie of affection and desire binds every married couple together, and Paul's Stoic contemporaries taught husbands to 'love'. But the verb they used was the weak word *phileō*; it was Christian teaching which introduced strong, sacrificial '*agapē*-love' into marriage. Paul uses two analogies to illustrate the tender care which a husband's love for his wife should involve.

The first is that the husband must love his wife as Christ has loved his church. Already in the Old Testament the gracious covenant which God made with his people Israel was many times referred to as a marriage covenant.[1] Jesus took over this teaching and boldly referred to himself as the Bridegroom.[2] Paul enlarges on the image here and in 2 Corinthians 11:1–3, while in the Revelation we are

[9] Barth, *Broken Wall*, p. 223.
[1] *E.g.* Is. 54:5–8; Je. 2:1–3; 31:31–32; Ezk. 23; Hos. 1–3.
[2] Mk. 2:18–20; *cf.* Jn. 3:29.

permitted glimpses of the glorified church 'prepared as a bride adorned for her husband' and of the coming 'marriage supper of the Lamb'.[3]

What stands out in Paul's development of the theme is the sacrificial steadfastness of the heavenly Bridegroom's covenant-love for his bride. It is this which husbands are to imitate: *Husbands, love your wives, as Christ loved the church and gave himself up for her, that he might sanctify her.*

It will be observed that Paul uses five verbs to indicate the unfolding stages of Christ's commitment to his bride, the church. He *loved* her, *gave himself up* for her, to *sanctify* her, having *cleansed* her, that he might *present* her to himself. The statement is so complete and comprehensive that some scholars think it may be a quotation from an early Christian confession, liturgy or hymn. It seems to trace Christ's care for his church from a past to a future eternity. Certainly the words *Christ loved the church*, preceding as they do his self-sacrifice on her behalf, seem to look back to his eternal pre-existence in which he set his love on his people and determined to come to save them. So, having loved the church, he *gave himself up for her*. The reference is, of course, primarily to the cross.

But why did Jesus Christ do it? What was the purpose of his sacrifice? It was *that he might sanctify her, having cleansed her*. Perhaps there is a deliberate allusion to the bridal bath which took place before both Jewish and Greek weddings. The tenses of the verbs suggest that the cleansing of the church precedes her consecration or sanctification. Indeed, the cleansing seems to refer to the initial purification or cleansing from sin and guilt which we receive when we first repent and believe in Jesus. It is accomplished *by the washing of water with the word*, or more simply 'by water and word' (NEB). The 'washing of water' is an unambiguous reference to baptism,[4] while the additional reference to 'the word' indicates that baptism is no magical or mechanical ceremony, but needs an explanatory word to define its significance, express the promises of cleansing and new life in the Spirit which it symbolizes, and arouse our faith.

[3] Rev. 19:6–9; 21:2,9.   [4] *Cf.* Acts 22:16.

True, some think 'the word' alludes to the candidate's confession of faith[5] or appeal for a clear conscience,[6] rather than to the minister's preaching of the gospel or formula of administration. But it seems more natural to take 'water' and 'word' together as being both administered *to* the candidate. So when Calvin reached this verse in his expository series, he urged care 'that we do not separate the sacraments from the Word at any time', for 'to have the sign without the promise added to it is but a frustratory and unprofitable thing'.[7] Markus Barth rather delightfully argues that in the context the word of promise can be no other than 'I love you'. He goes on: 'The Messiah as the Bridegroom . . . says this decisive "word" to his Bride and thereby privately and publicly, decently and legally binds himself to her and her to him.'[8] It is a solemn word of covenant love.

Having cleansed his bride by water and word, the heavenly Bridegroom's plan is to *sanctify* her and finally to *present* her to himself. The 'sanctification' appears to refer to the present process of making her holy in character and conduct by the power of the indwelling Spirit, while the 'presentation' is eschatological, and will take place when Christ returns to take her to himself. He will present her to himself *in splendour* (*endoxon*). The word may hint at the bride's beautiful wedding dress, since it is used of clothing.[9] But it means more than this. 'Glory' (*doxa*) is the radiance of God, the shining forth and manifestation of his otherwise hidden being. So too the church's true nature will become apparent. On earth she is often in rags and tatters, stained and ugly, despised and persecuted. But one day she will be seen for what she is, nothing less than the bride of Christ, 'free from spots, wrinkles or any other disfigurement' (JBP), *holy and without blemish*, beautiful and glorious. It is to this constructive end that Christ has been working and is continuing to work. The bride does not make herself presentable; it is the bridegroom who labours to beautify her in order to present her to himself. His love and self-sacrifice for her, his cleansing and

---

[5] Rom. 10:8–10,13.   [6] 1 Pet. 3:21.   [7] Calvin, pp. 583–584.
[8] Barth, *Ephesians*, II, p. 691.   [9] Lk. 7:25.

sanctifying of her, are all designed for her liberation and her perfection, when at last he presents her to himself in her full glory. Dr Lloyd-Jones writes: 'Dare I put it like this? The Beauty-Specialist will have put his final touch to the church, the massaging will have been so perfect that there will not be a single wrinkle left. She will look young, and in the bloom of youth, with colour in her cheeks, with her skin perfect, without any spots or wrinkles. And she will remain like that for ever and ever.'[1]

This, then, is Paul's exposition of the implications of Christ's headship. The church's head is the church's bridegroom. He does not crush the church. Rather he sacrificed himself to serve her, in order that she might become everything he longs for her to be, namely herself in the fullness of her glory. Just so a husband should never use his headship to crush or stifle his wife, or frustrate her from being herself. His love for her will lead him to an exactly opposite path. He will give himself for her, in order that she may develop her full potential under God and so become more completely herself.

After climbing with Paul to these sublime heights of romantic love, many readers sense an anti-climax in verse 28: *Even so husbands should love their wives as their own bodies.* For in his instruction to husbands to love their wives he seems to descend from the lofty standard of Christ's love to the rather low standard of self-love. This sense of anomaly has led some commentators to try to translate the sentence differently, but their attempts do not succeed because the next sentence stubbornly refuses to convey any meaning but the obvious one: *He who loves his wife loves himself.* The probable explanation for Paul's descent to the more mundane level of self-love is that he is always a realist. We cannot fully grasp the greatness of Christ's love; it 'surpasses knowledge', as he wrote earlier.[2] Nor do husbands find it easy to apply this standard to the realities of family life. But we all know from everyday experience how we love ourselves. Hence the practical usefulness of the 'golden rule' Jesus enunciated that we should treat others as we would ourselves like to be

[1] Lloyd-Jones, *Life in the Spirit*, pp. 175–176.   [2] 3:19.

229

treated.[3] For we all know this instinctively. It is after all the way we treat ourselves. *For no man ever hates his own flesh, but nourishes and cherishes it* (verse 29a). That is, he feeds it and (it may mean) clothes it, or at any rate looks after it.

This exhortation to a husband to 'nourish and cherish' his wife as he does his own body is more than a useful guide to daily behaviour, however. It also contains an inner appropriateness, since he and his wife have in fact become 'one flesh'. Yet God intends sexual intercourse not only to be a union of bodies, but to symbolize and express a union of personalities. It is when husband and wife become thus deeply one with each other that truly *he who loves his wife loves himself*.

This leads the apostle to return in his thought to Christ and so to reach the climax of his argument. So far he has used two analogies for a husband's love of his wife, namely Christ's loving sacrifice for his bride the church, and the husband's loving care of his own body. Now he fuses the two. Christ's bride and Christ's body are the same (see verse 23), *because we are members of his body* (verse 30).[4] He has incorporated us into himself, made us part of himself in a profound, indissoluble union. This leads Paul to quote Genesis 2:24: *For this reason a man shall leave his father and mother and be joined to his wife, and the two shall become one flesh* (verse 31) and to declare that *this mystery is a profound one* (verse 32).[5] There seems no reason to doubt that in the first instance he is referring to the mysterious and sacred depths of sexual union itself. But then he immediately goes on to its yet deeper symbolism: *I am saying that it refers to Christ and the church*. In doing so, he not only uses the *egō* of his

[3] Mt. 7:12.

[4] The AV 'of his flesh and of his bones' does not belong to the original text. It was doubtless added as an echo of Gn. 2:23.

[5] Jerome's Latin translation in the Vulgate is *sacramentum hoc magnum est*. He used *sacramentum* in its older meaning of a 'mystery' containing some hidden truth or sacred symbolism, as in 1 Tim. 3:16. He did not imply, nor does the Greek teach, that marriage is a 'sacrament' in the sense which later Roman Catholic theology gave it. It is 'sacramental' only in Paul's sense here, namely that the union of husband and wife symbolizes the union of Christ and his church.

apostolic authority but actually employs the very expression
egō de legō ('but I say') which Jesus himself used in the
six antitheses of the Sermon on the Mount.[6] It is appropriate
for him to do so because a 'mystery' is a revealed truth,
and the profound 'mystery' here, namely the church's
union with Christ, is closely akin to that of Jewish-Gentile
unity in the body of Christ, which had been revealed to
him and of which he has written in 3:1–6. He thus sees
the marriage relationship as a beautiful model of the
church's union in and with Christ. When applied to Christ
and his church, the 'one flesh' is identical with the 'one
new man' of 2:15. Indeed, the three pictures of the church
which Paul develops in Ephesians—the body, the building
and the bride—all emphasize the reality of its unity on
account of its union with Christ.

Verse 33 is a succinct summary of the fuller teaching
which Paul has been giving to husbands and wives: *Let
each one of you love his wife as himself*, for she and he
have become one, *and let the wife see that she respects her
husband*. It is true that 'respects' translates *phobētai*,
meaning literally 'fears', but this verb 'may express the
emotion of fear in all its modifications and in all its degrees
from simple respect through reverence up to adoration,
according to its object'.[7] The apostle began with one
couplet 'love' and 'submission'. He ends with another 'love'
and 'respect'. We have seen that the love he has in mind
for the husband sacrifices and serves with a view to
enabling his wife to become what God intends her to be.
So the 'submission' and 'respect' he asks of the wife express
her response to his love and her desire that he too will
become what God intends him to be in his 'leadership'.

4. Summary

Taking the husband first, what Paul stresses is not his
authority over his wife, but his love for her. Rather, his
authority is defined in terms of loving responsibility. To
our minds the word 'authority' suggests power, dominion

[6] See Mt. 5:22,28,32,34,39,44.   [7] Hodge, p. 353.

and even oppression. We picture the 'authoritative' husband as a domineering figure who makes all the decisions himself, issues commands and expects obedience, inhibits and suppresses his wife, and so prevents her from growing into a mature or fulfilled person. But this is not at all the kind of 'headship' which the apostle is describing, whose model is Jesus Christ. Certainly, 'headship' implies a degree of leadership and initiative, as when Christ came to woo and to win his bride. But more specifically it implies sacrifice, self-giving for the sake of the beloved, as when Christ gave himself for his bride. If 'headship' means 'power' in any sense, then it is power to care not to crush, power to serve not to dominate, power to facilitate self-fulfilment, not to frustrate or destroy it. And in all this the standard of the husband's love is to be the cross of Christ, on which he surrendered himself even to death in his selfless love for his bride. Dr Lloyd-Jones has a striking way of enforcing this truth. 'How many of us', he asks, 'have realized that we are always to think of the married state in terms of the doctrine of the atonement? Is that our customary way of thinking of marriage? . . . Where do we find what the books have to say about marriage? Under which section? Under Ethics. But it does not belong there. We must consider marriage in terms of the doctrine of the atonement.'[8]

As for the wife's duty in the marriage relationship, it surprises me how unpopular this passage is among many women. When it is read at a wedding and it provokes a feminine outcry, I find myself wondering how carefully it has been read and in particular whether it has been read in its total context. Let me spell out five points which will, I hope, demonstrate that it is not the blueprint for oppression which many think, but rather a charter of genuine liberty.

a. The requirement of submission is a particular example of a general Christian duty

That is, the injunction 'wives submit' (verse 22) is preceded by the requirement that we are to 'submit to one another'

[8] Lloyd-Jones, *Life in the Spirit*, p. 148.

(verse 21). If, therefore, it is the wife's duty as wife to submit to her husband, it is also the husband's duty as a member of God's new society to submit to his wife. Submissiveness is a universal Christian obligation. Throughout the Christian church, including every Christian home, submissiveness is to be mutual. For Jesus Christ himself is the paragon of humility. He emptied himself of his status and his rights, and humbled himself to serve. So in the new order which he had founded he calls all his followers to follow in his footsteps. 'Clothe yourselves, all of you, with humility towards one another.'[9] Should not the wife even rejoice that she has the privilege of giving a particular demonstration in her attitude to her husband of the beauty of humility which is to characterize all members of God's new society?

This is specially so when it is seen that her self-humbling is not coerced but free. It must have been very obvious in the ancient world. The wife had no status and few rights, as we have seen. Yet the apostle addresses her as a free moral agent and calls upon her not to acquiesce in a fate she cannot escape, but to make a responsible decision before God. It is this which 'begins the revolutionary innovation in the early Christian style of ethical thinking.'[1] Voluntary Christian self-submission is still very significant today. 'Jesus Christ demonstrates rather than loses his dignity by his subordination to the Father. When a person is voluntarily amenable to another, gives way to him, and places himself at his service, he shows greater dignity and freedom than an individual who cannot bear to be a helper and partner to anyone but himself. Ephesians 5 supports anything but blind obedience or the breaking of the wife's will. Rather, this chapter shows that in the realm of the crucified Servant-Messiah, the subjects respect an order of freedom and equality in which one person assists another—seemingly by renouncing rights possessed, actually in exercising the right to imitate the Messiah himself . . . A greater, wiser, and more positive description of marriage has not yet been found in Christian literature.'[2]

[9] 1 Pet. 5:5   [1] Yoder, p. 174.
[2] Barth, *Ephesians*, II, pp. 714–715

b. The wife's submission is to be given to a lover, not to an ogre

The apostle's instruction is not 'Wives submit, husbands boss'; it is 'Wives submit, husbands love'. Of course there have been examples in every age and culture of cruel and tyrannical husbands, and there have been painful occasions in which in order to maintain the integrity of her conscience, a wife has been obliged to resist her husband's authority. But Paul is describing the Christian ideal, not hideous deviations from it. This has always been obvious to commentators. Back in the sixteenth century Calvin preached. 'Husbands . . . should not be cruel towards their wives, or think all things that they please to be permissible and lawful, for their authority should rather be a companionship than a kingship.' Three times the apostle repeats his fundamental charge: *husbands, love your wives* (verse 25); *husbands should love their wives* (verse 28); *let each one of you love his wife* (verse 33). If then the husband's headship is expressed in responsible love for his wife, why should she be reluctant to submit to him? And if a husband desires her to do so, he will know that it is only by loving her that he will succeed.

c. The husband is to love like Christ

Does the requirement of 'submission' sound hard to a wife? I think what is required of her husband is harder. This is not that he 'love' her with the romantic, sentimental and even aggressive passion which frequently passes for genuine love today; instead, he is to love her with the love of Christ. If the husband's obligation to love is repeated three times, so is the requirement to model his attitude and behaviour on Christ's. He is the head of his wife *as Christ is the head of the church* (verse 23); he is to love his wife *as Christ loved the church* (verse 25); and he is to nourish and cherish her *as Christ does the church* (verse 29). Thus his headship, his love and his care are all to resemble Christ's. The highest pinnacle of demand is reached in verse 25 where he is exhorted to love his wife *as Christ loved the church and gave himself up for her*. This is the totality of self-sacrifice. He is to love her with what is sometimes termed 'Calvary love'; no higher standard is conceivable. A Christian husband who even partially fulfils this ideal preaches the gospel without ever opening his lips, for people can see in him that quality of love which took Jesus Christ to his cross.

d. The husband's love, like Christ's, sacrifices in order to serve

We considered earlier the five verbs of verses 25 and 26. Christ 'loved' the church and 'gave himself' for her, in order to 'cleanse' her, 'sanctify' her, and ultimately 'present' her to himself in full splendour and without any defect. In other words, his love and self-sacrifice were not an idle display, but purposive. And his purpose was not to impose an alien identity upon the church, but to free her from the spots and wrinkles which mar her beauty and to display her in her true glory. The Christian husband is to have a similar concern. His headship will never be used to suppress his wife. He longs to see her liberated from everything which spoils her true feminine identity and growing towards that 'glory', that perfection of fulfilled personhood which will be the final destiny of all those whom Christ redeems. To this end Christ gave himself. To this end too the husband gives himself in love.

e. The wife's submission is but another aspect of love

We have seen that the essence of Paul's instruction is 'Wives submit, husbands love', and that these words are different from one another since they recognize the headship which God has given to the husband. Yet when we try to define the two verbs, it is not easy to distinguish clearly between them. What does it mean to 'submit'? It is to give oneself up to somebody. What does it mean to 'love'? It is to give oneself up for somebody, as Christ 'gave himself up' for the church. Thus 'submission' and 'love' are two aspects of the very same thing, namely of that selfless self-giving which is the foundation of an enduring and growing marriage.

Not that such self-giving is ever easy. I fear I may have

painted a picture of married life which is more romantic than realistic. The truth is that all self-sacrifice, although the way of service and the means to self-realisation, is also painful. Indeed, love and pain appear to be inseparable, especially in sinners like us, since our fallenness has not been obliterated by our re-creation through Christ. In marriage there is the pain of adjustment, as the old independent 'I' gives way to the new interdependent 'we'. There is also the pain of vulnerability as closeness to one another leads to self-exposure, self-exposure to mutual knowledge, and knowledge to the risk of rejection. So husbands and wives should not expect to discover harmony without conflict; they have to work at building a relationship of love, respect and truth.

The giving of oneself to anybody is a recognition of the worth of the other self. For if I give myself up, it can only be because I value the other person so highly that I want to sacrifice myself for his or her self, in order that he may develop his selfhood, or she hers, more fully. Now to lose oneself that the other may find his or her self—that is the essence of the gospel of Christ. It is also the essence of the marriage relationship, for as the husband loves his wife and the wife submits to her husband, each is seeking to enable the other to become more fully himself and herself, within the harmonious complementarity of the sexes.

11. Parents, children, masters and servants

Children, obey your parents in the Lord, for this is right.
[2]'Honour your father and mother' (this is the first
commandment with a promise), [3]'that it may be well with
you and that you may live long on the earth.' [4]Fathers,
do not provoke your children to anger, but bring them up
in the discipline and instruction of the Lord.

Paul now passes in his *Haustafeln* from the reciprocal
duties of husbands and wives to those of parents and
children. As he does so, it is immediately noteworthy that
he thinks of the local congregation as a 'church family',
consisting of both sexes and of all ages. Since he addresses
the children in this paragraph as well as their parents, he
evidently expects whole families to come together for public
worship not only to praise God but also to listen to his
Word. They would hear the Old Testament Scriptures and
the apostle's letters read aloud and expounded, and when
the apostolic *Haustafeln* were read out, they would learn
their own Christian duties and those of other members of
their family. That children should have been included in
the instructions, and given a section of their own, is an
indication of the already pervasive influence in the church
of him who had said, 'Let the children come to me, do
not hinder them; for to such belongs the kingdom of
God,'[1] and again, 'Whoever receives one such child in my

[1] Mk. 10:14.

237

name receives me.'[2] It was a radical change from the callous cruelty which prevailed in the Roman Empire, in which unwanted babies were abandoned, weak and deformed ones killed, and even healthy children were regarded by many as a partial nuisance because they inhibited sexual promiscuity and complicated easy divorce.

1. The duty of children (verses 1–3)

Children, obey your parents ... Here is another example of that general submissiveness which according to 5:21 is expected of all members of God's new society. But this time the requirement is stronger, namely obedience. For wives were not told to 'obey', and in my view the 1662 Prayer Book marriage service was wrong to include this verb in the bride's vows. The concept of a husband who issues commands and of a wife who gives him obedience is simply not found in the New Testament. The nearest approximation to it is the cited example of Sarah who 'obeyed Abraham, calling him lord'. But even in that passage the apostle Peter's actual instruction to wives is the same as Paul's, namely, 'Be submissive to your husbands.'[3] And, as we saw in the last chapter, a wife's submission is something quite different from obedience. It is a voluntary self-giving to a lover whose responsibility is defined in terms of constructive care; it is love's response to love.

Children, however, are to obey their parents. Although Paul goes on to restrict parental authority and to guide it into the channel of Christian education, it is still clear that parents' authority over their children is distinct from and stronger than the husband's 'headship' over his wife. Yet Paul does not take it for granted. His teaching is always rationally argued. As with the wife's submission, so with the child's obedience, he builds his instruction on a carefully laid foundation. He gives three grounds for the obedience of children in a Christian home: nature, the law and the gospel.

First, nature: *Children, obey your parents* ... , *for this is right,* or righteous (*dikaios*). Child obedience belongs to

[2] Mt. 18:5.   [3] 1 Pet. 3:1–6.

that realm which came in medieval theology to be called 'natural justice'. It does not depend on special revelation; it is part of the natural law which God has written on all human hearts.[4] It is not confined to Christian ethics; it is standard behaviour in every society. Pagan moralists, both Greek and Roman, taught it. Stoic philosophers saw a son's obedience as self-evident, plainly required by reason and part of 'the nature of things'. Much earlier, and in oriental culture, one of the greatest emphases of Confucius was on filial respect, so that still today, though centuries later, Chinese, Korean and Japanese customs continue to reflect his influence. Indeed, virtually all civilizations have regarded the recognition of parental authority as indispensable to a stable society. We experience no sense of surprise, therefore, when Paul includes 'disobedient to parents' as a mark both of a decadent society which God has given up to its own godlessness and of 'the last days' which began with the coming of Christ.[5]

If the obedience of children is part of the natural law which God has written on human hearts, it belongs also to the revealed law which God gave on stone tablets to Moses. So Paul goes on: *Honour your father and mother (this is the first commandment with a promise), that it may be well with you and that you may live long on the earth* (verses 2, 3). In his quotation Paul freely conflates the Greek text of Exodus 20:12 ('Honour your father and your mother, that your days may be long . . .') and Deuteronomy 5:16 ('that it may go well with you'). Since this is the fifth of the ten commandments and appears at first sight to concern our duty to our neighbour, many Christians have divided the decalogue into two uneven halves, the first four commandments specifying our duty to God and the remaining six our duty to our neighbour. But the Jews regularly taught that each of the law's two tablets contains five commandments. The significance of this arrangement is that it brings the honouring of our parents into our duty to God. And this is surely right. For at least during our childhood they represent God to us and mediate to us both his authority and his love. We

[4] Rom. 2:14–15.   [5] Rom. 1:28–30; 2 Tim. 3:1–2.

239

are to 'honour' them, that is, acknowledge their God-given authority, and so give them not only our obedience, but our love and respect as well. It is because parental authority is divinely delegated authority that respectful obedience to parents was invested with such great importance in the life of God's covenant people. Moses was commanded to say to Israel: 'You shall be holy, for I the Lord your God am holy. Every one of you shall revere his mother and his father . . . I am the Lord your God.'[6] Reverence for parents was thus made an integral part of reverence for God as their God and of their special relationship to him as his people. Hence the extremely severe penalty (death, in fact) which was to be inflicted on anyone who cursed his parents and on the 'stubborn and rebellious son' who refused to obey them, defied their warning discipline and proved to be incorrigible.[7]

The apostle Paul, however, prefers to enforce God's commandment with a promise than with a threat. He reminds his readers that the command to honour parents is *the first commandment with a promise*, and he goes on to quote the promise of prosperity and long life. This deceptively simple statement contains several problems. Some commentators beg to disagree with Paul, claiming that the fifth commandment is not, in fact, the first to have a promise attached to it, since the second commandment also has one, promising 'steadfast love to thousands' who love and obey God. A sufficient answer to this objection is that these last words 'are a declaration of God's character rather than a promise'.[8] Others express the opinion that in this case it is not the first but the only commandment with a promise, for no other commandment has one. To this F. F. Bruce aptly responds that Paul is thinking 'not only of the decalogue but of the whole body of Pentateuchal legislation which is introduced by the decalogue'.[9] This does not satisfy everybody, however. So some interpret 'first' as a reference to rank not order (as when the scribe asked 'Which commandment is the first of all?'),[1] and suggest that it means 'a commandment of foremost

[6] Lv. 19:1–3.　　　[7] Lv. 20:9; Dt. 21:18–21.
[8] Bruce, p. 121.　　　[9] Bruce, p. 121.　　　[1] Mk. 12:28.

significance, with a promise attached'[2] or 'the first in importance among those relating to our social duties'[3] or that 'this, for children, is a primary commandment, accompanied with a promise'.[4]

The promise concerned was material prosperity (*that it may be well with you*) and long life (*that you may live long*). During the time of the theocracy, when Israel was both a nation and a church over which God ruled, his covenant blessings were closely tied to the promised land, and to safety, health and good harvests in it. But now times have changed, and God's dealings with his people have also changed. This seems to be implied by Paul's deliberate alteration of the promise from the original 'in the land which the Lord your God gives you' to *on the earth*. The promised land fades from view. God's covenant people are now an international community, and his blessings are largely spiritual in Christ. At the same time, alongside his blessing 'in the heavenly places' (1:3), there is here a promised blessing 'on earth'. Probably we should interpret this in general rather than individual terms. Then what is promised is not so much long life to each child who obeys his parents, as social stability to any community in which children honour their parents. Certainly a healthy society is inconceivable without a strong family life.

Two practical questions arise from the requirement that children obey their parents. Is the command unconditional? And to whom is it addressed?

Many Christian young people, who are anxious to conform their lives to the teaching of Scripture, are perplexed by the requirement of obedience. Are they to obey absolutely everything their parents tell them to do? What if they have themselves come to know Christ, while so far as they know their parents remain unconverted? If their parents forbid them to follow Christ or to join the Christian community, are they obliged to obey? In reply to such questions, which are often asked in great pain and anxiety, I think I need first to say that during a young person's minority (and I have more to say about this later) obedience to parents should be the norm, and disobedience

[2] Hendriksen, p. 258.   [3] Hodge, p. 358.   [4] Hunter, p. 74.

the rare exception.

For example, supposing you are a young person who, having been brought up in a non-Christian home, have recently come to Christ and now desire to be baptized, but your parents are forbidding it. Personally, I would not advise you to go ahead in defiance of your parents' expressed wishes. Even baptism, though Jesus commanded it, can wait until you are older and the law of your country gives you a measure of independence. If, on the other hand, your parents were to forbid you to worship and follow Christ in your heart, this you could not obey. It must have been just such a situation as this that Jesus had in mind when he warned of family conflict in which parents and children would be opposed to one another and our enemies would belong to our own household. In such circumstances, however painful or perilous, our loyalty to Christ must come first. If we love even our parents more than him, he said, we are not worthy of him.[5] Not, of course, that we should ever seek family conflict or be guilty of fomenting it. On the contrary, all the followers of Jesus are called to be peacemakers and, so far as it depends on us, to live peaceably with everybody.[6] Yet sometimes tension and strife simply cannot be avoided.

It is quite true that in the parallel passage in Colossians children are told to obey parents 'in everything'.[7] But this is balanced in Ephesians by the command to obey them *in the Lord* (6:1). The latter instruction surely modifies the former. Children are not to obey their parents in absolutely everything without exception, but in everything which is compatible with their primary loyalty, namely to their Lord Jesus Christ.

This brings us to the second practical question: who are these 'children' who are to obey their parents? And when do they cease to be such? Is Paul addressing himself only to infants, and to young boys and girls? Or does he include all young people who are still unmarried and living at home, even though now they may be grown up and may long since have left their childhood and their teens behind? No single answer can be given to this question;

[5] Mt. 10:34–39.   [6] Mt. 5:9; Rom. 12:18.   [7] Col. 3:20.

for different answers would need to be given in different cultures. In most western countries the age at which young people attain their majority has in recent years been lowered from twenty-one to eighteen. At that age now they are no longer minors, they are given the vote, and they are free to marry without parental consent. At the opposite extreme, in the empire of Paul's day, 'the power of the Roman father extended over the child's whole life, so long as the father lived. A Roman son never came of age.'[8] In some third world countries today, especially in Asia, a similar custom prevails. All one can say in relation to such situations is that either law or custom in every society recognizes at least a measure of independence for young people, either when manhood or womanhood is reached, or when they attain a certain age, or when they leave home or marry. Christians should not defy the accepted convention of their own culture in this matter. So long as they are regarded in their culture as children or minors, they should continue to obey their parents.

One other important point. Even after we have attained our majority, are regarded in our culture as being no longer under the authority of our parents, and are therefore no longer under obligation to 'obey' them, we still must continue to 'honour' them. Our parents occupy a unique position in our lives. If we honour them as we should, we will never neglect or forget them. Many third world cultures, even non-Christian ones, care for elderly parents far more conscientiously and thoughtfully than most of us do, who live in the so-called Christian West. Although in some circumstances it may be unavoidable and in others even desirable, it is a sad reflection on the selfish western tradition of the nuclear family that instead of looking after our elderly relatives ourselves, we consign them to an old people's home. Thus to isolate, and even symbolically to reject, one's own parents can seldom be reconciled with the command to honour them.

So far we have been following Paul as he grounds the child's obedience to his parents on both nature and Scripture, on natural law and revealed law. That is, he

[8] Barclay, p. 208.

243

urges it first because it is right and secondly because it is written. His third argument introduces the gospel and the new day which dawned with Jesus Christ. This is implied in the injunction that children should obey their parents *in the Lord*, namely, in the Lord Jesus. Already we have seen that these words modify the parallel command in Colossians to obey parents 'in everything'. But this does not exhaust their meaning. They bring child-obedience into the realm of specifically Christian duty, and lay upon children the responsibility to obey their parents because of their own personal relationship to the Lord Jesus Christ. It is he who as Creator first established order in family and society, and in the new society which he is now building he does not overthrow it. There is an essential continuity between the old order and the new, between the original creation and the new creation in Christ. Families have not been abolished. Men and women still marry and have children. 'In the Lord' there are still husbands and wives, parents and children. What has changed relates to the ravages of the fall. For the family life which God created at the beginning and pronounced to be 'good' was spoiled by human rebellion and selfishness. Relationships fell apart. Society was fractured. Love was twisted into lust, and authority into oppression. But now *in the Lord*, by his reconciling work, God's new society has begun, continuous with the old in the fact of family life but discontinuous in its quality. For now all our relationships are transformed precisely because they are *in the Lord*. They are purged of ruinous self-centredness, and suffused instead with Christ's love and peace. Even obedience to parents is changed. It is no longer a grudging acquiescence in parental authority. Christian children learn to obey with gladness, 'for this pleases the Lord'.[9] They remember the loving submission which Jesus himself gave as a boy to his parents.[1] Now this same Jesus is their Lord and Saviour, and the creator of the new order, so they are anxious to do what pleases him.

[9] Col. 3:20.   [1] Lk. 2:51.

2. The duty of parents (verse 4)

The instruction to children to obey their parents presupposes, as we have seen, the fact of parental authority. Yet when Paul outlines how parents should behave towards their children, it is not the exercise, but the restraint, of their authority which he urges upon them.

The picture he paints of fathers as self-controlled, gentle, patient educators of their children is in stark contrast to the norm of his own day. 'At the head of the Roman family . . . was the *pater familias*, who exercised a sovereign authority over all members of the family. . . The autocratic character of the *patria potestas* manifested itself not only in the father's right to punish, but also in his *iuo vitae necisque*[2] (killing the newborn; exposure of children) . . . *The pater familias* has a full right of disposal over his children, as over slaves and things . . .'[3] William Barclay adds: 'A Roman father had absolute power over his family. He could sell them as slaves, he could make them work in his fields even in chains, he could take the law into his own hands, for the law was in his own hands, and punish as he liked, he could even inflict the death penalty on his child.'[4]

Completely different was the Christian father, especially if he remembered what Paul had written earlier, namely that his fatherhood was derived from the 'one God and Father of us all' (3:14–15; 4:6). The overarching theme of *Ephesians* is that through Christ's reconciling work there is now one multinational, multicultural family of God. So human fathers are to care for their families as God the Father cares for his. And incidentally mothers are surely included too. Although the word in verse 4 is, in fact, 'fathers' (*pateres*), yet it could be used for 'fathers and mothers', much as 'brothers' (*adelphoi*) meant 'brothers and sisters'. Certainly it is parents, both father and mother, who are referred to in verses 1–3, so that it is entirely legitimate for GNB to put 'parents' in verse 4.

[2] *I.e.* 'right of life and death'.
[3] From the article *Patria Potestas* in the *Oxford Classical Dictionary* (1949 edition), p. 653.   [4] Barclay, p. 208.

Negatively, they are told: *Do not provoke your children to anger* (verse 4), or 'do not exasperate your children' (NIV) or 'goad your children to resentment' (NEB). Paul recognizes how delicate a child's personality is. Some authors have speculated that in his own childhood he was comparatively deprived of love, and that in this instruction to parents there is a flashback to some early childhood reminiscence. We do not know. What we do know is that parents can easily misuse their authority either by making irritating or unreasonable demands which make no allowances for the inexperience and immaturity of children, or by harshness and cruelty at one extreme or by favouritism and over-indulgence at the other, or by humiliating or suppressing them, or by those two vindictive weapons sarcasm and ridicule. These are some of the parental attitudes which provoke resentment and anger in children. How many 'angry young men', hostile to society at large, have learned their hostility as children in an unsympathetic home? There is a place for discipline, as Paul goes on to say, but it must never be arbitrary (for children have a built-in sense of justice) or unkind. Otherwise, they will 'become discouraged'.[5] Conversely, almost nothing causes a child's personality to blossom and gifts to develop like the positive encouragement of loving, understanding parents. Indeed, just as a husband's love for his wife is expressed in helping her develop her full potential, so parents' love for their children is expressed in helping them develop theirs.

Behind this curbing of parental authority there lies the clear recognition that, although children are to obey their parents in the Lord, yet they have a life and personality of their own. They are little people in their own right. As such they are to be respected, and on no account to be exploited, manipulated or crushed. 'The dominant father of the Victorian novels', writes Sir Frederick Catherwood, 'who used his own authority for his own ends is no more entitled to claim Christian authority than the rebellious son. One is abusing authority, the other is flouting it. Both are wrong.'[6]

[5] Col. 3:21.
[6] *A Better Way* (Inter-Varsity Press, 1975), p. 59.

It is not only in the novels of Victorian England that oppressive parenthood is to be seen, however. Another example comes from more recent times in the United States. Edna Ferber's novel *Giant* tells the story of the Texan, Jordan Benedict. Owner of a two and a half million acre cattle ranch, he is furious because his infant son Jordy, aged three, does not take to horses. When set on one in full cowboy regalia, he cries to be taken down. His father is disgusted. 'I rode before I could walk', he says. 'All right', responds his wife Leslie, 'that was very cute, but that was you. This is another person. Maybe he doesn't like horses. . .' 'He's a Benedict,' his father retorts, 'and I'm going to make a horseman out of him if I have to *tie* him to do it'. 'You've been playing God so long you think you run the world'. 'I run the part of it that's mine'. 'He's not yours. He's yours and mine. And not even ours. He's himself. . .'[7]

Every child must be allowed to be himself. Wise parents recognize that not all the non-conforming responses of childhood deserve to be styled 'rebellion'. On the contrary, it is by experiment that children discover both the limits of their liberty and the quality of their parents' love. Moreover, in order to grow up, they have to develop their independence, not because they are resistant to their parents' authority but because they need to exercise their own.

Paul does not rest content with his negative instruction to parents not to provoke their children to anger. He complements it with this positive exhortation: *Bring them up in the discipline and instruction of the Lord.* The verb (*ektrephō*) means literally to 'nourish' or 'feed' and was used in 5:29 of the nourishment we give to our own bodies. But it is also used of the upbringing of children. Calvin's translation is, 'Let them be fondly cherished . . ., deal gently with them,'[8] and William Hendriksen's, 'Rear them tenderly.'[9] Here is an understanding, centuries before modern psychology emphasized the vital importance of the earliest years of life, that children are fragile creatures needing the tenderness and security of love.

[7] (Victor Gollancz, 1952), pp. 285–286.
[8] Calvin, p. 622.   [9] Hendriksen, p. 262

The implications of this insistence on the parental upbringing of children are many. One is that Christian parents should jealously guard their responsibility, delegating some of it indeed to both church and school, but never entirely surrendering it. It is their own God-given task; nobody can adequately or completely replace them. Another implication is that parents need to take time and trouble with their children. Failure to do so causes many problems later. As Dr Lloyd-Jones pertinently observes, 'If parents but gave as much thought to the rearing of their children as they do to the rearing of animals and flowers, the situation would be very different.'[1]

How then should parents rear their children? Answer: *in the discipline and instruction of the Lord.* The second word (*nouthesia*), whether translated 'instruction' or 'warning', seems to refer primarily to verbal education, while the first word (*paideia*) means training by discipline, even by punishment. '*Paideia* (*discipline*) is training with the accent on the correction of the young.'[2] It is the word used in Hebrews 12 both of earthly fathers and also of our heavenly Father who 'disciplines us for our good'.[3]

On the need for discipline and punishment the Old Testament was clear. 'He who spares the rod hates his son, but he who loves him is diligent to discipline him.' Again, 'Folly is bound up in the heart of a child, but the rod of discipline drives it far from him.'[4] Of course our Victorian ancestors used these verses from Proverbs to justify their excessively stern discipline. In our generation, on the other hand, we have witnessed an over-reaction leading to excessively *laissez-faire* permissiveness. To the one extreme we need to say: 'The opposite of wrong discipline is not the absence of discipline, but right discipline, true discipline.'[5] To the other extreme we need to say: 'The opposite of no discipline at all is not cruelty, it is balanced discipline, it is controlled discipline.'[6] Above all, parents must be clear about their motives. It is always dangerous

---

[1] Lloyd-Jones, *Life in the Spirit*, p. 290.
[2] Houlden, p. 336.   [3] Heb. 12:5–11.
[4] Pr. 13:24; 22:15. See also Pr. 23:13–14 and 29:15.
[5] Lloyd-Jones, *Life in the Spirit*, p. 268.   [6] *Ibid.*, p. 283.

for them to discipline their children when they are annoyed, when their pride has been injured, or when they have lost their temper. Let me quote Dr Lloyd-Jones again, for his exposition of these verses is full of practical wisdom: 'When you are disciplining a child, you should have first controlled yourself . . . What right have you to say to your child that he needs discipline when you obviously need it yourself? Self-control, the control of temper, is an essential pre-requisite in the control of others.'[7]

So far we have been thinking principally of the disciplining of children. But the Christian upbringing of children is mental as well as moral. It includes instruction too. One popular contemporary fashion is to urge parents to be totally 'non-directive' and to leave their children to find their own way. Paul is of a different mind. Certainly some parents are too directive, too domineering, and thereby inhibit their children from learning to make their own decisions and so grow into maturity. We have to distinguish between true and false education. False education is indoctrination, in which parents and teachers impose their mind and will on the child. True education, on the other hand, is stimulation, in which parents and teachers act as a catalyst, and encourage the child to make his own responses. This they cannot do if they leave the child to flounder; they have to teach Christian values of truth and goodness, defend them, and recommend their acceptance, but at the same time abstain from any pressure, still more coercion.

The discipline and instruction in which parents are to bring up their children, Paul writes, are 'the Lord's'. This has been taken by some to mean simply that the kind of instruction and discipline intended 'belong to a Christian upbringing' (NEB), and that Paul is specifying Christian as opposed to secular education. But I think it means more than this, namely that behind the parents who teach and discipline their children there stands the Lord himself. It is he who is the chief teacher and administrator of discipline. Certainly the overriding concern of Christian

---

[7] *Ibid.*, p. 279. His exposition of these four verses is given in five chapters and covers pp. 237–302.

parents is not just that their children will submit to their authority, but that through this they will come to know and obey the Lord. There is always much rejoicing and thanksgiving whenever the teaching and discipline of a Christian home leads, not artificially but naturally, to a child's acceptance of the teaching and discipline of the Lord Jesus himself.

3. The duty of slaves (verses 5–8)

Slaves, be obedient to those who are your earthly masters, with fear and trembling, in singleness of heart, as to Christ; [6]not in the way of eye-service, as men-pleasers, but as servants of Christ, doing the will of God from the heart, [7]rendering service with a good will as to the Lord and not to men, [8]knowing that whatever good any one does, he will receive the same again from the Lord, whether he is a slave or free.

Slavery seems to have been universal in the ancient world. A high percentage of the population were slaves. 'It has been computed that in the Roman Empire there were 60,000,000 slaves.'[8] They constituted the work force, and included not only domestic servants and manual labourers but educated people as well, like doctors, teachers and administrators. Slaves could be inherited or purchased, or acquired in settlement of a bad debt, and prisoners of war commonly became slaves. Nobody queried or challenged the arrangement. 'The institution of slavery was a fact of Mediterranean economic life so completely accepted as a part of the labour structure of the time that one cannot correctly speak of the slave "problem" in antiquity. This unquestioning acceptance of the slave system explains why Plato in his plan of the good life as depicted in *The Republic* did not need to mention the slave class. It was simply there.'[9]

To those of us who live in countries in which slavery has been abolished by law for one and a half centuries, it is hard to conceive how the ownership of one human being by another can have been countenanced in this way.

---

[8] Barclay, p. 212.   [9] Westermann, p. 215.

It is even harder to understand how slaves can have been regarded more as things than as persons. For all his intellect and culture Aristotle could not contemplate any friendship between slave and slave-owner, for, he said 'A slave is a living tool, just as a tool is an inanimate slave', although he could at least concede that 'a slave is a kind of possession with a soul'.[1]

This dehumanization of slaves in the public mind was mirrored in early Roman legislation. 'Legally they were only chattels without rights, whom their master could treat virtually as he pleased.'[2] 'The Roman state left the problem of the discipline of slaves to their owners . . . The *pater familias* had complete control over all slaves owned in his *familia*, the power of punishment by whipping and by confinement in the *ergastulum*, and the right of execution of the death penalty.'[3] Consequently, accounts of terrible atrocities have survived, especially from the pre-Christian era. Slaves were sometimes whipped, mutilated and imprisoned in chains, their teeth were knocked out, their eyes gouged out, they were even thrown to the wild beasts or crucified, and all this sometimes for the most trivial offences. The fact that some slaves ran away (risking, if caught, branding, flogging and even summary execution), while others committed suicide, is sufficient evidence that cruelty towards them was widespread.

At the same time, it would be a grave mistake to suppose that this kind of barbaric treatment was either habitual or universal, or that it continued unabated into the first century AD. Although the law at first prescribed no penalties for slave owners who illtreated their slaves, yet more often than not they were restrained by other factors, either by their own sense of responsibility, or by public opinion, or by self-interest. As for public opinion, Paul's Stoic contemporary Seneca was teaching the brotherhood of man and urging kindness to slaves. As for self-interest, masters

[1] *Nichomachian Ethics*, viii.11.6, and *Politics* 1.2,4.
[2] Salmon, p. 70.
[3] *The Slave Systems of Greek and Roman Antiquity* by W. L. Westermann (The American Philosophical Society, 1955), pp. 75–76. The *pater familias* was the head of the household, and the *ergastulum* a workhouse or prison for offending slaves.

251

knew that their slaves represented a high capital investment. It was, therefore, to their own advantage to take good care of their slaves, just as they did their farm animals and their furniture.

It is immediately remarkable that in his *Haustafeln* Paul should address himself to slaves at all. The simple fact that he does so indicates that they were accepted members of the Christian community and that he regards them as responsible people to whom, as much as to their masters, he sends a moral appeal. If children are to obey their parents, slaves are to obey their *earthly masters* (verse 5), and for the very same reason, namely that behind them they must learn to discern the figure of their *master . . . in heaven* (verse 9), namely the Lord Christ. In each of the four verses addressed to slaves Jesus Christ is mentioned. They are to be obedient *as to Christ* (verse 5), to behave *as servants* (literally, 'slaves') *of Christ* (verse 6), to render service *as to the Lord* rather than men (verse 7), knowing that they will receive good *from the Lord* (verse 8). The Christ-centredness of this instruction is very striking. The slave's perspective has changed. His horizons have broadened. He has been liberated from the slavery of 'men-pleasing' into the freedom of serving Christ. His mundane tasks have been absorbed into a higher preoccupation, namely *the will of God* (verse 6) and the good pleasure of Christ.

Exactly the same principle can be applied by contemporary Christians to their work and employment. Our great need is the clear-sightedness to see Jesus Christ and to set him before us. It is possible for the housewife to cook a meal as if Jesus Christ were going to eat it, or to spring-clean the house as if Jesus Christ were to be the honoured guest. It is possible for teachers to educate children, for doctors to treat patients and nurses to care for them, for solicitors to help clients, shop assistants to serve customers, accountants to audit books and secretaries to type letters as if in each case they were serving Jesus Christ. Can the same be said in relation to the masses of industrial workers with tedious routine machine-minding to do, and to miners who have to work underground? Surely yes. The presence of Christ in the mine or factory is certainly no excuse for bad conditions. On the contrary, it should be a spur to improving them. At the same time, their situation is not nearly as bad as slavery in the Roman Empire, so that if the work of Christian slaves could be transformed by doing it *as to the Lord*, the same must be true of Christian miners, factory workers, dustmen, road sweepers and public lavatory attendants.

Once Christian slaves were clear in their minds that their primary responsibility was to serve the Lord Christ, their service to their earthly masters would become exemplary. First, they would be respectful, obeying them *with fear and trembling* (verse 5), which implies not a cringing servility before a human master but rather a reverent acknowledgement of the Lord Jesus whose authority the master represents. This is plain not only from the usual contexts of the expression 'fear and trembling' but also from the fact that in the equivalent Colossians passage it is replaced by 'fearing the Lord'.[4] Next, they would obey *in singleness of heart* (5), with integrity or wholeheartedness, without hypocrisy or ulterior motives. Thirdly, they would be conscientious, not offering *eye-service as men-pleasers*, working only when the boss is watching in order to curry favour with him, but *as servants of Christ*, who is in any case watching all the time and is never deceived by shoddy work. Fourthly, their service would become willing and 'cheerful' (NEB) instead of reluctant or grudging. Because they would consciously be *doing the will of God*, they would do it *from the heart* (verse 6) and *with a good will* (verse 7). As we might say, their heart and soul would be in it. And all this because they know that their Lord is also their judge, and that no good work, whoever does it (*slave or free*), is ever left unrewarded by him (verse 8).

4. The duty of masters (verse 9)

Masters, do the same to them, and forbear threatening, knowing that he who is both their Master and yours is in heaven, and that there is no partiality with him.

Although the duties of Christian slaves are spelled out in

[4] Col. 3:22; *cf.* Eph. 5:21

253

some detail, Christian slave-owners are given only three principles, all of which however have far-reaching implications against the background of the middle of the first century AD. First, *do the same to them*. That is, if you hope to receive respect, show it; if you hope to receive service, give it. It is an application of the golden rule. However masters hope their slaves will behave towards them, they must behave towards their slaves in the same way. Paul admits no privileged superiority in the masters, as if they could themselves dispense with the very courtesies they expect to be shown.

Secondly, *forbear threatening*. As parents are not to provoke their children, so masters are not to threaten their slaves. That is, they are not to misuse their position of authority by issuing threats of punishment. Punishment was accepted in the Empire as the only way to keep slaves under control, and Christianity does not deny that in some circumstances punishment is legitimate, even necessary. But threats are a weapon which the powerful wield over the powerless. And a relationship based on threats is not a human relationship at all. So Paul forbade it.

Thirdly, the reason for these requirements is their *knowing that* Jesus Christ is *master* of both slave and slave-owner, *and that there is no partiality with him*. Slave-owners were used to being flattered and fawned upon, but they should not expect (for they will not receive) such discriminatory favouritism from the Lord Christ. Thus all three principles were designed to lessen the cultural and social gap between slave and slave-owner. Instead of regarding his relationship with his slaves as that of proprietor to chattels, or of superior to inferiors, he was to develop a relationship in which he gave them *the same* treatment as he hoped to receive, renounced the unfair weapon of threats, and recalled that he and they both shared the same heavenly master and impartial judge.

5. The abolition of slavery

The new relationship which Jesus Christ made possible between slave and slave-owner was something new and beautiful. Understandably, however, it has seemed to many critics an inadequate Christian response to an unmitigated evil. Did the gospel offer no more radical solution to slavery than an adjustment of personal relationships? Even if Paul held back from inciting slaves to rise up against their owners and seize their freedom (as some hotheads wish he had), why did he not at least command slave-owners to emancipate their slaves? Why are the New Testament writers so feeble and mealy-mouthed, instead of condemning slavery outright for the horribly inhuman thing it was?

In whatever way we Christians seek to defend ourselves and our faith against such criticisms, it must never be by condoning slavery. For if the New Testament does not explicitly condemn slavery, it does not condone it either. Although there have been varying degrees of degradation in slavery at different times and places, and although Afro-American slavery was worse than Roman, Roman than Greek and Greek than Hebrew, yet the Christian conscience must condemn slavery in every form. Its evil lies neither in the servitude it involves (for Jesus voluntarily made himself a slave of others,[5] and so did his apostle Paul),[6] nor even in the element of compulsion, but rather in the ownership by one human being of others which degrades them into subhuman goods to be used, exploited and traded, and in the cruelty which often accompanied this. This being so, we again ask why the New Testament did not call for its abolition.

The first answer is the pragmatic one, namely that Christians were at first an insignificant group in the Empire. Their religion was itself still unlawful, and they were politically powerless. Besides, slavery was at that time an indispensable part of the fabric of Roman society. In most cities there were many times more slaves than free people. It would therefore have been impossible to abolish slavery at a single stroke without the complete disintegration of society. Even if Christians had liberated their slaves, they would have condemned most of them to unemployment and penury. As G. B. Caird has put it, 'Ancient society was economically as dependent on slavery as modern

[5] *E.g.* Phil. 2:7; John 13:14–16. [6] *E.g.* 1 Cor. 9:19; 2 Cor. 4:5.

255

society is on machinery, and anyone proposing its abolition could only be regarded as a seditious fanatic.'[7] It had to be tolerated a while longer (although, to be sure, that 'while longer' lasted much, much too long) as a symptom of what Christians called 'this present evil age'.

There is a second reason why we do not find in the New Testament stronger expressions of indignation at the system. 'The lack in antiquity of any deep abhorrence of slavery as a social and economic evil may be explained in part', writes W. L. Westermann, by this fact that 'the change of legal status out of slavery into liberty by way of manumission was . . . constant and easy . . .'[8] 'The apostles' attitude is best explained by the unique way in which the Romans of the first century AD treated their slaves, and released them in great numbers.'[9] According to the results of Tenney Frank's research, between 81 and 49 BC 500,000 Roman slaves were freed. So 'The Roman slave, far from living in perpetual servitude, could look forward to a day of opportunity. It became the common practice of the Romans to free their slaves and then establish them in a trade or profession. Many times the former slave became wealthier than his patron.'[1] This evidence helps to explain both Paul's advice to Corinthian slaves, if they could gain their freedom, to seize the opportunity to do so, and his strong hint to Philemon that he should release Onesimus.[2]

A third point in alleviation of the New Testament's position is that by that time the legal status of slaves was beginning to be eased and showed signs of further improvement to come. 'Sweeping humanitarian changes had been introduced into the Roman world by the first century AD, which led to radically improved treatment of slaves.'[3] Steadily they were granted many of the legal rights enjoyed by free people, including the right to marry and have a family, and the right to own property. 'In AD 20 a decree of the Senate specified that slave criminals were to be tried

[7] Caird, p. 216. [8] Westermann, p. 215.
[9] From the article 'Slave, Slavery' by A. Rupprecht in *The Zondervan Pictorial Encyclopedia of the Bible*, ed. Merrill C. Tenney (Zondervan, 1975), vol. V, p. 458. [1] *Ibid.*, p. 459.
[2] 1 Cor. 7:21; Phlm. 16. [3] A. Rupprecht, *op. cit.*, p. 458.

in the same way as free men.'[4] Several emperors introduced
liberalizing measures. 'Claudius c. AD 50 enacted that sick
slaves who were deserted by their masters should be free
if they recovered. Under Vespasian c. 75 a female slave
could under certain circumstances obtain her freedom if
prostituted by her master, Domitian c. 90 forbade the
mutilation of slaves. Hadrian early in the second century
refused to countenance the sale of slaves for immoral or
gladiatorial purposes, and may have forbidden the execution
of slaves by their masters.'[5]

So more humane legislation was already being introduced
in the Empire at the time when the gospel arrived to
accelerate and extend the process. Nevertheless we Christians
cannot escape a sense of shame that slavery and the slave
trade were tolerated for so long, especially later in the
European colonies. Both should have been abolished
centuries before they were. And the best Christian minds
recognized this. Calvin, for example, in the middle of the
sixteenth century attributed slavery to original sin. He
deduced it to be 'a thing totally against all the order of
nature' that human beings 'fashioned after the image of
God' should ever be 'put to such reproach'.[6]

While we cannot defend the indolence or cowardice of
two further Christian centuries which saw this social evil
but failed to eradicate it, we can at the same time rejoice
that the gospel immediately began even in the first century
to undermine the institution; it lit a fuse which at long
last led to the explosion which destroyed it. This brings
us back to Paul's Ephesian letter and to the transformed
slave-master relationship which he described. Three aspects
of it may be mentioned.

The first is equality. Of course nobody could imagine
that in culture or in law, masters and slaves were equal.
Quite patently they were not, since the one owned the
other. Nevertheless, they were equal before God, because
they had the same Lord and judge, who showed no
partiality between them (verse 9). Roman law was still in
certain respects discriminatory; heavenly justice was not.
Paul reminded both slaves and masters of this fact. For

[4] *Ibid.*, p. 459.   [5] Salmon, p. 72.   [6] Calvin, p. 634.

this was the theological foundation on which he built his doctrine of equality. Slaves were to give their earthly masters good service with a good will, as if to their heavenly Master, *knowing that* he would honour and reward them. Masters were not to threaten but to respect their slaves, *knowing that* they had the same Master in heaven. Thus, it was their shared knowledge of the lordship and the judgment of Jesus Christ which made them equal. If they remembered that Jesus was their common Lord now and would one day be their common judge, their whole attitude to one another would change.

The second quality of their relationship was to be justice. What is implicit here in the general instruction to masters to *do the same to them* (verse 9) is made explicit in Colossians 4:1: 'Masters, treat your slaves justly and fairly, knowing that you also have a Master in heaven.' This injunction will have sounded extremely strange in the ears of those who first heard it. For although, as we have seen, Roman law was becoming gradually more humane, slaves were still popularly regarded as the property of their masters, who had absolute power over them. And of course where there are thought to be no rights, there can be no justice. So justice for slaves was a revolutionary new concept. Essentially it was the gospel which insisted that slaves had rights. This is made plain by the reciprocal nature of the slave-master relationship. For if slaves had duties to their masters, masters had duties to their slaves. Then the master's duties became the slave's rights, just as the slave's duties were the master's rights.

In labour relations today the same basic principle holds good of justice based on reciprocal rights. Employers and employees alike have duties—the employee to give good work and the employer to pay a just wage. Then each person's duty becomes the other person's right. If it is the employee's duty to give good work, it is the employer's right to expect it. If it is the employer's duty to pay a fair wage, it is the employee's right to expect it. The major human problem in management-labour disputes is that each side concentrates on securing its own rights, and on inducing the other side to do its duty. Paul, however, reverses the emphasis. He urges each side to concentrate on its responsibilities, not on its rights. Certainly if in modern industrial disputes the concern were for each side to fulfil its own duty and secure the other side's rights, labour relations would immediately be sweetened.

The third and highest aspect of the transformed slave-master relationship is brotherhood. It appears with conspicuous clarity in Paul's letter to Philemon, in which he urges him to receive back his fugitive but now converted slave Onesimus, and to welcome him 'no longer as a slave but more than a slave, as a beloved brother'.[7] The words would have sounded incredible to all but Christian ears. Seneca taught the universal brotherhood of mankind but I cannot find that he applied his doctrine to slaves. 'Comrades', he called them, and even 'friends', but not 'brothers'. The concept of the brotherhood was Paul's innovation and is one of the major themes of Ephesians. For God's new society is the Father's household or family, all of whose members are related to one another in Christ as brothers and sisters. Even in the first letter he wrote he could affirm with confidence that all who are in Christ are the sons and daughters of God, and that 'there is neither . . . slave nor free, . . . for you are all one in Christ Jesus'.[8] He then repeated this sentiment in the letter which parallels Ephesians: 'Here there cannot be . . . slave, free man, but Christ is all, and in all.'[9] A message which thus united master and slave as brothers *ipso facto* issued its radical challenge to an institution which separated them as proprietor and property. Thereafter it was only a matter of time. 'Slavery would be abolished *from within*'.[1]

[7] Phlm. 16.   [8] Gal. 3:26, 28.   [9] Col. 3:11.

[1] Hendriksen, p. 263. See also the chapter 'The Apostle Paul and the Roman Law of Slavery' by P. R. Coleman-Norton in *Studies in Roman Economic and Social History* (Princeton University Press, 1951), pp. 155–177.

6:10–20

12 Principalities and powers

Finally, be strong in the Lord and in the strength of his might. [11]Put on the whole armour of God, that you may be able to stand against the wiles of the devil. [12]For we are not contending against flesh and blood, but against principalities, against the powers, against the world rulers of this present darkness, against the spiritual hosts of wickedness in the heavenly places. [13]Therefore take the whole armour of God, that you may be able to withstand in the evil day, and having done all, to stand. [14]Stand therefore, having girded your loins with truth, and having put on the breastplate of righteousness, [15]and having shod your feet with the equipment of the gospel of peace; [16]besides all these, taking the shield of faith, with which you can quench all the flaming darts of the evil one. [17]And take the helmet of salvation, and the sword of the Spirit, which is the word of God. [18]Pray at all times in the Spirit, with all prayer and supplication. To that end keep alert with all perseverance, making supplication for all the saints, [19]and also for me, that utterance may be given me in opening my mouth boldly to proclaim the mystery of the gospel, [20]for which I am an ambassador in chains; that I may declare it boldly, as I ought to speak.

We have had occasion several times in our study of this letter to marvel at the breadth of Paul's horizons. He began by unfolding God's purpose, conceived in a past eternity before the foundation of the world, to create a single new human race through the death and resurrection

260

of Christ and ultimately to unite the whole church and the whole creation under Christ's headship. He has emphasized that a distinctive shape has been given to this divine plan by the inclusion in God's new society, on an entirely equal footing, of Jews and Gentiles. The old days of division and discrimination have gone. A brand new oneness has emerged, in which through union with Christ Jews and Gentiles are equal members of the same body and equal sharers in the same promise. So now the one Father has one family, the one Messiah-Saviour one people, and the one Spirit one body. These sure facts of what God has done through Christ and by the Spirit form the basis on which Paul went on to issue his eloquent appeal. His readers must live a life that is 'worthy' of their calling and 'fitting' to their status as God's new and reconciled society. They must demonstrate their unity in the Christian fellowship, while at the same time rejoicing in the diversity of their gifts and so of their ministries. They must put away all the uncleanness of their pre-conversion behaviour and live a life of 'true righteousness and holiness'. And they must learn to submit to one another in every kind of domestic relationship and so promote harmony in their homes. Unity, diversity, purity and harmony—these the apostle has stressed as major characteristics of the new life and the new society in Christ. It has seemed a beautiful ideal, an obviously desirable goal, and not so difficult to attain.

But now Paul brings us down to earth, and to realities harsher than dreams. He reminds us of the opposition. Beneath surface appearances an unseen spiritual battle is raging. He introduces us to the devil (already mentioned in 2:2 and 4:27) and to certain 'principalities and powers' at his command. He supplies us with no biography of the devil, and no account of the origin of the forces of darkness. He assumes their existence as common ground between himself and his readers. In any case, his purpose is not to satisfy our curiosity, but to warn us of their hostility and teach us how to overcome them. Is God's plan to create a new society? Then they will do their utmost to destroy it. Has God through Jesus Christ broken down the walls dividing human beings of different races

261

and cultures from each other? Then the devil through his
emissaries will strive to rebuild them. Does God intend
his reconciled and redeemed people to live together in
harmony and purity? Then the powers of hell will scatter
among them the seeds of discord and sin. It is with these
powers that we are told to wage war, or—to be more
precise—to 'wrestle' (verse 12, AV). This metaphor is not
necessarily incompatible with that of the armed soldier
which Paul goes on to develop, as if he 'changed the
scenery from that of the battlefield to that of the
gymnasium'.[1] He is simply wanting to emphasize the reality
of our engagement with the powers of evil, and the grim
necessity of hand-to-hand combat.

The abrupt transition from the 'peaceful homes and
healthful days' of the previous paragraphs to the hideous
malice of devilish plots in this section causes us a painful
shock, but an essential one. We all wish we could spend
our lives in undisturbed tranquillity, among our loved-ones
at home and in the fellowship of God's people. But the
way of the escapist has been effectively blocked. Christians
have to face the prospect of conflict with God's enemy and
theirs. We need to accept the implications of this concluding
passage of Paul's letter. 'It is a stirring call to battle . . .
Do you not hear the bugle, and the trumpet? . . . We are
being roused, we are being stimulated, we are being set
upon our feet; we are told to be men. The whole tone
is martial, it is manly, it is strong'.[2] Moreover, there will
be no cessation of hostilities, not even a temporary truce
or cease-fire, until the end of life or of history when the
peace of heaven is attained. It seems probable that Paul
implies this by his *Finally* . . . For the better manuscripts
have an expression which should be translated not 'finally',
introducing the conclusion, but 'henceforward' meaning
'for the remaining time'.[3] If this is correct, then the apostle
is indicating that the whole of the interim period between
the Lord's two comings is to be characterized by conflict.
The peace which God has made through Christ's cross is
to be experienced only in the midst of a relentless struggle

[1] Hendriksen, p. 273.   [2] Lloyd-Jones, *Warfare*, pp. 16, 22.
[3] Barth, *Ephesians*, II, pp. 759–60.

against evil. And for this the strength of the Lord and the
armour of God are indispensable.

1. The enemy we face (verses 10–12)

A thorough knowledge of the enemy and a healthy respect
for his prowess are a necessary preliminary to victory in
war. Similarly, if we underestimate our spiritual enemy,
we shall see no need for God's armour, we shall go out
to the battle unarmed, with no weapons but our own puny
strength, and we shall be quickly and ignominiously
defeated.

So in between his summons to seek the Lord's strength
and put on God's armour on the one hand (verses 10–11)
and his itemizing of our weapons on the other (verses
13–20) Paul gives us a full and frightening description of
the forces arrayed against us (verse 12). *For we are not
contending against flesh and blood,* he writes, *but against
the principalities, against the powers.* In other words, our
struggle is not with human beings[4] but with cosmic
intelligences; our enemies are not human but demonic.
Paul's Asian readers were quite familiar with this fact.
They doubtless remembered—or would have heard
about—the incident of the Jewish exorcists in Ephesus who
were rash enough to try to dismiss an evil spirit in the
name of Jesus without themselves knowing the Jesus whose
name they used. Instead of succeeding in their attempt,
they were overpowered by the demoniac and fled in panic,
naked and battered.[5] This kind of happening may have
been common. For Paul's Ephesian converts had previously
dabbled in the occult and then made a public bonfire of
their valuable books of magic. Such a direct challenge to
the forces of evil will not have gone unheeded.[6]

The forces arrayed against us have three main characteristics. First, they are powerful. Whether 'principalities'
and 'powers' refer to different ranks of evil spirits in the
hierarchy of hell we do not know, but both titles draw

---

[4] That 'flesh and blood' means 'human beings' in their present mortal
human nature is clear from Mt. 16:17; 1 Cor. 15:50; Gal. 1:16 and Heb.
2:14.
[5] Acts 19:13–17.   [6] Acts 19:18–20.

attention to the power and authority they wield. They are also called *the world rulers of this present darkness*. The word *kosmokratores* was used in astrology of the planets which were thought to control the fate of mankind, in the Orphic Hymns of Zeus, in rabbinical writings of Nebuchadnezzar and other pagan monarchs, and in various ancient inscriptions of the Roman emperor. All these usages exemplify the notion of a worldwide rule. When applied to the powers of evil they are reminiscent of the devil's claim to be able to give Jesus 'all the kingdoms of the world', of the title 'the ruler of this world' which Jesus gave him, and of John's statement that 'the whole world is in the power of the evil one'.[7] These texts do not deny our Lord's decisive conquest of the principalities and powers, but indicate that as usurpers they have not conceded defeat or been destroyed. So they continue to exercise considerable power.

Secondly, they are wicked. Power itself is neutral; it can be well used or misused. But our spiritual enemies use their power destructively rather than constructively, for evil not for good. They are the worldwide rulers *of this present darkness*. They hate the light, and shrink from it. Darkness is their natural habitat, the darkness of falsehood and sin. They are also described as *the spiritual hosts of wickedness*, which operate *in the heavenly places*, that is, in the sphere of invisible reality. They are 'spiritual agents from the very headquarters of evil' (JBP). So then 'darkness' and 'wickedness' characterize their actions, and 'the appearance of Christ on earth was the signal for an unprecedented outburst of activity on the part of the realm of darkness controlled by these world-rulers'.[8] If we hope to overcome them, we shall need to bear in mind that they have no moral principles, no code of honour, no higher feelings. They recognize no Geneva Convention to restrict or partially civilize the weapons of their warfare. They are utterly unscrupulous, and ruthless in the pursuit of their malicious designs.

Thirdly, they are cunning. Paul writes here of *the wiles*

[7] Mt. 4:8–9; Jn. 12:31; 14:30; 16:11; 1 Jn. 5:19. *Cf.* also Eph. 2:2.
[8] Bruce, p. 128.

of the devil (verse 11), having declared in a previous letter
'we are not ignorant of his designs' or (NIV) 'schemes'.[9]
G. B. Caird finds the English word *wiles* 'slightly
disparaging', as if Paul 'did not take the devil seriously',
and 'hardly in keeping with the sustained military metaphor'.
Instead, he suggests that ' "strategems" would give the
required combination of tactical shrewdness and ingenious
deception'.[1] It is because the devil seldom attacks openly,
preferring darkness to light, that when he transforms
himself into 'an angel of light'[2] we are caught unsuspecting.
He is a dangerous wolf, but enters Christ's flock in the
disguise of a sheep. Sometimes he roars like a lion, but
more often is as subtle as a serpent.[3] We must not imagine,
therefore, that open persecution and open temptation to
sin are his only or even his commonest weapons; he prefers
to seduce us into compromise and deceive us into error.
Significantly this same word 'wiles' is used in 4:14 of false
teachers and their crafty tricks. 'As in Bunyan's *Holy
War*', writes E. K. Simpson, the devil develops 'a twofold
infernal policy'. That is, 'the tactics of intimidation and
insinuation alternate in Satan's plan of campaign. He plays
both the bully and the beguiler. Force and fraud form his
chief offensive against the camp of the saints, practised by
turns.'[4]

The 'wiles of the devil' take many forms, but he is at
his wiliest when he succeeds in persuading people that he
does not exist. To deny his reality is to expose ourselves
the more to his subtlety. Dr Lloyd-Jones expresses his
conviction on this matter in the following terms: 'I am
certain that one of the main causes of the ill state of the
Church today is the fact that the devil is being forgotten.
All is attributed to us; we have all become so psychological
in our attitude and thinking. We are ignorant of this great
objective fact, the being, the existence of the devil, the
adversary, the accuser, and his "fiery darts".'[5]

In Paul's characterization of them, then, the powers of
darkness are powerful, wicked and cunning. How can we

[9] 2 Cor. 2:11.   [1] Caird, p. 92.
[2] 2 Cor. 11:14.   [3] 1 Pet. 5:8; Gn. 3:1.
[4] Simpson, pp. 144–145.   [5] Lloyd-Jones, *Warfare*, p. 292.

expect to stand against the assaults of such enemies? It is impossible. We are far too weak and too ingenuous. Yet many—if not most—of our failures and defeats are due to our foolish self-confidence when we either disbelieve or forget how formidable our spiritual enemies are.

Only the power of God can defend and deliver us from the might, the evil and the craft of the devil. True, the principalities and powers are strong, but the power of God is stronger. It is his power which raised Jesus Christ from the dead and enthroned him in the heavenly places, and which has raised us from the death of sin and enthroned us with Christ. True, it is in those same heavenly places, in that same unseen world, that the principalities and powers are working (verse 12). But they were defeated at the cross and are now under Christ's feet and ours. So the invisible world in which they attack us and we defend ourselves is the very world in which Christ reigns over them and we reign with him. When Paul urges us to draw upon the power, might and strength of the Lord Jesus (verse 10), he uses exactly the same trio of words which he has used in 1:19 (*dynamis, kratos* and *ischus*) in relation to God's work of raising Jesus from the dead.

Two exhortations stand side by side. The first is general: *Be strong in the Lord, and in the strength of his might* (verse 10). The second is more specific: *Put on the whole armour of God, that you may be able to stand against the wiles of the devil* (verse 11). Both commands are conspicuous examples of the balanced teaching of Scripture. Some Christians are so self-confident that they think they can manage by themselves without the Lord's strength and armour. Others are so self-distrustful that they imagine they have nothing to contribute to their victory in spiritual warfare. Both are mistaken. Paul expresses the proper combination of divine ennabling and human co-operation. The power is indeed the Lord's, and without *the strength of his might* we shall falter and fall, but still we need to *be strong* in him and in it, or more accurately to 'be strengthened'. For the verb is a passive present which could almost be rendered 'Strengthen yourselves in the Lord' or (NEB) 'Find your strength in the Lord'. It is the same construction as in 2 Timothy 2:1 where Paul exhorts

Timothy to 'take strength from the grace of God which is ours in Christ Jesus' (NEB). Similarly, the armour is God's, and without it we shall be fatally unprotected and exposed, but still we need to take it up and put it on. Indeed we should do so piece by piece, as the apostle goes on to explain in verses 13 to 17.

2. The principalities and powers

I have thus far assumed that by 'principalities and powers' Paul was alluding to personal, demonic intelligences. There is an increasingly fashionable theory among recent and contemporary theologians, however, that he was alluding rather to structures of thought (tradition, convention, law, authority, even religion), especially as embodied in the state and its institutions. Although a number of German theologians were debating this possibility in the 1930s, in the English-speaking world it has been a post-war discussion. So popular has it become that I think it is necessary first to trace its development and then to subject it to a critique.

In 1952 Gordon Rupp's book *Principalities and Powers* appeared,[6] sub-titled 'Studies in the Christian conflict in history'. Writing in the aftermath of World War 2 he contrasted modern man's 'failure of nerve' with the early Christians' 'exultant confidence' and 'stubborn truculence' in the face of evil,[7] and attributed the latter to their certainty about the victory of Jesus over the principalities and powers. By this expression, borrowed from late Jewish apocalyptic thought, Paul meant 'supernatural cosmic forces, a vast hierarchy of angelic and demonic beings who inhabited the stars and . . . were the arbiters of human destiny', enslaving men 'beneath a cosmic totalitarianism'.[8] But Dr Rupp went on to apply the concept to 'the little people' who in every era have 'felt themselves to be no more than the playthings of great historical forces',[9] now in the middle ages, now in the industrial revolution, and now in the twentieth century in which they feel the victims of 'great economic and sociological pressures'.[1] He con-

---

[6] Published by Epworth.   [7] *Op. cit.*, p. 9.
[8] *Ibid.*, p. 10.   [9] *Ibid.*, p. 11.   [1] *Ibid.*, p. 83.

cluded: 'Down the centuries the principalities and powers have assumed many disguises. Terrifying and deadly they are, sometimes sprawling across the earth in some gigantic despotism, at times narrowed down to one single impulse in the mind of one individual man. But the fight is on. For believers fighting there is the certainty of struggle to the end. But there is also the assurance of victory.'[2] Dr Rupp writes rather as a historian than a theologian. Without any exegetical argument he simply transfers the expression 'principalities and powers' to economic, social and political forces.

The following year the Dutch original of Hendrik Berkhof's monograph *Christ and the Powers* was published, following a lecture delivered in Germany in 1950. Its English translation by John Howard Yoder appeared in America in 1962.[3] Professor Berkhof's thesis is that, although Paul borrowed the vocabulary of the powers from Jewish apocalyptic, his understanding of them was different: 'In comparison to the apocalypticists a certain "demythologizing" has taken place in Paul's thought. In short, the apocalypses think primarily of the principalities and powers as heavenly angels; Paul sees them as structures of earthly existence.'[4] He concedes that Paul *may* have 'conceived of the Powers as personal beings', yet 'this aspect is so secondary that it makes little difference whether he did or not'.[5] So he expresses his conclusion that 'we must set aside the thought that Paul's "Powers" are angels'.[6] He identifies them with the *stoicheia tou kosmou* ('elemental spirits of the universe') of Galatians 4:3, 9, and Colossians 2:8 and 20, translates the expression 'world powers' and suggests that these are seen in human traditions and religious and ethical rules.[7]

Dr Berkhof goes on to elaborate his understanding of Paul's teaching on the Powers in relation to the creation, the fall, the redemption, and the role of the church. The Powers (tradition, morality, justice and order) were created by God, but have become tyrannical and objects of worship. So they both preserve and corrupt society. 'The

---

[2] *Ibid.*, p. 2.   [3] (Herald Press, 2nd edition, 1977).
[4] *Op. cit.*, p. 23.   [5] *Ibid.*, p. 24.
[6] *Ibid.*, pp. 25–26.   [7] *Ibid.*, pp. 20–22.

state, politics, class, social struggle, national interest, public opinion, accepted morality, the ideas of decency, humanity, democracy'—all these unify men, while separating them from the true God.[8] Yet Christ has overcome them, for by his cross and resurrection they have been 'unmasked as false gods', and 'the power of illusion' has been struck from their hands.[9] In consequence, Christians 'see through the deception of the Powers' and question their legitimacy,[1] while others emboldened by the church refuse to let themselves be enslaved or intimidated. Thus the Powers are 'christianized' (*i.e.* limited to the modest, instrumental role God intended) or 'neutralized'.[2] More particularly, 'the Holy Spirit "shrinks" the Powers before the eye of faith',[3] so that the discerning believer sees them in their true, creaturely proportions (whether nationalism, the state, money, convention or militarism) and avoids deifying the world. More positively, the church both announces to the Powers by the quality and unity of her life 'that their unbroken dominion has come to an end'[4] and wages a defensive war against them in order 'to hold . . . their seduction and their enslavement at a distance'.[5] This announcement is Dr Berkhof's explanation of Ephesians 3:10 and the defensive war of 6:10–17.

A third presentation of this view of the Powers was given in 1954 by G. B. Caird in a series of lectures in Canada which were published in 1956 as *Principalities and Powers, A Study in Pauline Theology.*[6] It is a more careful biblical study than either of the two previously summarized books, although I cannot personally approach with any high degree of confidence a work which can refer to Paul's 'faulty logic and equally faulty exegesis', not to mention 'the insufficiency of Paul's spurious arguments'.[7] Affirming in his Introduction that 'the idea of sinister world powers and their subjugation by Christ is built into the very fabric of Paul's thought',[8] Dr Caird goes on to isolate three principal 'powers'. The first is 'pagan religion and pagan

[8] *Ibid.*, p. 32. [9] *Ibid.*, pp. 38–39.
[1] *Ibid.*, p. 44. [2] *Ibid.*, p. 58.
[3] *Ibid.*, p. 49. [4] *Ibid.*, pp. 50–51.
[5] *Ibid.*, p. 52. [6] Oxford University Press.
[7] *Op. cit.*, pp. 20–21. [8] *Ibid.*, p. viii.

power', including the state, and he interprets Ephesians 3:10 as teaching that these have already begun to be redeemed through Christian social action.[9] The second power is the law which is good in itself because it is God's, yet when it is 'exalted into an independent system of religion, it becomes demonic'.[1] The third power concerns those recalcitrant elements in nature which resist God's rule, including wild animals, diseases, storms and the whole creation's bondage to corruption. So 'Paul's view of man's dilemma' is as follows: 'He lives under divinely appointed authorities—the powers of the state, the powers of legal religion, the powers of nature—which through sin have become demonic agencies. To expect that evil will be defeated by any of these powers, by the action of the state, by the self-discipline of the conscience, or by the processes of nature, is to ask that Satan cast out Satan. The powers can be robbed of their tyrannical influence and brought into their proper subjection to God only in the Cross'.[2]

In his commentary on Ephesians published twenty years after *Principalities and Powers*, Dr Caird seems more willing to concede that Paul was referring to 'spiritual beings who preside over all the forms and structures of power operative in the corporate life of men'.[3] Indeed, 'The real enemies are the spiritual forces that stand behind all institutions of government, and control the lives of men and nations.'[4]

The only other author I will mention by name is Dr Markus Barth, whose *The Broken Wall* (*A Study of the Epistle to the Ephesians*) was published in 1959 and whose monumental two volumes in the *Anchor Bible* followed in 1974. In the former book he identifies the principalities and powers 'by reference to four features of Paul's thinking and terminology', namely the state (political, judicial, ecclesiastical authorities), death, moral and ritual law, and economic structures including slavery. 'We conclude that by principalities and powers Paul means the world of axioms and principles of politics and religion, of economics

[9] *Ibid.*, pp. 27–30.   [1] *Ibid.*, p. 41.   [2] *Ibid.*, p. 101.
[3] Caird, p. 46.   [4] *Ibid.*, p. 91.

and society, of morals and biology, of history and culture', and therefore 'it is of the essence of the Gospel to include utterances concerning political, social, economic, cultural and psychological situations, dogmas and problems'.[5]

In his later two-volume work, however, I get the distinct impression that Dr Barth is willing to allow Paul a continuing 'mythological' or 'superstitious' (as he thinks it) belief in supernatural powers. He seems to be seeking some kind of uneasy compromise between the two interpretations. Thus, 'Paul denotes the angelic or demonic beings that reside in the heavens', although there is a 'direct association of these heavenly principalities and powers with structures and institutions of life on earth'.[6] Again, 'the "principalities and powers" are at the same time intangible spiritual entities and concrete historical, social or psychic structures or institutions'.[7]

My first reaction to this attempted reconstruction, of which I have given four examples, is to admire its ingenuity. The scholars concerned have used great skill in their determination to make Paul's obscure references to heavenly powers speak relevantly to our own earthly situations. Hence the attraction of this theory, which a number of authors of evangelical persuasion have also begun to adopt. But hence also its suspicious character. For some are sharing with us with great candour the two embarrassments which led them to embrace it. First, they say, the traditional interpretation reflected an archaic world-view, with angels and demons, not far removed from spooks and poltergeists. Secondly, they could find in the New Testament no allusion to social structures, which have become a significant modern preoccupation. Then suddenly a new theory is proposed which solves both problems simultaneously. We lose the demons and gain the structures, for the principalities and powers are structures in disguise!

It would be wrong, however, to reject the new theory because we may suspect the presuppositions which have led people to propound or accept it. What is needed on both sides is more serious exegetical work, for the new

[5] Barth, *Broken Wall*, pp. 82–83.
[6] Barth, *Ephesians*, I, p. 154.   [7] *Ibid.*, p. 800.

theory is 'not proven' and has failed, I would judge, to convince a majority of exegetes. All I can attempt here is an introductory critique. It is true that the vocabulary of 'principalities and powers' (*archai* and *exousiai*) is sometimes used in the New Testament of political authorities. For example, the Jewish priests sought some means to hand Jesus over 'to the authority and jurisdiction (*archē* and *exousia*) of the governor'.[8] In that verse the words are singular. Also Jesus warned his followers that they would be brought before 'the rulers and the authorities', while Paul told his readers to be 'submissive to rulers and authorities' or 'to the governing authorities',[9] in all of which verses the words *exousiai* and *archai* or *archontes* occur together and in the plural. Moreover, in each case the context makes it unambiguously clear that human authorities are in view.

In the other contexts, however, in which the same words are normally translated 'principalities and powers', it is by no means clear that the reference is to political structures or judicial authorities. On the contrary, the *a priori* assumption of generations of interpreters has been that they refer to supernatural beings. That they were given the same names and titles as human rulers need not surprise us, since they 'were thought of as having a political organization'[1] and are 'rulers and functionaries of the spirit world'.[2] I confess to finding the reconstructions of the new theorists not only ingenious, but artificial to the point of being contrived.

Take the three main references to the principalities and powers in Ephesians. The natural interpretation of 1:20–21 is not that God has exalted Jesus far above all earthly rulers and institutions, thus making him 'King of kings and Lord of lords' (though he is that, and this thought may be included), since the realm in which he has been supremely exalted is specifically said to be 'in the heavenlies' at God's right hand. Next, it is to me extremely far-fetched to suggest that in 3:10 Paul is really saying that it is to power structures on earth that God's manifold wisdom is made known through the church. For those

[8] Lk. 2:20.   [9] Lk. 12:11; Tit. 3:1; Rom. 13:1–3.
[1] AG on *archē*.   [2] AG on *exousia*

who interpret it in this way, the allusion to 'the heavenly places' is again an awkward addition. And thirdly, the Christian's spiritual warfare is specifically stated to be 'not with flesh and blood but with principalities and powers', which has till recent days been universally understood as meaning 'not with human but with demonic forces'. The allusions to 'the world rulers of this present darkness' and 'the spiritual hosts of wickedness', together with the armour and weapons needed to withstand them, fit supernatural powers much more naturally, especially in a context which twice mentions the devil (verses 11 and 16), while again there is the awkward addition of 'in the heavenly places'. In fact, I have not come across a new theorist who takes into adequate account the fact that all three references to the principalities and powers in Ephesians also contain a reference to the heavenly places, that is, the unseen world of spiritual reality. It is a stubborn fact, as if Paul were deliberately explaining who the principalities and powers are, and where they operate. Indeed, the six stages in the developing drama of the principalities and powers—their original creation, their subsequent fall, their decisive conquest by Christ, their learning through the church, their continued hostility and their final destruction[3]—all seem to apply more naturally to supernatural beings than to structures, institutions and traditions.

Turning now from exegetical to theological considerations, nobody can deny that the Jesus portrayed in the Gospels believed in both demons and angels. It was not inevitable that he should have done so, because the Sadducees did not. But exorcism was an integral part of his ministry of compassion and one of the chief signs of the kingdom. It is also recorded that he spoke without inhibition about angels.[4] So if Jesus Christ our Lord believed in them and spoke of them, it ill becomes us to be too embarrassed to do so. His apostles took this belief over from Jesus. Quite apart from the references to principalities and powers,

[3] For their creation see Col. 1:16; their fall is assumed since Christ needed to conquer them; for their conquest see Eph. 1:20–22; Col. 2:15; Rom. 8:38 and 1 Pet. 3:22; for their learning, Eph. 3:10; for their hostility, Eph. 6:12 and for their final destruction, 1 Cor. 15:24.
[4] E.g. Mt. 26:53; Mk. 12:25; Lk. 15:10; 16:22.

there are numerous other allusions to angels by Paul, Peter and the author of Hebrews.[5] Now commentators are free, if their theology permits them, to disagree with Jesus and his apostles, to dismiss their beliefs about supernatural intelligences as 'mythological' or 'superstitious', and to attempt to 'demythologize' their teaching. But this is a different exercise from the attempt to argue that our Lord and his apostles were not teaching what for centuries it has appeared to virtually all commentators they were teaching. Very strong exegetical reasons, and not just the appeal of the relevant, would be necessary to overthrow such an almost universal tradition of biblical understanding.

Finally, in reaffirming that the principalities and powers are personal supernatural agencies, I am not at all denying that they can use structures, traditions, institutions, *etc.* for good or ill; I am only wishing to avoid the confusion which comes from identifying them. That social, political, judicial and economic structures can become demonic is evident to anybody who has considered that the state, which in Romans 13 is the minister of God, in Revelation 13 has become an ally of the devil. Similarly, the moral law which God gave for human good led to human bondage and was exploited by 'the elemental spirits of the universe'.[6] Every good gift of God can be perverted to evil use. But if we identify 'the powers' with human structures of one kind and another, serious consequences follow. First, we lack an adequate explanation why structures so regularly, but not always, become tyrannical. Secondly, we unjustifiably restrict our understanding of the malevolent activity of the devil, whereas he is too versatile to be limited to the structural. Thirdly, we become too negative towards society and its structures. For the Powers are evil, dethroned and to be fought. So if the Powers are structures, this becomes our attitude to structures. We find it hard to believe or say anything good about them, so corrupt do they appear. Advocates of the new theory warn us against deifying structures; I want to warn them against demonizing them. Both are extremes to avoid. By all means

---

[5] *E.g.* Rom. 8:38; 1 Cor. 4:9; 11.10; 1 Tim. 5:21; 1 Pet. 1:12; 3:22; Heb. 1:4 – 2:9; 12:18–24.　　[6] Gal. 3:19 – 4:11.

let the church as God's new society question the standards and values of contemporary society, challenge them, and demonstrate a viable alternative. But if God blesses her witness, some structures may become changed for the good; then what will happen to the new theology of the Powers?

3. The armour of God (verses 13–20)

The purpose of investing ourselves with the divine armour is *that you may be able to stand against the wiles of the devil* (verse 11), *that you may be able to withstand in the evil day, and having done all, to stand. Stand therefore* ... This fourfold emphasis on the need to 'stand' or 'withstand' shows that the apostle's concern is for Christian stability. Wobbly Christians who have no firm foothold in Christ are an easy prey for the devil. And Christians who shake like reeds and rushes cannot resist the wind when the principalities and powers begin to blow. Paul wants to see Christians so strong and stable that they remain firm even against the devil's wiles (verse 11) and even *in the evil day*, that is, in a time of special pressure. For such stability, both of character and in crisis, the armour of God is essential.

The expression *the whole armour of God* translates the Greek word *panoplia*, which is 'the full armour of a heavy-armed soldier' (AG), although 'the divineness rather than the completeness of the outfit is emphasized'.[7] The point is that this equipment is 'forged and furnished' by God.[8] In the Old Testament it is God himself, the Lord of Hosts, who is depicted as a warrior fighting to vindicate his people: *e.g.* 'He put on righteousness as a breastplate, and a helmet of salvation upon his head.'[9] Still today the armour and weapons are his, but now he shares them with us. We have to put on the armour, take up the weapons and go to war with the powers of evil.

Paul details the six main pieces of a soldier's equipment—the belt, the breastplate, the boots, the shield, the helmet and the sword, and uses them as pictures of the truth, righteousness, good news of peace, faith, salvation

[7] Armitage Robinson, p. 132.   [8] Hendriksen, p. 272.   [9] Is. 59:17.

and word of God which equip us in our fight against the powers. Paul was very familiar with Roman soldiers. He met many in his travels, and as he dictated Ephesians he was chained to one by the wrist. He refers to his chain in verse 20. And although it would be unlikely that such a bodyguard would wear the full armour of an infantryman on the battlefield, yet the sight of him close by may well have kindled his imagination.

In 1655 the Puritan minister William Gurnall, 'pastor of the church of Christ at Lavenham in Suffolk' (as he styled himself), published his treatise *The Christian in Complete Armour*. Its elaborate sub-title, for which one needs to draw a deep breath, is: *The saints' war against the Devil, wherein a discovery is made of that grand enemy of God and his people, in his policies, power, seat of his empire, wickedness, and chief design he hath against the saints; a magazine opened, from whence the Christian is furnished with spiritual arms for the battle, helped on with his armour, and taught the use of his weapon; together with the happy issue of the whole war*. In his Dedication of the book to his parishioners he modestly refers to himself as their 'poor' and 'unworthy' minister and to his treatise as but a 'mite' and a 'little present' to them. Yet in my eighth edition of 1821 it runs to three volumes, 261 chapters and 1,472 pages, although it is an exposition of only eleven verses.

Let me give you a taste of Gurnall's spirituality. Regarding God's armour he writes: 'In heaven we shall appear not in armour but in robes of glory; but here they (*sc.* the pieces of armour specified) are to be worn night and day; we must walk, work and sleep in them, or else we are not true soldiers of Christ.'[1] In this armour we are to stand and watch, and never relax our vigilance, for 'the saint's sleeping time is Satan's tempting time; every fly dares venture to creep on a sleeping lion'.[2] He goes on to instance Samson (whose hair was cut by Delilah while he slept), King Saul (whose spear David stole while he was asleep), Noah (who was in some way abused by his son while he was in a drunken sleep) and Eutychus (who slept

[1] Gurnall, I, p. 67.   [2] *Ibid.*, p. 330

while Paul preached).

Dr Martyn Lloyd-Jones in our own day has written a very fine and full exposition of the same eleven verses in two volumes entitled *The Christian Warfare* and *The Christian Soldier*,[3] totalling 736 pages. His twenty-one chapters in the former volume on 'the wiles of the devil', which describe some of the devil's subtlest assaults upon the people of God (in the three realms of the mind, of experience and of practice or conduct) and how we need to be on our guard, are full of wise counsel from an experienced pastor.

The first piece of equipment which Paul mentions is the girdle of truth: *having girded your loins with truth* (verse 14). Usually made of leather, the soldier's belt belonged rather to his underwear than his armour. Yet it was essential. It gathered his tunic together and also held his sword. It ensured that he was unimpeded when marching. As he buckled it on, it gave him a sense of hidden strength and confidence. Belts and braces still do. To 'tighten one's belt' can mean not only to accept a time of austerity during a food shortage but also to prepare oneself for action, which the ancients would have called 'girding up their loins'.

Now the Christian soldier's belt is 'truth'. Many commentators, especially in the early centuries, understood this to mean 'the truth', the revelation of God in Christ and in Scripture. For certainly it is only the truth which can dispel the devil's lies and set us free,[4] and Paul has in this letter several times referred to the importance and the power of the truth.[5] Other commentators, however, especially because the definite article is absent in the Greek sentence, prefer to understand Paul to be referring to 'truth' in the sense of 'sincerity' or (NEB) 'integrity'. For certainly God requires 'truth in the inward being', and the Christian must at all costs be honest and truthful.[6] To be deceitful, to lapse into hypocrisy, to resort to intrigue and scheming, this is to play the devil's game, and we shall not be able to beat him at his own game. What he abominates is

[3] *The Christian Soldier, An Exposition of Eph. 6:10–20* (Banner of Truth, 1977).   [4] *Cf.* Jn. 8:31–36, 43–45.
[5] *E.g.* 4:21; 5:6,9.   [6] Ps. 51:6; Eph. 4:15, 25.

277

transparent truth. He loves darkness; light causes him to flee. For spiritual as for mental health honesty about oneself is indispensable.

Perhaps we do not need to choose between these alternatives. The judicious Gurnall writes: 'Some by *truth* mean *a truth of doctrine*; others will have it truth of heart, *sincerity*; they think best that comprise both . . . one will not do without the other.'[7]

The second item of the Christian's equipment is *the breastplate of righteousness* (verse 14). Some expositors have maintained that in God's armour, although there is a breastplate, no protection is provided for the back. They then go on to argue that we must face our enemy with courage and not run away from him, exposing our unguarded back. John Bunyan made this point in *Pilgrim's Progress*. When Christian reached the Valley of Humiliation, 'he espied a foul fiend coming over the field to meet him', whose name was Apollyon. 'Then did Christian begin to be afraid, and to cast in his mind whether to go back or to stand his ground. But he considered again that he had no armour for his back, and therefore thought, that to turn the back to him might give him greater advantage with ease to pierce him with his darts. Therefore he resolved to venture, and stand his ground.'[8] It is a good point of spiritual counsel, but remains a doubtful example of biblical exegesis, for the soldier's breastplate often covered his back as well as his front, and was his major piece of armour protecting all his most vital organs.

In a previous letter Paul has written of 'the breastplate of faith and love',[9] but here as in Isaiah 59:17 the breastplate consists of 'righteousness'. Now 'righteousness' (*dikaiosynē*) in Paul's letters more often than not means 'justification', that is, God's gracious initiative in putting sinners right with himself through Christ. Is this then the Christian's breastplate? Certainly no spiritual protection is greater than a righteous relationship with God. To have been justified by his grace through simple faith in Christ crucified, to be clothed with a righteousness which is not one's own

[7] Gurnall, I, p. 337.
[8] *The Pilgrim's Progress* (1678: Collins' Classics edition, 1953), p. 71.
[9] 1 Thes. 5:8.

but Christ's, to stand before God not condemned but
accepted—this is an essential defence against an accusing
conscience and against the slanderous attacks of the evil
one, whose Hebrew name ('Satan') means 'adversary' and
whose Greek title (*diabolos*, 'devil') means 'slanderer'.
'There is therefore now no condemnation for those who
are in Christ Jesus . . . Who shall bring any charge against
God's elect? It is God who justifies; who is to condemn?
It is Christ Jesus who died, yes, who was raised from the
dead, who is at the right hand of God, who indeed
intercedes for us.'[1] This is the Christian assurance of
'righteousness', that is, of a right relationship with God
through Christ; it is a strong breastplate to protect us
against Satanic accusations.

On the other hand, the apostle wrote in 2 Corinthians
6:7 of 'the weapons of righteousness for the right hand and
for the left', apparently meaning moral righteousness, and
has used the word in the same sense in Ephesians 4:24 and
5:9. So the Christian's breastplate may be righteousness of
character and conduct. For just as to cultivate 'truth' is
the way to overthrow the devil's deceits, so to cultivate
'righteousness' is the way to resist his temptations.

Alternatively, as with the two possible meanings of
'truth', so with the two possible meanings of 'righteousness',
it may well be right to combine them, since according to
Paul's gospel the one would invariably lead to the other.
As G. G. Findlay put it, 'The completeness of pardon
for past offence and the integrity of character that belong
to the justified life, are woven together into an impenetrable
mail.'[2]

The gospel boots come next in the list. According to
Markus Barth, there is agreement among the commentators
that Paul 'has in mind the *caliga* ("half-boot") of the
Roman legionary which was made of leather, left the toes
free, had heavy studded soles, and was tied to the ankles
and shins with more or less ornamental straps'. These
'equipped him for long marches and for a solid stance
. . . While they did not impede his mobility, they prevented
his foot from sliding.'[3]

[1] Rom. 8:1, 33–34 margin. [2] Findlay, p. 415.
[3] Barth, *Ephesians* II, p. 798.

Now the Christian soldier's boots are *the equipment of the gospel of peace* (verse 15). 'Equipment' translates *hetoimasia*, which means 'readiness', 'preparation' or 'firmness'. The uncertainty is whether the genitive which follows is subjective or objective. If the former, the reference is to a certain firmness or steadfastness which the gospel gives to those who believe it, like the firmness which strong boots give to those who wear them. NEB takes it this way and translates: 'Let the shoes on your feet be the gospel of peace, to give you a firm footing.' And certainly if we have received the good news, and are enjoying the peace with God and with one another which it brings, we have the firmest possible foothold from which to fight evil.

But the genitive may be objective, in which case the Christian soldier's shoes are his 'readiness to announce the Good News of peace' (GNB). There can be no doubt that we should always be ready to bear witness to Jesus Christ as God's peacemaker (2:14–15) and also—as Paul writes in a parallel passage in Colossians[4]—to give gracious though 'salty' answers to the questions which 'outsiders' put to us. Such tip-toe readiness has a very stabilizing influence on our own lives, as well as introducing others to the liberating gospel. For myself I veer slightly towards this explanation, partly because of the Colossians parallel and partly because of the faint echoes of 2:17 ('He came and preached peace') and of Isaiah 52:7 ('How beautiful upon the mountains are the feet of him who brings good tidings, who publishes peace'). As Johannes Blauw has written, 'Missionary work is like a pair of sandals that have been given to the Church in order that it shall set out on the road and *keep on going* to make known the mystery of the gospel.'[5]

In either case the devil fears and hates the gospel, because it is God's power to rescue people from his tyranny, both us who have received it and those with whom we share it. So we need to keep our gospel boots strapped on.

Our fourth piece of equipment is *the shield of faith* (verse 16) which we are to take up not so much 'above

[4] Col. 4:5–6.
[5] *The Missionary Nature of the Church* by Johannes Blauw (1962: Eerdmans, 1974), p. 125.

all' (AV), as if it were the most important of all weapons, but rather *besides all these*, as an indispensable addition. The word Paul uses denotes not the small round shield which left most of the body unprotected, but the long oblong one, 'measuring 1.2 metres by 0.75, which covered the whole person. Its Latin name was *scutum*. It 'consisted . . . of two layers of wood glued together and covered first with linen and then with hide: it was bound with iron above and below.'[6] It was specially designed to put out the dangerous incendiary missiles then in use, specially arrows dipped in pitch which were then lit and fired.

What, then, are *all the flaming darts of the evil one*, and with what shield can Christians protect themselves? The devil's darts no doubt include his mischievous accusations which inflame our conscience with what (if we are sheltering in Christ) can only be called false guilt. Other darts are unsought thoughts of doubt and disobedience, rebellion, lust, malice or fear. But there is a shield with which we *can quench* or extinguish all such fire-tipped darts. It is *the shield of faith*. God himself 'is a shield to those who take refuge in him',[7] and it is by faith that we flee to him for refuge. For faith lays hold of the promises of God in times of doubt and depression, and faith lays hold of the power of God in times of temptation. Apollyon taunted Christian with the threat, 'Here will I spill thy soul.' 'And with that,' Bunyan continues, 'he threw a flaming dart at his breast; but Christian had a shield in his hand, with which he caught it, and so prevented the danger of that.'[8]

The Roman soldier's helmet, which is the next piece of armour on the list, was usually made of a tough metal like bronze or iron. 'An inside lining of felt or sponge made the weight bearable. Nothing short of an axe or hammer could pierce a heavy helmet, and in some cases a hinged vizor added frontal protection.'[9] Helmets were decorative as well as protective, and some had magnificent plumes or crests.

According to an earlier statement of Paul's, the Christian soldier's helmet is 'the hope of salvation',[1] that is, our

[6] Armitage Robinson, p. 251.   [7] Pr. 30:5.
[8] *The Pilgrims' Progress*, p. 74.   [9] Barth, *Ephesians*, II, p. 775.
[1] 1 Thes. 5:8.

281

assurance of future and final salvation. Here in Ephesians it is just *the helmet of salvation* (verse 17) which we are to take and wear. But whether our head piece is that measure of salvation which we have already received (forgiveness, deliverance from Satan's bondage, and adoption into God's family) or the confident expectation of full salvation on the last day (including resurrection glory and Christ-likeness in heaven), there is no doubt that God's saving power is our only defence against the enemy of our souls. Charles Hodge wrote: 'that which adorns and protects the Christian, which enables him to hold up his head with confidence and joy, is the fact that he is saved'[2] and, we might add, that he knows his salvation will be perfected in the end.

The sixth and last weapon to be specified is *the sword* (verse 17). Of all the six pieces of armour or weaponry listed, the sword is the only one which can clearly be used for attack as well as defence. Moreover, the kind of attack envisaged will involve a close personal encounter, for the word used is *machaira*, the short sword. It is *the sword of the Spirit*, which is then immediately identified as *the word of God*, although in the Revelation it is seen issuing from the mouth of Christ.[3] This may well include the words of defence and testimony which Jesus promised the Holy Spirit would put into his followers' lips when they were dragged before magistrates.[4] But the expression 'the word of God' has a much broader reference than that, namely to Scripture, God's written word, whose origin is repeatedly attributed to the inspiration of the Holy Spirit. Still today it is his sword, for he still uses it to cut through people's defences, to prick their consciences and to stab them spiritually awake. Yet he also puts his sword into our hands, so that we may use it both in resisting temptation (as Jesus did, quoting Scripture to counter the devil in the Judean wilderness) and in evangelism. Every Christian evangelist, whether a preacher or a personal witness, knows that God's word has cutting power, being 'sharper than any two-edged sword'.[5] We must never

---

[2] Hodge, pp. 387–388.   [3] Rev. 1:16; 2:12; 19:15; *cf*. Is. 11:4; Ho. 6:5.
[4] Mt. 10:17–20.   [5] Heb. 4:12.

therefore be ashamed to use it, or to acknowledge our confidence that the Bible is the sword of the Spirit. As E. K. Simpson wrote, this phrase sets forth 'the trenchant power of Scripture . . . But a mutilated Bible is what Moody dubbed it, "a broken sword" '.[6]

Here, then, are the six pieces which together make up the whole armour of God: the girdle of truth and the breastplate of righteousness, the gospel boots and the faith shield, salvation's helmet and the Spirit's sword. They constitute God's armour, as we have seen, for he supplies it. Yet it is our responsibility to take it up, to put it on and to use it confidently against the powers of evil. Moreover, we must be sure to avail ourselves of every item of equipment provided and not omit any. 'Our enemies are on every side, and so must our armour be, on the right hand and on the left.'[7]

Finally, Paul adds prayer (verses 18–20), not (probably) because he thinks of prayer as another though unnamed weapon, but because it is to pervade all our spiritual warfare. Equipping ourselves with God's armour is not a mechanical operation; it is itself an expression of our dependence on God, in other words of prayer. Moreover, it is prayer *in the Spirit,* prompted and guided by him, just as God's word is 'the sword of the Spirit' which he himself employs. Thus Scripture and prayer belong together as the two chief weapons which the Spirit puts into our hands.

Prevailing Christian prayer is wonderfully comprehensive. It has four universals, indicated by the fourfold use of the word 'all'. We are to pray *at all times* (both regularly and constantly), *with all prayer and supplication* (for it takes many and varied forms), *with all perseverance* (because we need like good soldiers to *keep alert,* and neither give up nor fall asleep), *making supplication for all the saints* (since the unity of God's new society, which has been the preoccupation of this whole letter, must be reflected in our prayers). Most Christians pray sometimes, with some prayers and some degree of perseverance, for some of God's people. But to replace 'some' by 'all' in each of

[6] Simpson, p. 151.   [7] Gurnall, p. 60.

these expressions would be to introduce us to a new dimension of prayer. It was when Christian 'perceived the mouth of hell . . . hard by the wayside' in the Valley of the Shadow of Death, and saw flame and smoke and heard hideous noises, that 'he was forced to put up his sword, and betake himself to another weapon, called All-prayer: so he cried in my hearing, "O Lord, I beseech thee, deliver my soul." '[8]

Perhaps most important is the command to stay awake and therefore alert (verse 18). It goes back to the teaching of Jesus himself. He emphasized the need for watchfulness in view of the unexpectedness both of his return[9] and of the onset of temptation.[1] He seems to have kept repeating the same warning: 'I say to you, Watch!' The apostles echoed and extended his admonition. 'Be watchful!' was their general summons to Christian vigilance,[2] partly because the devil is always on the prowl like a hungry lion, and false teachers like fierce wolves,[3] and partly lest the Lord's return should take us unawares,[4] but especially because of our tendency to sleep when we should be praying.[5] 'Watch and pray', Jesus urged. It was failure to obey this order which led the apostles into their disastrous disloyalty; similar failure leads to similar disloyalty today. It is by prayer that we wait on the Lord and renew our strength. Without prayer we are much too feeble and flabby to stand against the might of the forces of evil.

Pray *also for me*, Paul begged (verse 19). He was wise enough to know his own need of strength if he was to stand against the enemy, and humble enough to ask his friends to pray with him and for him. The strength he needed was not just for his personal confrontation with the devil, however, but for his evangelistic ministry by which he sought to rescue people from the devil's dominion. This had been a part of his original commission when the risen Lord Jesus had told him to turn people 'from darkness to light, and from the power of Satan to God'.[6]

[8] *The Pilgrim's Progress*, p. 77.
[9] *E.g.* Mk. 13:33 ff; Lk. 12:37 ff.   [1] Mk. 14:34–38.
[2] 1 Cor. 16:13; *cf.* Rev. 3:2–3.   [3] 1 Pet. 5:8; Acts 20:31.
[4] 1 Thes. 5:1–8; Rev. 16:15.   [5] verse 18; Col. 4:2.   [6] Acts 26:18.

Hence the spiritual conflict of which he was aware. Moreover he had not left the battlefield now that he was under house arrest and unable to continue his missionary expeditions. No, there were those soldiers to whom one by one, each for a shift of several hours on end, he was chained, and there were his constant visitors. He could still witness to them, and he did so. There must have been other individuals beside the fugitive slave Onesimus whom he led to faith in Christ. Luke tells of Jewish leaders who came to him at his lodging 'in great numbers', and who heard him expound 'from morning till evening' about the kingdom and about Jesus. 'Some were convinced,' Luke added.[7] Thus Paul's evangelistic labours went on. For 'two whole years' he 'welcomed all who came to him', he proclaimed 'the kingdom of God and . . . the Lord Jesus Christ', and he did it 'quite openly and unhindered'.[8]

It is those last words which we need specially to notice. For 'quite openly' translates the Greek phrase 'with all *parrēsia*'. The word originally denoted the democratic freedom of speech enjoyed by Greek citizens. It then came to mean 'outspokenness, frankness, plainness of speech, that conceals nothing and passes over nothing', together with 'courage, confidence, boldness, fearlessness, especially in the presence of persons of high rank' (AG). And this is precisely what Paul asks the Ephesians to pray that he may be given. Freedon is what he longs for—not freedom from confinement, but freedom to preach the gospel. So he uses the word *parrēsia* twice (first as a noun, then as a verb) in the expressions *opening my mouth boldly* (verse 19) in preaching the gospel, and *that I may declare it boldly*, as I ought to speak (verse 20). The good news he announces he still calls the *mystery*, because it has become known only by revelation, and centres on the union of Jews and Gentiles in Christ; and the two major qualities he wants to characterize his preaching of it are 'utterance' (verse 19) and 'boldness' (verses 19–20).

The first of these two words seems to refer to the clarity of his communication, and the second to his courage. He is anxious to obscure nothing by muddled speech and to

[7] Acts 28:17, 23–24.   [8] Acts 28:30–31.

hide nothing by cowardly compromise. Clarity and courage remain two of the most crucial characteristics of authentic Christian preaching. For they relate to the content of the message preached and to the style of its presentation. Some preachers have the gift of lucid teaching, but their sermons lack solid content; their substance has become diluted by fear. Others are bold as lions. They fear nobody, and omit nothing. But what they say is confused and confusing. Clarity without courage is like sunshine in the desert: plenty of light but nothing worth looking at. Courage without clarity is like a beautiful landscape at night time: plenty to see, but no light by which to enjoy it. What is needed in the pulpits of the world today is a combination of clarity and courage, or of 'utterance' and 'boldness'. Paul asked the Ephesians to pray that these might *be given* to him, for he recognized them as gifts of God. We should join them in prayer for the pastors and preachers of the contemporary church.

It was for the gospel that he had become *an ambassador in chains* (verse 20). Earlier in the letter he has designated himself both 'a prisoner . . . on behalf of you Gentiles' and 'a prisoner for the Lord' (3:1; 4:1). Thus he gives the gospel, the Lord and the Gentiles as three reasons for his imprisonment. Yet these three are one. For the good news he preached was of the Gentiles' inclusion in the new society, and it had been entrusted to him by the Lord. So by communicating it in its fullness he was being simultaneously faithful to the gospel itself, to the Lord who had revealed it to him and to the Gentiles who received its blessings. His faithfulness to these three had cost him his freedom. So he was a prisoner for all three. Perhaps now he was sometimes tempted to compromise in order to secure his release. For 'imprisonment brings its own special temptation to bow to the fear of man'.[9] But if so, he was given grace to resist. 'Paul thinks of himself as the ambassador of Jesus Christ, duly accredited to represent his Lord at the imperial court of Rome'.[1] How could he be ashamed of his King or afraid to speak in his name? On the contrary, he was proud to be Christ's

---

[9] Foulkes, p. 180.   [1] Bruce, p. 134.

ambassador, even if he was experiencing the anomaly of being an 'ambassador in chains'. It is possible even that he deliberately plays on this paradox. Markus Barth writes: 'The term "chain" (*alusis*) signifies among other things the (golden) adornment(s) worn around the neck and wrists by rich ladies or high ranking men. On festive occasions ambassadors wear such chains in order to reveal the riches, power and dignity of the government they represent. Because Paul serves Christ crucified, he considers the painful iron prison chains as most appropriate insignia for the representation of his Lord.'[2] What concerns Paul most, however, is not that his wrist may be unchained, but that his mouth may be opened in testimony; not that he may be set free, but that the gospel may be spread freely and without hindrance. It is for this, then, that he prays and asks the Ephesians to pray too. Against such prayer the principalities and powers are helpless.

[2] Barth, *Ephesians*, II, p. 782.

6:21–34

Conclusion

Now that you also may know how I am and what I am doing, Tychicus the beloved brother and faithful minister in the Lord will tell you everything. [22]I have sent him to you for this very purpose, that you may know how we are, and that he may encourage your hearts.

[23]Peace be to the brethren, and love with faith, from God the Father and the Lord Jesus Christ. [24]Grace be with all who love our Lord Jesus Christ with love undying.

Paul has reached the end of his letter, which he has been dictating. Perhaps at this point he takes the pen from his scribe and writes an authenticating sentence or two in his own handwriting. He certainly did this at the conclusion of his letters to the Galatians,[1] the Thessalonians,[2] the Corinthians[3] and the Colossians.[4]

To whom, then, has he been dictating? Probably to *Tychicus*, whom he now mentions affectionately by name. Tychicus was a native of Asia. Luke not only describes him as an 'Asian',[5] but also brackets him with Trophimus, whom he later calls an 'Ephesian'.[6] So Tychicus may have come from Ephesus too. Paul certainly sent him there during his second imprisonment in Rome,[7] and reading between the lines of the Ephesian and Colossian letters Paul seems to assume that his readers know him already.

What is clear, whether or not Tychicus was Paul's scribe,

---

[1] Gal. 6:11. [2] 2 Thes. 3:17. [3] 1 Cor. 16:21.
[4] Col. 4:18. [5] Acts 20:4.
[6] Acts 21:29. [7] 2 Tim. 4:12.

is that Paul entrusts the letter to him to deliver, together with the Colossian Letter.[8] For the apostle evidently has complete confidence in his younger colleague. *Beloved brother*, he calls him, and also *faithful minister in the Lord* (verse 21). He will rely on him not only to deliver the letters safely, but also to supplement their message with some personal news. He is sending him, he says, *that you also may know how I am and what I am doing*; he *will tell you everything* (verse 21). Indeed, *I have sent him to you for this very purpose, that you may know how we are* (verse 22). Thus three times Paul reiterates his intention that Tychicus will bring his readers up to date with news of him. This no doubt explains the unusual absence at the end of the letter of personal messages and greetings. Tychicus will convey them by word of mouth.

Then there is another reason for the visit of Tychicus to Ephesus and its neighbouring cities. He will deliver the letter, he will tell the church members how Paul is, and in addition Paul is sending him *that he may encourage your hearts*, (verse 22). It is touching to see the apostle's desire to forge stronger personal links between himself and these Asian Christians. His exposition of God's new society is no mere theological theory; for he and they are members of it themselves. So they must deepen their fellowship with one another—by praying for one another (he has recorded two of his prayers for them, in chapters 1 and 3, before requesting their prayers for him in verses 19 and 20), by his letter to them, and through Tychicus who would both bring them information about Paul and seek to encourage them. Prayer, correspondence and visits are still three major means by which Christians and churches can enrich one another and so contribute to the building up of the body of Christ.

It was the custom in the ancient world for correspondents to end their letters with a wish—usually a secular wish, even if the gods were invoked—for the reader's health or happiness. Paul sees no reason to abandon the convention in principle. But as he has Christianized the opening greeting, so now he Christianizes the final wish. Indeed,

[8] Col. 4:7–8.

what he writes is half wish, half prayer. For the blessings he desires for his readers will come *from God the Father and the Lord Jesus Christ*. What blessings are these?

Paul's first prayer-wish is this: *Peace to the brethren, and love with faith* (verse 23). Peace has been a characteristic word of this letter. In the doctrinal section at the beginning he has explained how Jesus Christ 'is our peace' since he has broken down the dividing wall and created a single new humanity, 'so making peace', and how he then 'came and preached peace'.[9] Consequently, in the ethical section which follows Paul has begged them both to 'maintain the unity of the Spirit in the bond of peace' and to 'forbear one another in love' (4:2–3), indeed to 'walk in love as Christ loved us' (5:2). Peace and love belong together, for peace is reconciliation and love is its source and outflow. Paul paints a beautiful picture of the church fellowship and the Christian home pervaded with love and peace, even though no peace treaty can ever be negotiated with the principalities and powers of evil. When he adds to 'love' the words 'with faith', he is probably thinking of faith as a characteristic they already have, rather than as another he wants them to be given. For 'faith they had; Paul's prayer was that love might be connected with it'.[1]

Paul's second prayer-wish is this: *Grace be with all who love our Lord Jesus Christ with love undying*. By this expression he characterizes his Christian readers in terms of their love for Christ. The letter's final words in the Greek sentence mean simply 'in incorruption' (*en aphtharsiā*). Most commentators understand them as a qualification of people's love for Christ and so as a restriction on the grace of God. In this case, the prayer is that God's grace may accompany those who love Christ *with love undying* or 'with unfailing love' (NEB). Other commentators have not felt such a limitation to be congruous with Paul's conclusion. They therefore suggest attaching the phrase rather to God's grace than to Christians' love. In this case, the prayer is that all who love our Lord Jesus Christ may experience God's grace 'in immortality' or 'for ever'. If this is correct, then 'the epistle which

[9] 2:14–17. [1] Hendriksen, p. 396.

opened with a bold glance into the eternal past closes with the outlook of an immortal hope'.[2]

Of the four words 'peace', 'love', 'faith', and 'grace' which are included in the apostle's final greeting, the two which stand out as particularly appropriate are 'grace' and 'peace'. The apostle began his letter by wishing his readers 'grace . . . and peace from God our Father and the Lord Jesus Christ' (1:2); he now ends it with a similar reference to grace and peace. No two words could summarize the message of the letter more succinctly. For 'peace' in the sense of reconciliation with God and one another is the great achievement of Jesus Christ, and 'grace' is the reason why and the means by which he did it. Moreover, both are indispensable to all members of God's new society. Hence Paul's wishing of peace to 'the brethren' (verse 23), who belong to each other as brothers and sisters in the family of God, and of grace to 'all' those who love Christ, without discrimination, whatever their race, rank, age or sex. It is a wish, a prayer, that the members of God's new society may live in harmony as brothers and sisters in his family, at peace and in love with him and with each other, together with a recognition that only by his grace can this dream come true.

I venture, then, as we conclude our study of this letter to the Ephesians, to make Paul's words my own and address them to you my readers: 'Peace be to the brothers and sisters' and 'grace be with you all'.

[2] Armitage Robinson, p. 138.